To A

All Life's
a
Game

Best wishes

Trevor Threckmorth
2011

The Brian Clough philosophy that transformed a region

All Life's a Game

Words by Trevor Frecknall
Pictures by Nottingham Post

BREWIN BOOKS

First published by
Brewin Books Ltd, 56 Alcester Road,
Studley, Warwickshire B80 7LG in 2010
www.brewinbooks.com

ISBN: 978-1-85858-471-3

A Cataloguing in Publication Record
for this title is available from the British Library.

Typeset in Arno Pro
Printed in Great Britain by
by Information Press Ltd.

Contents

· · · · · · · · · · · · · ·

Introduction

· · · · · · · · · · · · · · · · · · · ·

MANY BOOKS have been written about Brian Clough, the only football manager to lead two provincial English clubs from second-tier obscurity to League titles. Some are factual. Some fictional. Some not quite one nor the other.

But none like this one; the memoirs of a journalist who was plucked from a mundane career in features and found himself reporting on Clough's Nottingham Forest enjoying the glory-glory days of successive European Cup triumphs and, almost a decade later, the glory days of historic domestic victories at Wembley.

It was far from as idyllic as it sounds. Not even the unique manager's closest allies knew exactly which Brian Clough would reveal himself at the City Ground daily. So imagine how his enemies (real or perceived) were treated.

The author was kicked-out of the City Ground by Clough the first time they met, caught in the middle of a dispute that was typical of the 1970s, when the ideologies of Capitalism and Socialism clashed frequently and ferociously. Yet the relationship changed over the years to such an extent that, on the last occasion he covered a Cup Final at Wembley, Clough asked him to carry Forest's freshly-won trophy out of the stadium.

Did he enjoy the ups and downs of his working relationship with the most out-spoken manager pre-Jose Mourinho? Yes and No. But you'll love it…

1

Like throwing an anchor through a sinking ship

• •

BRIAN CLOUGH'S arrival at Nottingham Forest fitted perfectly into the history of Nottingham, the East Midlands "city of pretty girls" that was built on the cornerstones of bicycles, cigarettes, drugs and lace. All were beginning to struggle to survive.

The bicycles wheeling off the Raleigh production lines in Radford in the west of Nottingham were being under-cut by imports from the Far East even while the company was sponsoring a team to victories in the prestigious *Tour de France*. Ditto the intricate creations of the thousands who toiled in the labyrinth of factories making up the Lace Market adjacent to the city centre. Even the less expensive dresses and lingerie created more cheaply in the plethora of textile factories around the city were losing the same economic battle.

As if that wasn't enough of a headache for a city that never quite made it into the big league industrially, over-the counter drugs such as pain-killers created by Boots the Chemist in their laboratories beside Nottingham Midland Railway Station and in the nearby suburb of Beeston were being replicated by rivals across the world.

And while it was still considered "big" to smoke, John Player & Son were becoming increasingly aware – and defensive – of a small but vocal medical lobby claiming their products were killers. It must have been coincidence, surely, that John Player began manufacturing his cigarettes just three months before Jesse Boot opened his first chemist's shop less than a mile away, in 1877.

And then, aloof from all of this unseemly competition, there was T. Bailey Forman Limited, chaired by Colonel Thomas E. Forman Hardy C.B.E., M.C., T.D., D.L., the head of a family of the landed gentry who had served with the South Notts Hussars in the Second World War, survived having his horse shot from beneath him in North Africa, and was now Chairman of the family company that had printed and published the *Nottingham Evening Post* for more than a century.

Quiet and kindly though he always was to his underlings, "Colonel Tom" was a ruthless businessman. He had already got rid of the competition, the *Nottingham Evening News*, by buying it from the UK-wide Westminster Group and merging it with the *Post*; and was therefore the sole purveyor of news (and advertisements) to some 750,000 households. When a rival began to deliver a paper full of advertisements free to most households in the Greater Nottingham conurbation, TBF (as the family firm became known in a nod to modern trends) responded by closing its centuries-old traditional paid-for weekly paper, the Guardian, and replacing it with a free paper called *The Weekly Post* with a mix of 20 per cent news and 80 per cent advertisements.

Not content with his high rank among the Capitalists of Great Britain, the Colonel had emphasised his Conservative tendencies in the early 1970s by appointing as his Managing Director a retired Naval commander, Christopher Pole-Carew, to carry out the modernisations. Along the way, the highly combative PC was to become legendary as the man who out-fought the printing unions and dragged the newspaper industry into the technological revolution, first at the *Post* in Nottingham and then at the *Sun* in London.

The stage was set: Clough, the People's Champion of the Underdog, and his fellow Yorkshire firebrand Arthur Scargill, Chairman of the National Union of Mineworkers and leader of the most ferocious groups of flying pickets ever seen, versus the inappropriately nicknamed PC and his scabs (as strike-breakers were called) – with a newly-appointed *Evening Post* Sports Editor called Trevor Frecknall caught in the cross fire.

The *Post* hierarchy reasoned that they didn't need a big-hitter to head their Sports Department: The retiring Sports Editor, Harry E. Richards, was quick to tell me that while the *Post's* circulation area stretched from the Lincolnshire coast to the Derbyshire Peaks, our sphere of interest lay only in the half-mile triangle that covered Meadow Lane, Trent Bridge and the City Ground. Richards was able to argue that it contained virtually all the spectator sports; and they were the sports that generated big readerships.

It was hardly a golden triangle. Despite boasting of being the oldest football league club in the world, Notts County had not been in the top flight for half a century. Nottinghamshire's cricketers had won nothing for 40 or more summers. Forest's Trophy Room – the size of a comprehensive school classroom beneath the Main Stand where Clough gave his players their pre-match briefings – had seen no new silverware (apart from the County Cup) since the 1959 FA Cup Final. Pole-Carew, his 6ft 6in frame made to seem even taller by his slimness, wondered why it required 10 journalists in the Sports Department to fill two pages each night. The Editor, Bill Snaith, a much more traditional newspaperman whose baldness, rimless spectacles and tendency to blush beetroot when riled forced unfavourable comparisons with Captain Mainwaring of *Dad's Army* on the television, considered sport to be of little more consequence than a round of golf on his home course at Wollaton Park on his day-off.

So I believe that with me – 33 years old and in charge of a team of ten for the first time – the plan was that the Sports Department would soon be stripped for more economic action.

After all, Forest's Championship triumph of 1977-78, only 12 months after they scraped promotion to the top Division, was merely a fluke further than usual … wasn't it?

The outspoken Clough would soon be put in his place … wouldn't he?

And his footballers would be returned from the ranks of sporting icons and part-time pop stars to their Saturday afternoon role as entertainers in between pub opening times … wouldn't they?

Then, four or five people could easily fill the sports pages that stopped the much more valuable classified advertisements spilling out of the back of the paper … couldn't they?

Well … no, actually.

This book explains how the novice *Nottingham Evening Post* Sports Editor and the Manager with the grandest ego in the sporting world came to work closely, but warily, together as the socio-political battle that brought Margaret Thatcher to power raged around us … and as Clough…

- ended our nine-month feud by rescuing me from a freezing night in Sweden;

- made me change seats in the Press Box to help Forest out of a losing run;

- used a £40 newspaper column to help off-load a £1 million misfit;

- needed all his persuasive powers to avoid a trip to a police station after a stash of alcohol was found on his team bus;

- remained faithful to his favourite club chairman after a prison term;

- locked an entire team of opposing players in a bus while he plied their manager with alcohol;

- discovered to his shock that his most fearless captain was prone to "going Commando";

- fretted over whether to gamble professional contracts on two apprentices who went on to international careers;

- thumped supporters, welcomed their apologies, accepted a record fine from the FA, and let me make-up most of his quotes of contrition;

- piloted his young team through the traumas of the Hillsborough Disaster and an FA Cup semi-final he never wanted while winning two Wembley finals;

- raged because Nelson Mandela could not remain incarcerated in South Africa for another 90 minutes while Forest played a televised match;

- fretted about Roy Keane's preference for black furnishings in Forest's lodgings for their apprentices;

- rued missing the big chance to send Alex Ferguson back to Scotland as a managerial failure before he had won any silverware at Manchester United;

- asked me to carry a trophy out of Wembley after yet another Forest victory.

2

Brian Clough, Brian Clough and his Merry Men...

FROM TIME immemorial, the only man readily associated with Nottingham was Robin Hood, the outlaw who, according to legend, lived in Sherwood Forest (a massive woodland that sprawled from Nottingham into Yorkshire in the Middle Ages) and spent his every waking moment robbing the rich to feed the poor. The modern day fable that brought adventurous men to Nottingham was that it was "the city of pretty girls" – housing

The Master-Manager prowls the Forest training ground accompanied by his daughter's dog, Del Boy, with squash racket ready to add emphasis to his judgements.

three of the fair sex for every male. Quite how many red-blooded footballers were seduced to Forest and Notts County by this statistic from the 1961 census is not known; but many a fair maiden spent Sunday mornings chatting contentedly with her most trusted *confidantes* about the Saturday night she had enjoyed with this goalkeeper or that winger at entertainment emporia such as the *Palais de Dance*. This was, after all, the city known to other Britons only because of the success of the *Saturday Night and Sunday Morning* opus written by Alan Sillitoe in 1958.

As the world changed, Nottingham Forest FC withstood all suggestions that they should drop tradition and move with the times. While every other Football League club was run by a board of directors (and most were owned by a Chairman who was the richest, most egotistical man in town), Forest remained in the control of a committee elected by its 250 members. And every time the players trotted out of the City Ground tunnel for a home match, the Tannoy blared:

> *Robin Hood, Robin Hood*
> *Riding through the glen.*
> *Robin Hood, Robin Hood*
> *With his band of men.*
> *Feared by the bad*
> *Loved by the good*
> *Robin Hood, Robin Hood, Robin Hood…*

And then came Brian Clough to transform this modest, under-achieving city – never mind a football club – almost at a stroke and to bring undreamed-of fame to a bunch of footballers who had every right to believe fortune had passed them by.

Not that even the successful footballers dreamt of becoming tycoons in the 1970s. Pub licensees? Yes. Mansion owners? Never! Paying-off the mortgage on a semi-detached equalled life-long security. Their wages had been restricted to £30 a week until the previous decade.

Agents had yet to consider getting their feet in the door of football grounds, preferring to concentrate on easing 10% from the somewhat more laden bank balances of whichever pop group was flavour of the week. They were astute enough to know that football managers were waiting to give them a hard time when they did move in.

Clough, for example, asked a player who wanted an agent involved in discussions in the early 1980s: "How much do you pay him?"

"Ten per cent," replied the player.

"OK," Clough conceded. "He can listen to one word in 10 of our conversation."

The negotiations with the player came to nought. Clough concluded: "If he can't make his mind up whether to play for me, how's he going to decide when to win the ball, who to pass it to, whether to head it?"

So by and large, the players were happy to take what was offered by any manager good enough to let them pursue their sporting dream.

Sponsors? Well, stars such as Johnny Haynes (a Fulham midfield international who became the English game's first £100 a week player) and, before him, Tommy Lawton (the only striker to average a goal a game for England) picked up a few bob from advertisements urging men to grease their hair with Brylcreem.

Sponsored cars? In the 1950s when the ball itself was genuine leather and not waterproof so that it became as heavy as lead, Lawton was happy to travel from Notts County's home matches at Meadow Lane on the trolley buses to his home in the leafy suburb of Sherwood because "the fans could tell me how I'd played in the second half; I had no idea because I was suffering from concussion from heading the ball and the centre half's elbows in the first half." This from the most famous header of a football of all time.

Besides, playing football for 90 minutes (no substitutes were allowed in those days) was thirsty work so a pint or two with the Forest fans in the Jubilee Club after a home match (especially a win) was preferable to driving home to the missus even when the Ford Cortina was the height of luxury in the 1970s.

It truly was a man's game. The supporters tended to work on the production lines (Nottingham's alphabet, remember, began Aspirin, Bikes, Cigarettes) from Monday to Friday and until noon on Saturday, and then drifted down to the match via one or two of the pubs along the way to the ground. At the City Ground or Meadow Lane, the fan would stand on concrete terraces, trusting that the man fidgeting next to him would make it to the urinal at half-time before those two pints began to reappear. The Jubilee Club at the City Ground – so-named because it was modernised at the time of Queen Elizabeth II's Silver Jubilee in 1977 – was vital for the after-match pints in the days when pubs were closed from 2.30pm to 6pm.

The post-match drink was generally needed to drown sorrows. When Clough took charge of his first match on 6 January 1975, Forest were languishing sixth from bottom of the old Second Division and facing two fears: one, that they would be relegated; two, that they would finish below County.

This being under-achieving Nottingham, the cynical (though thankfully minority) fear was that Forest had got a man to help them on the way down. Clough had reached the heights westward along the A52 at Derby County. He had taken them up from the Second Division, won the League Championship in 1971-72 and been eliminated from the following year's European Cup at the semi-final stage only by some strange refereeing decisions. Indeed, Clough went to his grave insisting his Rams had been "cheated" by refereeing decisions in the semi-final against Juventus – a unique situation because, out-spoken though he was on all other aspects of his game, he maintained throughout his career that the match officials were always right ... especially when they had been wrong. His reason was simple: "We face eleven opponents every time we step onto the pitch.

There's no point in goading the referee to become our 12th opponent. Not that any of them help us for making their lives that little bit easier."

Thereafter, though, the master manager with a reputation for having a motor-mouth went into self-destruct mode. He argued so severely with the Derby County Chairman Sam Longson – a dangerous thing to do in the era when self-made men like Longson owned the clubs they chaired – that he found himself managing Third Division[1] Brighton and Hove Albion. Some critics considered this to be an incongruous seaside retirement home for an out-spoken Teessider endlessly proud of his Yorkshire roots; and so it proved.

He could not resist an invitation to leave Taylor on the South Coast and succeed his arch-enemy Don Revie as Manager of Leeds United. He marched into Elland Road determined to change the philosophies of a dozen or more tough cookies who had won most of the baubles on offer but had failed at the final hurdle more often than any other club in history. Clough lasted just 44 days. His biggest victory was to emerge with a pay-off of £100,000 which (a) tells everything there is to reveal about the low level of football rewards at the time and (b) was sensibly invested so that he, his loyal, patient and loving wife Barbara and their three children, Simon, Nigel and Elizabeth had a secure future, no matter what.

So he arrived at the City Ground with a reputation as a hard drinker who had imploded in two of his previous three jobs – just the man for a club like Forest accustomed to yo-yoing between the First and Third tiers of the Football League. It was like throwing an anchor through a sinking ship in the view of the masochists who spent good money watching their team under-achieve.

What Nottingham folk did not instantly spot was that Clough was far from "shot" (to use one of his favourite words to describe anyone past their best). On the contrary, this invariably contrary man was re-energised. It was as if he was starting his managerial life all over again. And he persuaded Peter Taylor to once again become his faithful assistant. Taylor had been goalkeeper at Middlesbrough when Clough was centre forward. When Clough launched his managerial career at Hartlepool United, the first thing he did was ask Taylor to become his assistant. They got on so well that they moved to Derby together and transformed both club and city. Now Taylor was back in the city in which he was born; Clough was defiantly fired-up by his string of disappointments; and they made miracles look so simple …

Clough's questions about prospective signings were basic:

- Can he win a ball (i.e., tackle)?
- Can he trap a ball (i.e., control it)?
- Can he pass a ball (i.e., keep it for his team)?
- Can he head a ball (i.e., dominate his immediate opponent)?

---

[1] The Third Division in which Brighton played at the time is now called League One.

If the answers were 'Yes', Clough took it for granted that he would teach even the wildest, most spoilt brat how to "live properly" with the help of his coaching staff, who frequently worked overtime as spies in a range of temptations such as nightclubs and greyhound stadia; and he would then give Taylor the task of finding players whose specific skills would be capable of improving the jigsaw that was his template for a team.

Clough always knew exactly how he wanted each player in his team to perform – "in an open, attacking way that will put a smile on supporters' faces". It was such a fluid and free-flowing 4-4-2 format that it frequently became 4-3-3 and, during spells of special magic, 4-2-4. In a nutshell, every team Clough ever selected was expected to perform like this...

1 **Goalkeeper**: Strong and vocal enough to dominate 6-yard area; agile enough to be top shot-stopper; sensible enough to distribute ball to team-mate.			
2 **Right back**: swift as rival winger; good timer of tackles; constructive passer.	5 **Centre half**: strong in the air; stronger on ground; always up for battle.	6 **Sweeper**: physically equal to 5; able to anticipate danger and cope.	3 **Left back**: swift as rival winger; good timer of tackles; constructive passer.
7 **Right winger**: speed, close control; accurate crosser; mobility length of pitch	4 **Midfielder**: disrupt opposition; win the ball; find a team-mate.	8 **Midfielder**: use the ball won by 4; move forward; pass ball again.	11 **Left winger**: stretch opposition; hold ball from, say, 8; feed 9 and/or 10.
9 **Centre Forward**: be stronger, more mobile than opponent; be first to near post for crosses; never shoot wildly and give ball away.		10 **Striker**: use speed and mobility to open-up opposition; be first to far post for crosses; never tire – it only takes a second to score.	

Taylor was so instinctively adept at recognising which player would fit each specific slot in the Clough team jigsaw that, between them, they fashioned squads that scraped promotion from the Second Division almost by a fluke in 1976-77 and then immediately ran away with the First Division Championship in 1977-78 (wresting the League Cup from the European Champions almost as an aside along the way). Little wonder the supporters couldn't believe their luck!

The 1977 promotion came about because Bolton Wanderers lost their last two matches of the season, presenting Forest with third place in the final table. The success took them so much by surprise that Clough and Taylor were on family holidays in Spain by the time Bolton lost their last match; and Forest's celebratory sheet of heroes' autographs looked like this...

Note the simplicity of it all, compared with the tendency of clubs these days to celebrate beginning each season out of bankruptcy by producing a fresh replica kit for supporters to pay through the noses for. This is a basic A4 sheet of paper with the club's letterhead changed on a manual typewriter because the Information Line has a new telephone number. Oh, and the typist has helpfully printed the appropriate name under each autograph in case a player's hand-writing is illegible.

This is the 1976-77 Second Division table that brought about the autograph souvenir:

Pos	P	W	D	L	F	A	Pts
1 Wolverhampton W	42	22	13	7	84	45	57
2 Chelsea	42	21	13	8	73	53	55
3 Nottingham Forest	42	21	10	11	77	43	52
4 Bolton Wanderers	42	20	11	11	75	54	51
5 Blackpool	42	17	17	8	58	42	51
6 Luton Town	42	21	6	15	67	48	48
7 Charlton Athletic	42	16	16	10	71	58	48
8 Notts County	42	19	10	13	65	60	48
9 Southampton	42	17	10	15	72	67	44
10 Millwall	42	15	13	14	57	53	43
11 Sheffield United	42	14	12	16	54	63	40
12 Blackburn Rovers	42	15	9	18	42	54	39
13 Oldham Athletic	42	14	10	18	52	64	38
14 Hull City	42	10	17	15	45	53	37
15 Bristol Rovers	42	12	13	17	53	68	37
16 Burnley	42	11	14	17	46	64	36
17 Fulham	42	11	13	18	54	61	35
18 Cardiff City	42	12	10	20	56	67	34
19 Orient	42	9	16	17	37	55	34
20 Carlisle United	42	11	12	19	49	75	34
21 Plymouth Argyle	42	8	16	18	46	65	32
22 Hereford United	42	8	15	19	57	78	31

And this is what the players had contributed to promotion and the Anglo-Scottish Cup triumph that Clough always hailed as the trigger for Forest's trophy-winning spell (in the order in which their autographs were pasted onto the souvenir):

John McGovern led the team in 39 League matches, seven Anglo-Scottish ties, two FA Cup ties and two League Cup ties without scoring a goal but breaking-up innumerable attacks by the opposition.

Ian Bowyer was the second-highest scorer in the promotion drive with 12 goals in 41 matches. He also contributed fully to the Anglo-Scottish Cup triumph with nine appearances (and a goal).

Terry Curran was the fleet-footed right winger in only 13 League matches yet scored six times and also rattled in four goals (including a penalty) in five Anglo-Scottish ties.

John Middleton earned England Under 21 honours while keeping goal in 49 matches through the season, 38 of them in the League.

Martin O'Neill contributed 11 goals from various parts of midfield in 38 League matches and a couple of League Cup ties; and also figured in six Anglo-Scottish ties.

John Robertson racked-up 57 appearances on the left wing; not bad for a chubby lad who wasn't the hardest trainer on the books. Of his 11 goals, five were penalties and most of the others rocket-like free-kicks.

Viv Anderson played in 35 League games (and was a substitute in another three), all five FA Cup ties and all six Anglo-Scottish Cup ties.

Frank Clark carried his old legs through all 42 League games and 14 Cup ties: seven in the Anglo-Scottish, five in the League Cup and two in the FA Cup.

Colin Barrett scored five goals in 17 starts – 10 League matches, five Anglo-Scottish Cup ties and two League Cup matches – not bad for a full back.

Kenny Burns signed for Forest after promotion was confirmed. He replaced a local hero, Sammy Chapman, who had toiled for years in the centre of defence, finishing with 31 League matches and six Anglo-Scottish ties at the heart (and as the heart) of the Forest defence.

Tony Woodcock scored 11 goals in 30 League appearances as the second striker once he had taken over from Barry Butlin (who had scored three times in 10 matches).

Larry Lloyd was signed in time to figure in 26 League games and three Anglo-Scottish ties, contributing four goals as well as his brick wall defence.

Peter Withe did what the Centre Forward should do and led the scoring chart: 16 goals in 33 League starts was a fine ratio in the context of the way the game was played – though Forest were a much more attacking-minded team than most.

Sean Haslegrave made only five League appearances but figured in midfield in six Anglo-Scottish ties.

Garry Birtles' contribution – one appearance on the wing – was so insignificant that even his Christian name was spelt wrong.

There is one more hero whose autograph did not appear on that modest souvenir but whose contributions were pivotal to the successes: the increasingly versatile John O'Hare played in 19 League matches and six Anglo-Scottish ties.

3

League Champions at the first attempt

· ·

ADOPTING TACTICS that could have come straight out of the industrial anarchy handbook, English football reigned supreme. It was not always pretty. To be honest, some of it was as ugly as the battles between strikers and police in real life, not to mention the rucks between rival gangs of supporters on trains and the ritual taunting between supporters and police on the roads to and from matches.

It seemed as if the top clubs from mainland Europe had the artistic players. Ours had the enforcers. No defence worked without a "hard man" … Norman "Bite yer legs" Hunter at Leeds; Tommy "the tank" Smith at Liverpool; Ron "Chopper" Harris at Chelsea. Tackling from behind was as common as attempting to cut a goalkeeper in half as he leapt to catch a high cross; after all, forwards who were faster than defenders had to be challenged somehow … stopped anyhow. No striker had a chance of surviving if he showed pain; diving was acceptable only in the communal bath after a bloody, hard-fought win.

So while Liverpool were winning the European Cup finals of 1977 (3-1 against West German champions Borussia Moenchengladbach in Rome's Olympic Stadium with Tommy the tank Smith scoring one of the goals) and 1978 (1-0 v the Belgian underdogs of FC Bruges at Wembley with a skilful chip by Kenny Dalglish), Clough and Taylor were honing a Forest squad to prove their successes at Derby County had been no fluke.

When Clough arrived at the City Ground, Anderson, O'Neill, Bowyer, Woodcock and Robertson were already there. Clough and Taylor were to help all five become European Cup-winners. But first Clough had to persuade O'Neill and Robertson to withdraw transfer requests they had made before his arrival. They were far from the last arguments he won. He frequently said that, when faced with a player who disagreed with him, "I listen to what he has to say and then we decide that I was right all along."

**Brian Clough with the League Championship trophy
and League Cup that Forest won in 1977-78.**

Anderson, born on 29 August 1956, the right back reared on the massive Clifton estate half-a-mile up-stream from the ground and nicknamed 'Spider' because his lean legs seemed to be telescopic when he swooped into a tackle, went on to become the first black player to play for England and won 30 caps.

O'Neill, born on 1 March 1952, a law graduate who cost £27,000 from Derry City, became Forest's vibrant right winger, formed a formidable and fast partnership with

Anderson, and played for Northern Ireland 64 times. He went on to become by far the most successful Manager among former Clough players, working his way up from Grantham Town in non-League through Wycombe Wanderers and Leicester City to Aston Villa where, as recently as February 2010, he rallied his team for the Carling Cup Final against Manchester United by using a Clough phrase: "The best trophy you'll ever win is your first one." Alas, United won 2-1.

Bowyer, born on 6 June 1951 on Merseyside, had moved down the Divisions from Manchester City to Leyton Orient in 1971, but was sufficiently impressive as an attacking midfielder for the then Forest manager Allan Brown to fork out £40,000 for him two years later. Bowyer repaid the fee time and again during two spells as a player (spanning 419 games) and another on the coaching staff at the City Ground.

Woodcock, born at Eastwood towards the Derbyshire border on 6 December 1955, was sent out by Clough on loan to Lincoln City and Mansfield Town to learn his scoring trade; and did so with such success that he went on to score 36 in 129 games for Forest, 16 in 42 England internationals, 39 in 130 in two spells in Germany with Cologne and 56 in 131 back in the First Division with the Arsenal before becoming a respected coach in Germany.

Robertson, born on 20 January 1953, an apprentice at Forest from the age of 17, was transformed from a midfielder into a left winger and set-piece specialist by Clough and won 28 Scotland caps. He then went into management as assistant to O'Neill with great success.

Clough's first additions to the squad, not surprisingly, were Jimmy Gordon, the coach who had served him at Derby and Leeds plus two players he knew equally well.

John McGovern, born on 28 October 1949, had played under him at Hartlepool United, Derby County and during his 44 days at Leeds United. At the City Ground, he instantly became "The Captain", as Clough called his on-field mouthpiece. Yet to many opposing teams, he was the frail-looking figure they hardly noticed as he pottered about, repeatedly nicking the ball in midfield and off-loading it to someone who could use it for the benefit of the team.

John O'Hare, another Scot, born on 24 September 1946, had scored 65 goals in 258 League games for Clough at Derby and another one in seven Leeds matches. Now he was to become a loyal and lethal super-substitute.

Then came 'the old Mr. Reliable', Frank Clark, a left back born on 9 September 1943. Newcastle United thought he was over the footballing hill when they gave him away in 1975. He went on to play 155 times for Forest (and even received the kiss of death when Clough insisted he be the club's next manager – but that's another story). Early on in his unexpected Forest career, Clark was vying for the No.3 shirt with Colin Barrett, born on 3 August 1952 in Stockport, a versatile and immensely mobile defender signed from Manchester City for £30,000 in 1976.

In July 1975, Peter Taylor had resigned as manager of Brighton and Hove Albion to reunite with Clough as assistant manager of Forest. Within a year there were two gambles of the kind that set Clough and Taylor apart from their contemporaries: the signings of Larry Lloyd from Liverpool and Kenny Burns from Birmingham City to pair-up as centre halves. Both were playing reserve team football when Taylor persuaded Clough that their enormous talents could be harnessed.

Lloyd, born on 6 October 1948, cost Forest a meagre £60,000 after losing his Liverpool place to Phil Thompson. He was to pay almost as much in fines – if club folklore is to be believed – in a row with the Gaffer over his failure to wear the club blazer after Forest's 1979 European Cup win. His refusal to bow down to Clough in that argument was typical of this battering-ram whose style explained why defenders were called markers. Big Larry left his mark on every striker.

Burns, born on 23 September 1953, moved from Birmingham for £150,000 with a reputation as a versatile player – striker or central defender – with a wild streak on and off the field. He was tamed to such an extent that he was voted the Football Writers' Association Player of the Year during Forest's League Championship season – much to the chagrin of Lloyd, who was prone to complain: "I take the knocks for making the challenges. He takes the honours for tidying up." Burns had won the first of his 20 Scottish caps as a striker while with Birmingham, but thrived on being Clough's No.1 stopper – a glowing example of The Gaffer making things simple even for his most talented players. Needless to say, Clough also harnessed his image as a 'wild man' in such a way that Burns never attracted adverse publicity while at the City Ground yet was never known to shirk a tough tackle, either.

To supplement their muscle, David Needham was signed from Queen's Park Rangers just before Christmas of 1977. Born in Leicestershire on 21 May 1949, he had begun his career as a Notts County apprentice and spent 11 years at Meadow Lane before moving to QPR in the summer of 1977 for £90,000. Six months later, Clough paid £150,000 for him – and he joined the unlikely squad that earned honours beyond its dreams.

Behind them, John Middleton seemed to have the world at his feet as the England Under 21 goalkeeper as season 1977-78 began with him the Forest No.1 for their first five matches. But Clough had his doubts and made his unexpected world record £270,000 swoop for the finished product, Peter Shilton, who was to make a record 125 appearances for England. The instant up-shot: Forest conceded only 24 goals in the 42 games of their Championship season.

Next came Archie Gemmill, who was already well aware of Clough's Canadian Mountie-like ability to get his man. Born on 24 March 1947 in Scotland (for whom he was to play 43 internationals between 1971 and 1981), Gemmill was playing for Preston North End in 1970 and contemplating a move to First Division Everton when Clough/Taylor decided they could fit his busy passing style into Derby's jigsaw. There was no room for agents and prolonged transfer negotiations between clubs' chief executives in those days. Clough drove to Gemmill's house to make an offer that the ambitious Scotsman refused, knowing Everton's pedigree and potential was immeasurably better than Derby's. So Clough announced he would sleep in his car outside their front door and ask him again next morning. "But my wife invited him and he stayed the night," Gemmill recalled. After manager and player shared a fried breakfast the following morning, Clough got his man for £60,000. After 261 games for Derby, Gemmill came even cheaper to Forest in September 1977: £25,000. His job during 58 appearances was to make good use of the ball that been won by the defenders or McGovern.

Strangely considering what a prolific striker he had been, Clough never had a really settled scoring spearhead in his Forest team. Peter Withe, born in Liverpool on 30 August 1951, was signed from Birmingham City for £40,000 in 1976 and was Forest's leading scorer with 19 goals in the 1977-78 season when they succeeded his native city club as League Champions and League Cup holders.

The Cup came first… This the route to Forest's 1977-78 League Cup triumph:

Date	Opposition	Venue	F	A	Scorers
30 Aug	West Ham United	Home	5	0	Withe, Bowyer 2, O'Neill, Woodcock
25 Oct	Notts County	Home	4	0	Bowyer 2, Woodcock, Robertson pen.
29 Nov	Aston Villa	Home	4	2	Withe, Woodcock, Anderson, Lloyd
17 Jan	Bury	Away	3	0	Robertson, Bowyer, O'Neill
8 Feb	Leeds United	Away	3	1	Withe 2, O'Hare
22 Feb	Leeds United	Home	4	2	Withe, Woodcock, Bowyer, O'Neill
18 Mar	Liverpool	Wembley	0	0	
22 Mar	Liverpool	Old Trafford	1	0	Robertson pen.

Appearances: 8 – Viv Anderson, Kenny Burns, Martin O'Neill, Ian Bowyer, Peter Withe, Tony Woodcock, John Robertson. 7 – Chris Woods, John McGovern. 6 – Larry Lloyd. 5 – Colin Barrett. 4 – Frank Clark. 3 – John O'Hare. 1 – John Middleton.

And then the major prize was secured. This was Forest's run to the 1977-78 League title, known at the time as the First Division Championship:

Date	Opposition	Venue	F	A	Scorers
20 Aug	Everton	Away	3	1	Withe, Robertson, O'Neill
23 Aug	Bristol City	Home	1	0	Withe
27 Aug	Derby County	Home	3	0	Withe 2, Robertson
3 Sep	Arsenal	Away	0	3	
10 Sep	Wolves	Away	3	2	Withe, Bowyer, Woodcock
17 Sep	Aston Villa	Home	2	0	Woodcock, Robertson
24 Sep	Leicester City	Away	3	0	O'Neill, Woodcock, Robertson pen.
1 Oct	Norwich City	Home	1	1	Burns

4 Oct	Ipswich Town	Home	4	0	Withe 4
8 Oct	West Ham United	Away	0	0	
15 Oct	Manchester City	Home	2	1	Woodcock, Withe
22 Oct	QPR	Away	2	0	Bowyer, Burns
29 Oct	Middlesbrough	Home	4	0	Anderson 2, Bowyer, McGovern
5 Nov	Chelsea	Away	0	1	
12 Nov	Manchester United	Home	2	1	Burns, Gemmill
19 Nov	Leeds United	Away	0	1	
26 Nov	West Bromwich Alb	Home	0	0	
3 Dec	Birmingham City	Away	2	0	O'Neill, Woodcock
10 Dec	Coventry City	Home	2	1	O'Neill, McGovern
17 Dec	Manchester United	Away	4	0	Greenhoff og, Woodcock 2, Robertson
26 Dec	Liverpool	Home	1	1	Gemmill
28 Dec	Newcastle United	Away	2	0	McGovern, Needham
31 Dec	Bristol City	Away	3	1	Needham, Woodcock, O'Neill
2 Jan	Everton	Home	1	1	Robertson pen.
14 Jan	Derby County	Away	0	0	
21 Jan	Arsenal	Home	2	0	Needham, Gemmill
4 Feb	Wolves	Home	2	0	Woodcock, McGovern
25 Feb	Norwich City	Away	3	3	Withe, Barrett, O'Neill
4 Mar	West Ham United	Home	2	0	Needham, Robertson pen.
14 Mar	Leicester City	Home	1	0	Robertson pen.
25 Mar	Newcastle United	Home	2	0	Robertson pen., Anderson
29 Mar	Middlesbrough	Away	2	2	Woodcock, O'Neill
1 Apl	Chelsea	Home	3	1	Burns, O'Neill, Robertson
5 Apl	Aston Villa	Away	1	0	Woodcock
11 Apl	Manchester City	Away	0	0	
15 Apl	Leeds United	Home	1	1	Withe
18 Apl	QPR	Home	1	0	Robertson pen
22 Apl	Coventry City	Away	0	0	
25 Apl	Ipswich Town	Away	2	0	Clark, own goal
29 Apl	Birmingham City	Home	0	0	
2 May	West Bromwich Alb	Away	2	2	Bowyer, Robertson pen.
4 May	Liverpool	Away	0	0	

Forest hit the top of the table with their 4-0 home win over Ipswich on 4 October, were five points clear by the turn of the year and were never seriously threatened. As Clough said: "We bombed it for as long as we could and when we were knackered we just held on." Simple as that, eh!

Hello, old friend! Clough and Taylor reunited with the Football League Championship Trophy they had also won at Derby. By coincidence, Clough's chosen successor, Frank Clark, smiles between trophy and Taylor.

Clough made his philosophy even simpler for his players: "This is the ball. Keep it. Play with it. Treasure it. Look after it. If you do, it will come back to you. The most you ever do is lend it to somebody else." To emphasise the importance of possession, he would readily fine players who gave the ball away by, for example, shooting from long range and either having the ball saved or conceding a goalkick.

And when he was about to make a signing on the recommendation of one of his staff, the questions would always be the same: "Can he win a ball? Can he pass a ball? Can he trap a ball?"

This was the 1977-78 First Division final table that stunned the football world:

Pos.		P	W	D	L	F	A	Pts
1	Nottingham Forest	42	25	14	3	69	24	64
2	Liverpool	42	24	9	9	65	34	57
3	Everton	42	22	11	9	76	45	55
4	Manchester City	42	20	12	10	74	51	52
5	Arsenal	42	21	10	11	60	37	52
6	West Bromwich Albion	42	18	14	10	62	53	50
7	Coventry City	42	18	12	12	75	62	48
8	Aston Villa	42	18	10	14	57	42	46
9	Leeds United	42	18	10	14	63	53	46
10	Manchester United	42	16	10	16	67	63	42
11	Birmingham City	42	16	9	17	55	60	41
12	Derby County	42	14	13	15	54	59	41
13	Norwich City	42	11	18	13	52	66	40
14	Middlesbrough	42	12	15	15	42	54	39
15	Wolverhampton W	42	12	12	18	51	64	36
16	Chelsea	42	11	14	17	46	69	36
17	Bristol City	42	11	13	18	49	53	35
18	Ipswich Town	42	11	13	18	47	61	35
19	Queens Park Rangers	42	9	15	18	47	64	33
20	West Ham United	42	12	8	22	52	69	32
21	Newcastle United	42	6	10	26	42	78	22
22	Leicester City	42	5	12	25	26	70	22

Appearances in the run to the League title: 42 – John Robertson. 41 – Kenny Burns. 40 – Peter Withe. 38 – Martin O'Neill. 37 – Viv Anderson, Peter Shilton. 36 – Tony Woodcock. 31 – Colin Barrett, John McGovern. 30 – Archie Gemmill. 26 – Larry Lloyd. 25 – Ian Bowyer. 16 – David Needham. 12 – Frank Clark. 10 – John O'Hare. 5 – John Middleton.

League scorers: 12 each – Withe, Robertson (including 6 penalties). 11 – Woodcock. 8 – O'Neill. 4 each – Bowyer, Burns, McGovern, Needham. 3 each – Anderson, Gemmill. 1 each –Barrett, Clark.

4

Forest will be out of Europe before anybody notices

• •

IT WAS all too much for even the Forest faithful to take in, accustomed as they were to yo-yoing twixt Divisions One to Three. So much too much that when Forest were drawn to meet holders Liverpool in the first round of the 1978-79 European Cup, almost half of the advertisers tried to back out of a celebratory supplement I was working on called *Forest into Europe*.

"They'll be eliminated before anyone notices they're in," said one motor dealer, whom I had got to know well during my previous incarnation as *Post* Motoring Correspondent. He was not being destructive, you understand; merely articulating the consensus of those who had been hoping to thrive on the back of the club's success.

"Shall we scrap it?" asked the *Post's* Advertisement Manager, Lenny Simmons, who was on such a successful roll personally that he eventually became TBF's Chief Executive (after the departure to London of PC and the retirement of his surprise successor, Charlie Wright, who had been the Chief Electrician responsible for wiring-in all the computer terminals; hardly the pedigree expected of a man set to head a business financed by advertising acumen and dependent on quality journalism, one might think. But Charlie was always ready to cheerfully explain: "They've got to keep me happy cos I'm the only one who knows where your computers plug-in.").

"Well, first let's tell the reluctant advertisers we'll have to explain to Mr. Clough that we've had to drop the venture because certain businesses have got no confidence in him and his team; and he'll want to know which ones," I suggested.

Blackmail? All's fair in newspaper advertising! There was no way I could have explained anything to Mr. Clough. He had no idea I existed as Sports Editor-in-waiting as he holidayed in Spain during the summer of 1978 with his family plus sundry friends and hangers-on. But the wavering advertisers did not know that; and enough of them blanched at the prospect of an ear-bashing from Motor-mouth for the supplement – 48 tabloid pages, in glorious colour (the most spectacular in the history of the newspaper) – to survive by the skin of its commercial teeth.

Here's the front cover, with Clough, utterly refreshed by his winter successes and summer holiday, superimposed on a crowd scene from the 1978 League Cup Final at Wembley...

The discerning reader will notice Clough is not wearing either his trademark green jersey or a Forest tracksuit top for the picture. The sartorially-minded will further realise that his choice of attire is not a design one would readily associate with him. This is because he did not really want to cooperate with this project (and not just because he and PC were at an uneasy truce in their Battle of Ideologies). He realised the supplement was little more than a money-spinner and he was not going to get a share. But he felt obliged to help the *Post's* Forest correspondent John Lawson, whom he trusted like no other journalist in the world and so gave him a few words plus the somewhat bizarre photo opportunity.

And what successes both the paper and the club enjoyed despite the political rivalry! Forest saw-off Liverpool in two epic first round ties and went on to make history in several ways when they defeated Malmo 1-0 in the 1979 European Cup Final (and retained the League Cup that they had also wrested from Liverpool). Their successes were infectious. These are the triumphs Nottingham savoured – and the increasingly incredulous *Evening Post* sports team covered – in the next few frantic, fabulous years as the city's rugby union club and Mansfield Town joined the glory, glory parade…

1979: Forest retained the League Cup with a thrilling 3-2 victory at Wembley over Southampton to follow their 1-0 success over Liverpool in the Final replay 12 months earlier. Forest achieved the ultimate prize – the European Cup – with a 1-0 victory over Malmo in the Final in Munich.

1980: Forest defeated Cup-Winners Cup holders Barcelona 2-1 on aggregate to win the UEFA Super Cup – and then returned to Spain to retain the European Cup, defeating Hamburg 1-0 in Madrid. Peter Shilton was named the Professional Footballers' Association (PFA) Player of the Year for his successes with Forest. Nottinghamshire CCC's Derek Randall was named a Wisden Cricketer of the Year. Nottingham Panthers ice hockey club was reborn – and instantly packed the Ice Stadium on Saturday evenings.

1981: Notts County won promotion to the First Division, completing an amazing journey from the Fourth Division under the same chairman, Jack Dunnett MP, the same team captain, Don Masson, the same trainer, Jack Wheeler – and the same manager, Jimmy Sirrel. Nottinghamshire CCC won the County Championship for the first time since 1929 and their captain, Clive Rice, was named a Wisden Cricketer of the Year. Jayne Torvill and Christopher Dean won the first of their four ice dance titles at World Championships, in Hartford, Connecticut, USA.

1982: Richard Hadlee completed a hat-trick of Wisden Cricketer of the Year accolades for Notts even though the county imploded in the Benson & Hedges Cup Final at Lord's, losing by nine wickets to Somerset. Torvill and Dean skated to their second World Championships gold medals in Copenhagen.

1983: Forest were robbed of a UEFA Cup Final spot by some awful refereeing decisions in their semi-final against Anderlecht in Belgium. Torvill and Dean completed their World Championships hat-trick in Helsinki.

1984: Torvill and Dean set ice dance history by scoring a perfect 6 from every judge in the free dance section at the Winter Olympics in Sarajevo, Yugoslavia. Nottingham RFC, who had produced only one England international in their first 50 years, celebrated the first of flanker Gary Rees's 23 caps, little dreaming five of his colleagues would follow him into the Five Nations Championship before the end of the decade.

1985: Notts CCC reached the NatWest Trophy Final but lost by one run to Essex even though Randall smashed 16 from the last over. Nottingham RFC fly half Rob Andrew made his England debut.

1986: Tim Robinson, being groomed as Rice's successor at Trent Bridge, batted so well for England that he became the fourth Notts player this decade to win a Wisden Cricketer of the Year Award.

1987: Nottingham RFC hooker Brian Moore made his England debut. Notts completed a cricket double, winning the County Championship for the second time in seven summers and defeating Northamptonshire by three wickets in the NatWest Trophy Final. Nottingham Panthers made their first contribution to the city's silverware, winning ice hockey's Autumn Cup, a feat the club repeated four times between 1992 and 1999.

1988: Forest reached the FA Cup semi-finals, but went down 1-0 to Liverpool (who were sensationally defeated by the same score by Wimbledon in the Final). Nottingham RFC's Chris Oti made his England debut.

1989: Forest achieved a unique Wembley 'double', defeating holders Luton Town 3-1 in the Littlewoods League Cup Final and Everton 4-3 in an epic Simod Cup Final. In between came the Hillsborough Disaster to put a whole new perspective on football and Forest lost 3-1 to Liverpool in the replayed semi-final at Old Trafford. Notts CCC won the Benson & Hedges Cup, defeating Essex by three wickets in the Final. Brian Moore became the first-ever Nottingham rugby player to earn a place in a British Lions touring party. Nottingham RFC full back Simon Hodgkinson made his debut for England; his club-mate Chris Gray, a lamp-post sized line-out specialist burst into the Scotland XV.

1990: Forest retained the League Cup with a 1-0 win over Oldham Athletic in the Final – and collected the League's Fair Play Award, a significant achievement at a time when football appeared to be descending into anarchy on and off the field.

1991: Forest suffered agony in the FA Cup Final, a 2-1 defeat by Tottenham Hotspur. Most neutrals remembered the match for an horrific knee injury to Paul Gascoigne, the Spurs and England midfielder, that put him out of action for a full year at a time when he was poised to move to Lazio in Italy. Few recalled that Gascoigne sustained his injury fouling a Forest player, Gary Charles, so recklessly that, in any other game than an FA Cup Final, he would have been sent off. As it was, Spurs were allowed to send on a substitute and triumph in extra time, meaning that the FA Cup remained the only major trophy to elude Clough. It was little consolation a few months later when Nottinghamshire won cricket's Sunday League for the first (and only) time.

1992: Forest tasted more glory at Wembley, defeating Southampton 3-2 in the Zenith Data Systems Cup Final.

There was, however, at Christmas 1978 a massive dark cloud over my elevation from the Features Department to my dream job as Sports Editor. The *Evening Post* was embarking on the latest (and, as it transpired, the last) massive confrontation with the massed militant forces of the Trades Union movement in the uncompromising campaign master-minded by its Manager Director, Christopher Pole-Carew, to modernise newspaper production globally.

The biggest battle had been won a few years earlier. The power of the print unions had been decimated during a strike that had lasted for months yet never stopped production of the *Evening Post* or its Saturday night little brother, the *Football Post*. Now, as 1978 drew to an end, the opportunity arose to rid the Forman Street fortress of the National Union of Journalists. A national strike began among weekly newspaper journalists. It was joined by 28 *Evening Post* reporters and sub editors. PC instantly dismissed them for breaking their contracts, arguing that the dispute was not theirs. They explained they were striking in sympathy with their union brothers. Mayhem was instant.

The back of the *Post's* 200-metre square building was adjacent to the Guildhall law courts and city police headquarters, meaning our defenders did not have far to travel to protect us against pickets who flocked from the length and breadth of the country. The ritual became almost as boring as it was frightening to those of us having to run the gauntlet of hate. The strikers would be allowed to mass in Forman Street, which contained the main entrances to the Victorian building that had been gutted and refitted to house all the requirements of a newspaper eager to meet the new challenges of regional television and local radio. It now became virtually our prison; and I was far from the only loyalist to the *Evening Post* cause to liken it to Colditz, the German castle made famous by the exploits of British prisoners in the Second World War.

The 15-foot high iron gates would be locked, padlocked and defended from within by a private army recruited by PC from we-knew-not-where. Suffice to say that they looked fit enough to put "Bite yer legs" Hunter and company in their places. And they proved they were one Saturday afternoon in particular when two flying pickets suddenly appeared in the Editorial Department, on the second floor of our supposedly secure building. They hardly had time to recognise that they were within a few strides of the hated computer terminals before whooping and hollering along the corridors heralded the arrival of PC's cavalry. In the next few seconds, I realised why night club defenders were called "bouncers". Our intruders were literally bounced down the stone steps of the spiral staircase from the Editorial Floor past the Production Floor past the Ground Floor down to the Basement and then back up to the Ground Floor, whence they were – er – helped through the gates to rejoin their mates. Complaints of brutality were, of course, thoroughly investigated by the police but no charges were preferred. As for the visit to the basement, PC explained that the intruders were unfamiliar with the lay-out of the building and were travelling down the stairs so quickly that initially they missed the Ground Floor exit.

PC's campaign would have more repercussions worldwide than even Clough's successes on playing fields, dragging newspapers kicking and screaming away from the traditions of restrictive practices into the technological world of computers. But that did not mean Clough was at all ready to accept the inevitable. Being a dedicated Socialist – he was being touted at the time to stand as the Labour candidate for Parliament in the Leicestershire constituency of Loughborough – Clough took understandable exception to this rampant capitalist in the midst of his fiefdom scything through over-staffing in the interests of bloated profits. And he made sure that the authorities at Meadow Lane and Trent Bridge took equally hostile stances against the *Evening Post*.

All of which meant that I had to stop dreaming about how I was about to fulfil a childhood ambition to be "a sports reporter" and grow accustomed instantly to the ruthless realities of our Winter of Discontent. Politicians and trades unions fell out to such an extent that power workers went on strike, causing long cuts in electricity supplies and forcing factories into part-time production. Dustmen joined in with the result that stinking refuse housed growing infestations of vermin in many streets. The mineworkers lent their mighty muscle to a variety of strikers, with the result that pitched battles between massed ranks of police and flying pickets were commonplace every time an individual – never mind a laden van – ventured through the gates.

5

Hello Young Man, you're barred

· ·

THE REPORT of my elevation to Sports Editor of the *Evening Post* and Editor of the *Football Post* appeared on Thursday 29 December 1978. It pretty much coincided with the arrival of protesting masses waving banners and chanting: "Reinstate the 28." Among the 28 journalists dismissed by the *Evening Post* were John Lawson, the Forest football and Notts cricket correspondent who hailed from the North-East and therefore spoke the same language as Clough, and Terry Bowles, the Notts County correspondent. He had built a good working relationship with the club's Chairman, Jack Dunnett, who in turn was the President of the Football League and, more pertinent to the political situation, the Labour MP for Nottingham Central and therefore honour-bound to support strikers in this ultra-politicised era.

Because the 28 had broken their contracts, they were summarily dismissed by PC even though he knew that this could result in walk-outs "in sympathy" by members of the other print unions that dominated the newspaper industry at the time. His gamble that he would still have enough staff to produce an *Evening Post* paid-off, by the skin of his teeth. But his pedigree as a pioneer of computerised newspaper production – meaning many fewer typesetters and compositors would be employed – made him a target of many militant trade union leaders, chief among them Arthur Scargill's miners.

So on Friday 30 December 1978, I drove through a picket line outside the fortified *Evening Post* offices in Forman Street, to my first meeting with Clough at the City Ground. It was arranged by the Vice-Chairman of Forest, Stuart Dryden, whose profession as manager of the Post Office in the nearby village of Ruddington was immeasurably out-weighed by his part in attracting the world's best goalkeeper of the era, Peter Shilton, into the Forest team that won the Championship in 1978. A month into the 1977-78 season,

Clough had phoned Dryden and asked him if he would be free to drive him that night. Knowing that several reserve teams were in action that night, Dryden duly arranged cover at the Post Office and headed off to collect Clough from his home before driving on across the Derbyshire Dales towards the M6. To his surprise, Clough directed him into Stoke-on-Trent rather than to a spying mission at an actual match. To his utter astonishment, he found himself agreeing a then world record fee for a goalkeeper, £250,000. Still in a state of shock, he then had the jobs of driving Clough home and explaining to the Club Chairman, a genial but generally feared barrister called Brian Appleby QC that he had just taken an arbitrary decision that no single member of the Forest Committee was entitled to take. I should explain that, at this time, Forest was the only one of the 92 League clubs to be run by a Committee, which was elected by annual democratic votes by its 250 paid-up Members. Appleby – and, I suspect, all of his colleagues – were pragmatic enough to realise that in reality Clough was running the club and they might as well enjoy the ride for as long as it contained more ups than downs.

So Dryden survived – and thrived as the link between Clough and Committee. Not an easy fence to sit upon, but his ready smile, easy-going nature and dedication to the club he had supported all his life meant his occasional interjections were respected by Clough.

So now, Dryden met me at the double doors as I entered the Forest office area for the first time. "Hope you've got your flak jacket on," he said as he ushered me through a door to the right of the entrance, past doors marked 'Manager' on the left and 'Secretary' on the right, on past Peter Taylor's office on the left and into the Chairman's Room on the right. There was nobody else in sight: it was as if all potential witnesses to the slaughter of the innocent had been spirited away. The appointment was for 11.30am. I was on time. "He'll be at training," said Dryden, offering me a cigarette that I took eagerly. We'd probably smoked a couple more before the door at the end of the corridor banged open and Clough appeared, preceded by his trademark squash racket but, unusually, not accompanied by any of his henchmen – notably assistant manager Peter Taylor nor even the quietest member of the backroom staff, first team trainer Jimmy Gordon, who was bald, permanently beaming and looked like every player's favourite grandfather.

I made sure to keep eye contact and smile as Dryden introduced us. Clough maintained the eye contact but most certainly did not smile as he said: "So you're the young man who's just sacked my best friend in journalism."

I laughed: "Christ, I'm not that important!"

He persisted: "But you've let it happen to one of your staff. Two of your staff, in fact, from what I've heard."

I held my fluttering nerve and the eye contact and kept my voice quietly even: "Not quite, Brian. John and Terry made it happen to themselves."

Quick as a flash, Dryden coughed on his John Player cigarette, suggesting: "Shall we sit down?" He slipped between us, ushering Clough round the coffee table in the centre of the room with his right arm, and shoving me towards the chair closest to the door with his left lever. It didn't occur to me at the time but it has done frequently since that Dryden probably reacted as a boxing referee would to protect an underdog from undue punishment.

I sank into the cold but comfortable leather. Clough stood, his racket swinging from one hand, his face and eyes inscrutable while Dryden poured us drinks: vodka for the Manager, Scotch and ginger for me.

"Cheers," I said, half-rising so my glass moved towards his. Clough ignored the salutation, even forsook the opportunity to sip his drink, preferring to ask: "So tell me why you're here at the time when I usually meet my friend, my trusted reporter friend Mr. Lawson to tell him what my team is for tomorrow's match."

Stubbing out my ciggie in one of the two ashtrays on the coffee table, I leaned back (a) to look as relaxed as I could in the most nerve-wracking situation of my life and (b) to be at the easiest angle to maintain eye contact with him as he stood over me with only an oblong coffee table between us. To be fair to him, he let me go on for probably 10 minutes about how the *Evening Post* was leading the newspaper world in the inevitability of computerisation saving the industry from suffocation by over-manning and multi-union regulation; and that his friend Mr. Lawson and Mr. Lawson's friend Mr. Bowles had both broken their legally-signed contracts by joining a strike that had nothing to do with evening newspaper journalists.

"But they work for a weekly newspaper called the *Football Post*," drawled Clough, his squash racket still swinging like a pendulum at about the height of my head.

"No, like the rest of us at T. Bailey Forman Limited they are employed to work on the *Evening Post*," I persisted.

"So they do their *Football Post* articles out of the goodness of their hearts?" Clough drawled.

"I think we all do, Brian – I certainly only get one wage," I said, risking a smile.

"But they won't get any wage next week," he responded. "Nothing to buy food for their wives and bairns."

"Not unless they work for it – you don't pay players not to work, do you?"

"It's not me who's sacked anybody," he shot back.

"Nor me," I persisted. "And I've got a wife and a couple of bairns at home who need feeding, too."

At last, he could resist his drink no longer. As he stooped to pick up his glass, I took the opportunity to add: "Look, I'm not a posh union-basher, Brian. My Dad works six and a half days a week on the railway as a platelayer. My Mum went pot-washing in the village pub to buy my school uniform when I passed my 11-plus. The only advice they gave me was, 'Work with your brain. Don't be a slave.' And that's why I'm convinced newspapers have got to modernise. As things stand, we can't print more than 48 pages a day. With computerisation, we'll be able to produce bigger papers, which means we'll make more from advertising, which means we'll afford more journalists …."

"But not my friend Mr. Lawson," he interjected, putting his empty glass back down on the table.

At no time was either of our voices raised above sparring level, but the mutual intransigence was not lost on Dryden: "I think we're going round in circles here."

"No Vice-Chairman, we're going," Clough said, gesturing towards me with his left arm (the one not holding his squash racket). I stood and he guided me back down the corridor.

With every step, I could feel his hand in the middle of my back, propelling me; and I was quite surprised when he said: "Don't take this personally, Trev. I think in any other circumstances me and you could have got on. Just remember all life's a game."

"Yes Brian, thanks, and you remember I'm playing to win as well," I said as we reached the double doors that led out into the car park.

"Good lad, now f*** off – you're barred," he said, without raising his voice, but adding emphasis by sticking the sole of his football boot against my backside to propel me outside. "And so are all your f***ing colleagues," he shouted – almost screamed – as the doors flapped back and forth and would-be autograph hunters wondered what on earth was going on.

Mustering as much dignity as I could, I marvelled at how his limb had retained its strength despite a knee injury ending his goal-scoring career cruelly prematurely, regained my balance and feigned indifference as I strolled to my company Ford Sierra and headed back to another foray through the picket-line to give the expected news to my besieged workmates.

Once I'd stopped shaking, I sat down to compose my first 'Editor's View' column for the *Football Post* – and set out to goad Clough into talking to me (even if it was more of a rant than I had been granted at our meeting). I wrote on the subject of 'money madness' in football…

> Consider the intriguing case of Nottingham Forest. For most of this season, manager Brian Clough and his talent-spotting assistant Peter Taylor have been ready to break the club's transfer record. They have failed thus far – and I emphasise *thus far* because they are rather like the Mounties in their pursuit of the men they want – because nobody seems to want their money.
>
> Wouldn't it be pleasant if Clough and Taylor decided to give a vote of confidence to the present squad of players and called off what seems to be an increasingly frantic, rather undignified, scramble for a new star?
>
> Don't the players deserve a show of confidence from the bosses in whom they have the utmost confidence? After all, those players have got Forest into the favourites' position in the European Cup and onto the edge of Wembley Way again in the League Cup, while overcoming terrible injury problems to stay on the verge of the League Championship race. Oh, and they did win the League Championship and League Cup together last season.

This is the golden opportunity for Clough and Taylor to emphasise to their critics – of whom there are still plenty – that their skills are, without question, more than chequebook deep.

Come Saturday night, I sat by my home phone confident I'd get a call, if only so that he could swear at me, remind me what he'd done at Derby, force me to apologise … My theory was that it would generate an atmosphere in which he felt in control, letting him realise that mine was a conciliatory stance amid a growing number of entrenched, embittered positions. It didn't. My ploy fell on stony ground. No call came.

But the Editor-in-Chief, Bill Snaith, had his plan: "Let's ignore Nottingham Forest. Give all the publicity to Notts County, to Nottingham Rugby Club, to Mansfield Town … to anyone but bloody Forest. Clough will soon come round. He needs publicity more than he needs his drink. It's his elixir of life."

Mr. Snaith, I should add, did not like anything or anyone to rock his boat. "Steady as you go" was a motto made for his conservative approach. His use of "bloody" as a swear word was dramatic evidence that all was not well in his world. "We've always done it this way" was his mantra; a concept at odds with my tendency to try to treat every new news day with a fresh approach. So not surprisingly he was the Editor who had considered me one of his most dangerous enemies a few years earlier when I had created such a good impression as Editor of the *Weekly Post* free newspaper that I had been promoted to the newly-created position of Editorial Assistant to the Managing Director, the revolutionary PC. This grand title meant that I got to drive a company car of my own (a Ford Cortina) in a colour of my choice (British Racing Green) but was little more than a messenger as PC pitched-up suggestions how to change the Editorial Department and Mr. Snaith stone-walled every one. It quickly became so tiresome that I craved a move back to the writing I loved.

Yet Mr. Snaith (for he was a member of the final generation of newspaper professionals to address even his biggest friends among the staff as Mr. …) had continued to treat me with suspicion when my love of writing had over-ridden my lust for power and I had jumped at a menial job in the Features Department, sub-editing features, testing cars and, in my spare time, joining forces with another cricket-mad journalist, John Lucy, to launch a club cricket news page in the *Post's* sister morning paper, the *Guardian Journal*.

So I had been stunned when Mr. Snaith offered me the Sports Editor's job. Indeed, when his demure secretary, a shapely little blonde called Mavis Brand, informed me I was required in The Editor's Office, my first instinct was to wonder what I had done seriously wrong … Had he rumbled that I was only test-driving cars so that I had a nice motor each weekend?

When he invited me to be Sports Editor, he misinterpreted my gasp of surprise as hesitance to accept, and assured me: "You don't have to know anything about sport. That's the reporters' job. They just need organising so that they emerge from the ruts they seem to be in…" Ruts…? I bit my tongue with "pot, kettle, black" bursting to pop out of my mouth.

And as for not knowing anything about sport … Mr. Snaith obviously had no idea of my many accomplishments outside the office. Not quite as sensational as Clough's but…

In the very same winter in which the teenage Brian Clough was banging in goals for Middlesbrough Schools, I was already multi-tasking in football: playing matches for Bathley, South Muskham and Little Carlton, usually against the massed forces of neighbouring villages Kelham and Averham; and then cycling home before dark to write my match report and note the League results as they were announced on *Sports Report* on the wireless, after which I would spend my Saturday night designing my own sports pages.

A few short winters later, while Clough was beginning to make his name as Middlesbrough's prolific centre forward, I was big enough to sit on the shoulders of the tallest under-18s in North Muskham Juniors' XI and perform the important task of hooking the nets on the crossbars for matches in the Newark Minor League before patrolling the touchline, cheering on my pals and then rushing home to turn them into the heroes of my reports.

As my luck would have it, North Muskham Juniors closed down just as I became old enough to play in the Minor League; but the team I joined, Carlton Juniors, won a trophy in my first season – the wooden spoon for holding up the rest of the table – at about the time Sunderland were getting together the princely sum of £45,000 to buy Clough.

By this time, though, I had played cricket for Nottinghamshire Schools Under-15s and had taken all 10 wickets (for only 8 runs) in an adult match for North Muskham and Bathley CC against Fiskerton. Never heard of Fiskerton? Shame on you! They were the Trentside village club that nurtured Paul Todd, who went on to open the batting for Nottinghamshire from 1972-82. Not him but his Dad was in the team that I bowled out on a humid Saturday afternoon when my seamers were swinging like bananas. Mr. Todd and his team-mates were so displeased to have been humiliated by a ginger-haired up-start of a kid that they refused to let our captain, a bulldog of a builder's labourer called Cyril Marriott, take home the match ball so that he could have it inscribed and mounted for me. Cyril, Clough-like in his reluctance to accept a defeat readily, even offered to buy the ball. Fiskerton mumbled something about needing something to play with tomorrow, to which Cyril responded: "Bugger you lot, then. You can stuff your ball and your teas. We're going home now." And so we trundled home, pride intact, sucking on cigarettes to quell the hunger gnawing at our stomachs. If I wasn't already on course for a career in journalism – for this drama took place in the summer I left school and joined the Nottingham News Service as a cub reporter – the story of my bowling feat that appeared in the local weekly paper, the *Newark Advertiser*, would have given me pause for thought. Here is the cutting I found screwed in my Dad's wallet after his death in April 1980…

You may have noticed the odd flaw … My first name was wrong. I suddenly became two years older – a point made much more sore because my Dad had thrown me out of

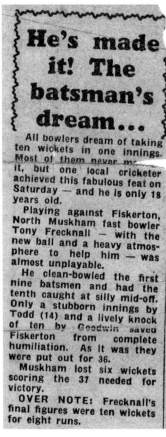

He's made it! The batsman's dream...

All bowlers dream of taking ten wickets in one innings. Most of them never m. it, but one local cricketer achieved this fabulous feat on Saturday — and he is only 18 years old.

Playing against Fiskerton, North Muskham fast bowler Tony Frecknall — with the new ball and a heavy atmosphere to help him — was almost unplayable.

He clean-bowled the first nine batsmen and had the tenth caught at silly mid-off. Only a stubborn innings by Todd (14) and a lively knock of ten by Goodwin saved Fiskerton from complete humiliation. As it was they were put out for 36.

Muskham lost six wickets scoring the 37 needed for victory.

OVER NOTE: Frecknall's final figures were ten wickets for eight runs.

the village pub personally when he caught me celebrating with a half-pint of shandy and a packet of crisps. And as for the heading calling my feat 'the batsman's dream', my usually quiet and dignified little Mum was moved to get on her bike, pedal the four miles into Newark and berate the Sports Editor of the *Advertiser* in person for the "absolute rubbish" that had persuaded her never to believe a word in his paper ever again.

As life rolled on, Saturday 19 March 1966 was memorable for two occasions. Nigel Clough, the middle of Brian and Barbara's three children, was born. And Gillian Mary Weaver was married to Trevor Frecknall.

As my appreciation of cricket evolved, while Clough was establishing his motor-mouth and managerial reputations at Derby County, I became the founding secretary of the Newark Club Cricket Alliance in the 1970s. At a time when many clubs were struggling to emerge from the rut of endless friendly fixtures, I helped them take the plunge into competitions in much the same way that Clough tended to rage against traditionalism if it was past its usefulness.

As my responsibilities as a parent increased in the mid-1970s, while Clough stormed out of Derby, spent a brief time at Brighton and Hove Albion and his famous 44 days at Leeds United, I became the founding secretary of Muskham United Football Club; and we ran teams for Under-14s and Under-12s. While he wrestled with the egos of Billy Bremner and company, I failed miserably to find 11-year-old wingers brave enough to run through the nettles that encroached over the touchlines of our ex-cow meadow of a pitch. I can, however, confess now that this was one of the reasons why I was happy to take on the role of the *Evening Post* motoring correspondent at this time. I managed to test drive all kinds of large motors at weekends – especially when I knew I had half a team or more to cart to an away match. Not that motoring was a job I knew anything about!

But sport? I loved it. Even so, I had a sneaking suspicion that, by inviting me to become Sports Editor, Mr. Snaith saw me as a successor to the anti-hero in Evelyn Waugh's *Scoop*, in which a gardening columnist was let loose to cover a war in Africa. Or could strait-laced Mr. Snaith be a better schemer than I had imagined? Was this his way of repaying me for helping the union-bashing PC to push through the reactionary ideas that changed newspaper production forever? Now, as I drove through a cacophony of sound and a barrage of umbrellas beating on my car roof and windscreen in the midst of a Nottingham winter, I realised that *Scoop* might be my most favourite book ever but it was suddenly too close to reality to be as funny as I had always thought.

For the flaw in Mr. Snaith's cunning "black them back" plan was that Forest were on the way to winning the European Cup, retaining the League Cup and finishing second in the First Division[2]. My view was that we could not stop informing their supporters (home crowds were above 30,000 for many matches) what was happening at what was England's highest-profile club-of-the-moment; and even if we did, Clough would still receive the publicity he craved from national newspapers, local radio and regional television. In addition, the 28 strikers had set up their own newspaper, the *Nottingham News*, which appeared only weekly rather than nightly but always had a biting column "exclusive by Brian Clough" ghost-written by John Lawson.

As luck (of a dubious kind) would have it, my view was supported by the fact that Clough also helped Lawson and Bowles start their own freelance agency, appointed Lawson as Forest's official spokesman, persuaded County Chairman Jack Dunnett to give Bowles similar roles at Meadow Lane – and obtained office space for them at Trent Bridge cricket ground.

With 'the golden triangle' more of a no-go war zone to the *Evening Post*, the only thing going in our favour was the weather. There was so much snow and frost that there were no matches to report on anyway. Imagine the daily struggle to fill a back page with the kind of stories expected by supporters of Forest and Notts when both clubs were officially 'blacking' the *Post* in support of the strikers and their fixtures were being routinely called-off even while we were striving to sell editions carrying previews.

Inspired (and I use that word deliberately) by Clough's assertion that "all life's a game", I let Dryden know my superiors were quite happy to 'black' Forest if push came to shove. Whether he took the scenario to the Forest Committee I know not; but he made many calls over the coming days and weeks to ensure there was a regular flow of stories from the City Ground, though we never revealed who was leaking them. In this respect, one of the sports reporters I inherited, David Stapleton, proved as useful as he was fearless. He would take the phoned tip-offs from Dryden and then do his best to check them, usually with Peter Taylor, whom he had known through covering Derby County for the *Post* when Clough and Taylor were winning the League Championship in 1974-75. Taylor frequently cursed David but, as he was the ace football spy who frequently put on disguises to check-up on potential transfer targets, I have no doubt that he enjoyed the subterfuge as much as, and maybe even more than, Dryden.

Notts County were equally ambivalent. Club Secretary Dennis Marshall had been as helpful as Manager Sirrel in the early months of the season, when I was "shadowing" the out-going Sports Editor. Even Chairman Dunnett had invited me to his place in The Park, Nottingham's historically poshest address in the shadow of the Castle, one Friday night

---

[2] The First Division of the 1970s is now known as the Premier League.

to explain one or two important rules. By this time – a few weeks before the strike broke out – I was swimming in the 'important rules' that local sports journalists were expected to follow when covering their League football clubs. The most pressing of these, I had been told by a member of the Football League Management Committee, was: "Whenever a transfer takes place, clubs never divulge financial details officially but you will hear rumours of two fees. Always use the rumour that emanates from your local club, whether it be us, them across the river or Mansfield." *Why?* "Our supporters read your newspaper … and so may our tax inspector."

A few weeks later, Mr. Dunnett, true to his Labour supporters' wishes, announced that he would not be cooperating with the *Post* until the 28 strikers were reinstated – something that was, of course, not possible from the moment he helped Clough provide Lawson and Bowles with alternative employment.

To my surprise, the first time Notts County did not have a match snowed-off in 1979, Sirrel phoned me in the office: "I'm nae talking to a journalist, y'understand?"

"Is that right, Jimmy?" I was mystified … intrigued.

"I'm talking to a friend."

"Oh, right, Jimmy!"

"So can I tell this friend what my team is for tomorrow, my friend?"

"My pen is poised Jimmy."

"Aye, I thought it would be."

Years later he told me why he had taken this unexpected rebellious action. Sitting in his cramped office under the old Meadow Lane stand, he had overheard Bowles briefing Marshall about the developments in the dispute – and had bristled silently when Bowles summed-up: "Just my luck to finish up with the manager who never says anything!"

Sirrel the Manager never said anything to the *Evening Post* Sports Department while the dispute raged (and there was a war with the pickets every Saturday teatime until the end of the football season in May) but he frequently phoned this new friend called Trevor he had made in the early months of that football season and talked of turning points in last Saturday's or last night's match, who the outstanding performers had been, whether anyone was injured … the kind of information the Sports Department would love to have. And he'd always include in the conversations the caveat: "I'm nae talking to a journalist, y'understand? I'm talking to a friend."

"Of course, Jimmy." So all of the juicy quotes from "the manager who never said anything" remained unattributed on the back page of the *Post*.

But all this furtive work almost exploded before it got properly underway on the night of 17 January when Forest's pitch was playable enough for them to entertain Watford in the first leg of a League Cup semi-final. As we were barred from the Press Box (and Lawson was in residence to report any *Post* incursion) and Mr. Snaith insisted we would not demean ourselves by buying a ticket to stand on the terraces, Dryden came up with a blinding plan. He would smuggle me past the gatemen who had been threatened with a fate worse than death by squash racket if I got in. He would take me into the Committee Box as his special guest. It worked a treat: I was such a new-boy to the scene that none of his fellow committee members showed any interest in the bloke in Hank Marvin spectacles peering at the action from the back corner of the away club's side of the Committee Box and occasionally scribbling in the margins of his match programme. I could have been one of the Watford Chairman's musical hangers-on for all they cared; Elton John was not at all like the hauliers or factory owners or lawyers who owned clubs in the 1970s. Even John, the long-serving doorman in the inner sanctum of the City Ground on match days, mistook me for a visiting Watford VIP.

So all went wonderfully until I decided to leave about an hour after the final whistle. Dryden had carried out a reconnaissance of my exit route and come back with a surreptitious "all-clear" (i.e., a thumbs up followed by fingers crossed and a shrug of the shoulders). So, pausing only to finish my second Scotch and ginger (for courage, you understand), I stepped out into the 50-yard long corridor from deep under the Main Stand to the double doors through which Clough had kicked me when we first met. There were people milling all over the place; after all, Forest had won 3-1 (with two goals from Garry Birtles and one by John Robertson) so the whiff of another Wembley trip was much more agreeable than a journey home along freezing roads.

Alas, too late I realised that one of the knots of people consisted "the Midland mafia" (as the national newspaper journalists covering Midland clubs were affectionately known by we locals) gathered around Clough, who was giving a spontaneous press conference at the door to the staff car park. I thought about reversing but instantly realised Lawson, at Clough's shoulder, had spotted me. I tried to shrink and accelerate past the throng but Lawson's nudge and whisper stopped Clough's monologue. The 'mafia' parted instinctively so that the Manager's gaze was uninterrupted.

"Where have you been?" he asked me.

"Watching you're wonderful team," I said quietly, trying to smile, struggling to keep moving when my legs turned to such jelly that I was almost frozen in the headlight of his stare and his fury.

"From where? From the Committee Box? But you're banned! Get out!!"

By this time, I was almost past him but felt obliged to say: "But I've got a job to do."

"It's not your job, it's his," shouted Clough, almost knocking Lawson off his feet in his eagerness to embrace his mate. To emphasise his partisanship, Clough snatched someone's BIC pen and hurled it at me. I swayed to avoid it and it pinged into one of the pictures idolising Clough along the wall, shattered into its six sides and flared around me.

"And don't dare come back!" he added as I made it to the door with a measured stride, rather than the panicky sprint I would have favoured, to be ushered out by an incredibly startled doorman John.

I didn't even mention the incident back at the office. I saw no point. It would merely have taken the dispute up a notch; and it was nasty enough already with flying pickets clashing with massed ranks of police every time we produced an edition – especially on a Saturday afternoon when the *Football Post* hit the streets. Mr. Snaith would have reiterated his preference for us to ignore Forest "and that bloody egotist". We would have bitten our own nose off to spite our face.

Not that I slept for a couple of nights, worrying that both Dryden and Taylor would no longer continue their surreptitious support. Which just went to show how little I knew! It became apparent years later that both of them had quietly faced up to Clough with what they considered the facts of life. They argued that Forest needed the *Post* as much as the *Post* needed Forest – especially to sell tickets for all the extra European and League Cup ties they were playing. They respected Clough's revulsion at the thought of dealing with such job-destroying capitalists but argued that if they kept giving us a basic news service, Forest would have the best of both worlds. Clough's principles would remain intact; the club's need to speak nightly to a quarter of a million or more readers would be satisfied.

Clough must have agreed because we not only continued to receive virtually daily news from Taylor and Dryden but were also told we would have access to the Press Box restored, and our photographers would be able to return to their positions beside the goals – provided none of us attempted to interview any player or official.

We were given the silent treatment to the extent that few other journalists dared acknowledge our presence. The stark exception was a veteran freelance from Leicester called Roly Orton, who cheerfully and loudly advised me: "Keep a diary of all that happens to you down here. You'll have enough for a book even if you only last a month!"

He was right, of course. All I lacked was the time to write it all up.

6

Francis to Munich on the quiet

· · · · · · · · · · · · · · · · · ·

MY FIRST boss in journalism, Eric Bradshaw at the Nottingham News Service, laid down two rules in 1961 which, for the rest of my life, I have continued to strive to respect:

1 – If you must use clichés, invent your own.
2 – Always get the expert's view into your story; it will be more authoritative than your guess.

The greatest regret of my career is that I covered the five ties in early 1979 that finished with Nottingham Forest Kings of Europe without ever being able to substantiate my guesses with the views of management or players. Not being known to the players, I suppose I could have hung around the area at the City Ground between the changing room exit and the Jubilee Club entrance – as did 'the Midland mafia' – and pretend I was an autograph-hunting fan, asking players what they thought of the match they'd just starred in. But I had no wish to embroil the players in a dispute that had nothing to do with them. I just wished their Manager had taken the view that a newspaper strike had nothing to do with him, either!

So task No.1 was to cover English football's first £1 million transfer without going anywhere near the ground. Trevor Francis was the Wayne Rooney of the era; the fleet-footed super-hero every manager coveted. Born near the English Riviera in Devon on 19 April 1954, there was something of the international heart-breaker about him. His dark good looks were framed by a mass of dark curls. Yet the innocence from his up-bringing in the South-West meant there was never anything sinister or scheming about him. What you saw was what you got. To be fair, dour Birmingham City got him first.

He was only 16 when City gambled with him in their first team in 1971 and over the next eight years he scored 119 goals in 280 games. He also proved himself a tireless young man by adding to his pay-packet (and his status) in the summers of 1978 and 1979 as football entrepreneurs such as Jimmy Hill (former Fulham midfielder, by the 1970s an out-spoken BBC pundit) tried to teach the USA to appreciate real football rather than their rugby-based version of it. Francis scored 39 goals in 38 games for Detroit Express.

So when word spread that Birmingham might just be ready to sell their Boy Wonder (he was on the way to his 25th birthday but still a youngster in England development terms) providing they collected £1 million – more than any footballer had ever cost an English club – everyone sat back and waited for him to sign for the General Manager at Coventry City, one Jimmy Hill… Everyone, that is, except Clough and Taylor. Although he already had the fleet-footed Northern Ireland international Martin O'Neill in his squad, Clough always wanted a speedy scorer on the right of his midfield. Taylor had to agree that Francis fitted the bill perfectly.

And so it came to pass that Francis signed for Forest in the Jubilee Club just before 2.00pm on Friday 9 February 1979. From our 'District Edition' that went to the presses at 1.10pm, we had our front page report of the historic move. Re-reading it now, it's fair to say that our unattributed sources did us proud because the signing was due to be completed at 1pm. What nobody expected was that Clough, being more important than even the most expensive signing in the history of English football, would delay the deal so that he could finish his usual lunchtime squash match at Trent Bridge cricket ground. It was also, of course, the Master Manager's way of putting Boy Wonder in his place from the outset of their relationship.

If Francis had been a less placid character and asked his manager-wife Helen to drive him back to Birmingham rather than wait the extra hour for Clough to exercise his racket, the *Evening Post* would have made the biggest boob in its cautious history. This is what we wrote about the historic deal:

> Francis took less than 24 hours to decide to join Forest after spending five hours at the City Ground yesterday talking terms with manager Brian Clough and his assistant, Peter Taylor. And while the intricacies of the move have still to be revealed, informed sources in the West Midlands today insisted Clough had offered Francis the massive incentive of continuing to play summer football in America. If this is so, it marks a master-stroke change of mind by Clough, who has always insisted his leading players should spend the English close season resting from, and for, the rigours of the Football League and its appendages.
>
> The theory all this week, while Forest have battled with Coventry City for Francis' signature, has been that the American connection would decide the

EVENING POST

No. 31,281   NOTTINGHAM, FRIDAY, FEBRUARY 9, 1979   PRICE 8p

£1m. PLAYER SIGNS FOR FO

By Trevor Frecknall

BRITAIN's first £1m footballer, Trevor Francis was this afternoon signing for Nottingham Forest — to become twice as expensive as any other player in the Football League.

Francis took less than 24 hours to decide to join Forest after spending five hours at the City Ground yesterday talking terms with manager Brian Clough and his assistant, Peter Taylor.

And while the intricacies of the £1m-plus deal have still to be revealed, informed sources in the West Midlands today insisted Clough had offered Francis the massive incentive of continuing to play summer football in America.

If this is so, it marks a master-stroke change of mind by Clough, who has always insisted his leading players should spend the English close season resting from, and for, the rigours of the Football League and its appendages.

The theory all this week, while Forest have battled with Coventry City for Francis's signature, has been that the American connection would decide the issue.

GLORY CHASE

On the face of it, Coventry's offer was much more attractive than Forest's.

Forest could offer Francis only a one-quarter share in the unprecedented glory as they chase the European Cup and three domestic trophies this season.

For Francis has already played for Birmingham in the League Cup and FA Cup this season; and he will be ineligible for the European Cup until the final.

Coventry were content to allow him to seek to renew his England career — he has won 12 caps — and to chase his fortune in America, where he earned over £50,000 last summer.

He earned his cash in dollars playing for Detroit Express, who are run by Jimmy Hill, the Coventry general manager.

But Francis was as aware as anyone even before he spoke to Clough and Taylor yesterday that he stands more chance of keeping in the English spotlight with Forest than with Coventry.

He is already highly regarded by England manager Ron Greenwood, who considers him to be potentially the next Kevin Keegan, currently the European Footballer of the Year.

But when Greenwood made the assessment, he was quick to add: "It depends on where he goes and with whom he works."

INSPIRATION

And Clough's inspirational qualities are second to none in football.

He has rescued Forest from the relative obscurity of the Second Division, "tamed" Kenny Burns — Francis's old team-mate at Birmingham — and built the most successful side Nottingham has ever known.

Clough clinched the deal in his own inimitable style — first, making Francis wait until he had finished a game of squash, then virtually dotting every i and crossing every t before they parted last evening.

And Clough's reputation as the manager who always gets his man was confirmed today when a Birmingham City official announced that Francis had chosen Forest.

The signing is Clough's first since he paid Queen's Park Rangers £140,000 for defender David Needham 14 months ago.

PROMISING

But both Clough and Taylor have been promising all season that they would smash all the transfer fee records to get the right man.

And it is ironic that this "scoop" has occurred after months of frustration for the pair.

Frar joi Re

They have been repeatedly th sign players such as Peter Daley at Wolves, and Ian W ho both play for Coventry, Even their quest for Franci nings. Their first bid was re and it seemed Birmingham minds whether they wanted part-exchange.

COMMIT

Cash suits Clough, because o ments in the weeks to com small size of his first team p But it's a massive amount — Francis's cut of £45,000 becaï move, plus £45,000 for the F Fund, plus VAT.

As Greenwood said: "It is ; around your neck . . . reb stadium and admission mone chance of recouping the cash The £1m footballer, see back p

FRANCIS — joined the League cham- r deciding their offer was too good to refuse.

issue. On the face of it, Coventry's offer was much more attractive than Forest's.

Forest could offer Francis only a one-quarter share in the unprecedented glory as they chase the European Cup and three domestic trophies this season. For Francis has already played for Birmingham in the League Cup and FA Cup this season; and he will be ineligible for the European Cup until the Final.

Coventry were content to allow him to seek to renew his England career – he has won 12 caps – and to chase his fortune in America, where he earned over £50,000 last summer. He earned his cash in dollars playing for Detroit Express, who are run by Jimmy Hill, the Coventry general manager.

But Francis was as aware as anyone even before he spoke to Clough and Taylor yesterday that he stands more chance of keeping in the English spotlight with Forest than with Coventry.

He is already highly regarded by England manager Ron Greenwood, who considers him to be potentially the next Kevin Keegan, currently the European Footballer of the Year. But when Greenwood made the assessment, he was quick to add: "It depends on where he goes and with whom he works."

And Clough's inspirational qualities are second to none in football. He has rescued Forest from the relative obscurity of the Second Division, "tamed" Kenny Burns – Francis's old team-mate at Birmingham – and built the most successful side Nottingham has ever known.

Clough clinched the deal in his own inimitable style – first, making Francis wait until he had finished a game of squash, then virtually dotting every i and crossing every t before they parted last evening.

And Clough's reputation as the manager who always gets his man was confirmed today when a Birmingham City official announced that Francis had chosen Forest.

The signing is Clough's first since he paid Queen's Park Rangers £140,000 for defender David Needham 14 months ago. But both Clough and Taylor have been promising all season that they would smash all the transfer fee records to get the right man. And it is ironic that this "scoop" has occurred after months of frustration for the pair. They have been repeatedly thwarted in their attempts to sign players such as Peter Ward of Brighton, Steve Daley at Wolves, and Ian Wallace and Mike Ferguson, who both play for Coventry.

Even their quest for Francis had unpromising beginnings. Their first bid was rejected earlier this week – and it seemed Birmingham could not make up their minds whether they wanted a cash deal or players in part-exchange.

Cash suits Clough because of Forest's heavy commitments in the weeks to come and the comparatively small size of the first team pool. But it's a massive amount – £975,000 plus Francis's cut of £45,000 because he did not ask for the move, plus £45,000 for the Football League Provident Fund plus VAT.

As Greenwood said: "It is a terrible debt, a noose around your neck … relative to the size of your stadium and admission money – whether you have a chance of recouping the cash."

And that was it – except for a single column picture on the right-hand side of the story. I am sure the readers would have expected it to be of Clough but Editor Snaith would have none of that. The image he chose was of the spy whose phone calls kept us abreast of developments and the caption was Mr. Snaith's tacit put-down of Clough:

Peter Taylor – pulled off the biggest-ever deal in British soccer.

But note my creep in the report to our political enemy at the City Ground: "Clough's inspirational qualities are second to none in football." Francis doubtless took issue with that statement twice in the next few weeks.

First, he was sent out onto the snow and ice of a park pitch on the morning after he signed to make his Forest debut among the hopeful teenagers of the A team in the Midland Intermediate League. As our luck would have it, the opposition was provided by Notts County A. As my luck would have it, no *Evening Post* photographer was available to risk being kicked off the touchline by Clough. No matter; we had a comprehensive report under the heading…

County hold star-studded Forest A

Million pound investment Trevor Francis made his debut in a Forest shirt today – playing for the A-team against Notts County A.

Forest manager Brian Clough made the surprise move of naming his new super star for a testing Midland Intermediate League match at Grove Farm, Clifton.

Clough, assistant Peter Taylor and club vice-chairman Stuart Dryden were among those watching Francis make a quiet opening to his four-year contract.

Francis was lucky not to be on the losing side as County's inexperienced youngsters took a shock two-goal first half lead and Forest only rallied with a late burst in the second half to clinch a 2-2 draw.

There was much more to the report; but, looking back, the team Clough sent out spoke volumes for his psychology. Once he had signed Francis for what many people considered to be an obscene amount of money, he set about making him "one of the lads" rather than the "super star" to which we referred.

"We're all in it together," was one of the manager's mantras; and so he lined Francis alongside Chris Woods, the understudy goalkeeper to the imperious Shilton who went on to win England caps of his own; plus Frank Clark, David Needham, Colin Barrett and John O'Hare from the European Cup-winning squad. Needham's inclusion was particularly significant: he had made his reputation during more than 450 first team appearances for Notts.

Francis's second lesson in Clough psychology during the early weeks and months, when ice and snow forced the postponement of many matches, came on the rainy evening of 3 March 1979, on the way back from his full Forest first team debut in a 1-1 draw at Ipswich Town. He had obtained Clough's agreement that he could alight from the team coach at a specific spot on the A1 near Peterborough, whence Helen would drive him to London for a television or promotional appearance the following day. The Forest bus driver, an ebullient and obliging veteran called Albert, knew better than to take his time on the way home, especially when The Gaffer was brooding on a victory getting away as Forest strove to keep pace with Liverpool at the top of the First Division table.

So he reached Francis's drop-off point a good half-an-hour earlier than the estimated time of arrival. Eager not to upset The Gaffer, Francis was at the bus doorway as Albert pulled it up and activated the door opener. Only when he began to descend the bus steps, did it dawn on the £1m man just how hard the rain was persisting.

"It's pouring down, Boss," he said.

"I know," yawned Clough.

"And Helen's not here yet."

"But you are – good night!" And out shot the Clough foot that had propelled me out of the City Ground to complete Francis's exit from the bus.

"Off we go, Albert – put your foot down please," he added, resuming his seat (the second one behind the driver) and dropping off back to sleep.

Not that the *Post* was welcome on Clough's bus in those days. Pickets were still going through the ritual of trying to halt the Saturday night *Football Post* though the vast majority of the 28 who had left TBF were now in new, gainful employment. The NUJ made sure that we remained "blacked" by all freelance journalists who would normally sell us news about teams about to play against Forest, Notts and Mansfield, etc. and who historically had hired to us telephone lines in Press Boxes so that we could dictate our reports back to the office as the matches happened. That hardly added to our problems for home matches; we simply accepted nobody dared talk to us. But it meant reporters had to take "runners" with them to away matches to dash out and search of public phones from which to dictate running reports. And it gave us (usually photographer Trevor Bartlett and me) some pretty memorable European adventures once the Cup competition resumed on Wednesday 7 March.

Forest had, of course, already come through two rounds of their first European Cup campaign. It's time to savour the full run...

Fittingly, it was heralded by a massive surprise. Peter Withe, chief scoring hero of the previous two seasons, never got the chance to face Liverpool in the European Cup first round epic. After the opening League game in 1978-79 (a 1-1 draw at home to Tottenham Hotspur) he was summarily sold to Newcastle United, who gambled £200,000 on him shooting them out of Division Two.

It was an even bigger gamble by Clough/Taylor – one that arguably cost them the defence of the League title. Without a ready-made replacement No.9 to operate alongside Woodcock, Forest won only one and drew six of their first seven Division One matches. And then came Garry Birtles, a carpet fitter born on 27 July 1965 in Chilwell, an outer suburb of Nottingham best known as the venue of a bomb making factory that had blown up during the First World War with the loss of many lives.

Birtles' impact was suitably explosive. He had been bought from a local non-League club, Long Eaton United for £2,000 on Taylor's say-so. Clough was so unimpressed that he frequently said of his own scouting trip: "The half-time Bovril was better than him." With Withe sold, ex-Forest apprentice Stephen Elliott played in the next three League matches without making the necessary impact. Then Clough threw the untried Birtles into the home League match against Arsenal. He did not score in the 1-1 draw. But he did enough to retain his place for arguably the most glamorous match of Forest's history, the home leg of the European Cup first round tie against Liverpool, European Cup winners for the previous two years and still smarting from the loss of the League Cup to Forest five months earlier.

The least-known player on the pudding of a pitch – the City Ground always seemed to be a morass in those days – made the biggest impacts. Birtles tapped in Forest's first goal in the 26th minute. And with only two minutes left and the Koppites already chanting their optimism for the second leg, Birtles hustled Liverpool's international defenders into an uncharacteristic mistake and crossed the ball into the middle. Woodcock knocked it down and who should be rushing into the six yard box but the left back, the flaxen-haired Colin Barrett. As his flying volley ballooned the net, Liverpool's hopes of a European hat-trick imploded. What was overlooked in the euphoria of the moment was that Barrett had suffered a knee injury that would make him a pained and, at best, peripheral figure for the rest of the glory season.

Huff and puff as Liverpool's seasoned battlers did in the return leg at Anfield a fortnight later, there was no way Shilton and his defenders were going to be any more generous than they had been in the previous season when they achieved shut-outs against Liverpool in the League Cup Final and replay plus the First Division match at Anfield.

But the impassioned atmosphere on Merseyside prepared Forest perfectly for the home supporters in the first leg of the second round against AEK Athens in the Greek capital. In the era before mobile phones, never mind emails. Without realising this would be the only European Cup match he would cover for the *Evening Post* from the mainland of the continent, John Lawson dictated this report of Forest's 2-1 victory:

> Nottingham Forest carried their class, composure and coolness across Europe last night to take charge of this European Cup tie. The Reds faced everything – a hostile crowd, intimidatory tackling and an appalling penalty decision – to bring back a vital lead to the City Ground. And although they played against ten men for almost 70 minutes, make no mistake that Brian Clough's side deserved their memorable victory. Uruguayan midfield man Viera was sent off for flooring Kenny Burns with a Henry Cooper-style left hook. But it is doubtful whether his presence would have helped AEK achieve a better result.

His full report covered a broadsheet page with the help in the first edition of stock pictures of the Forest team. By the time the main editions were printed in the afternoon of 19 October, the plane chartered by the Forest Supporters' Club had landed at East Midlands Airport (now called Nottingham East Midlands to the doubtless exasperation of users in Derby and Leicester, which are just as close) so our photographer, Trevor Bartlett, was able to replace the stock photographs with action shots, notably of skipper McGovern nudging in the first goal after 10 minutes and Birtles adding the second (his seventh goal in his first ten games!) after a sprightly run and cross by veteran full back Clark.

It was a landmark experience for Trevor B – his first venture outside the British Isles. Like me, he never expected his travels to stretch far beyond Skegness and the rest of the bracing resorts on the East Coast of England. He had been brought-up in the Nottingham suburb of St Ann's, famous for its back-to-back streets of modest terraced houses and, in the 1960s, some of the first race riots ever witnessed in Nottingham. With typical St Ann's humour, Trevor B always dismissed the seriousness of the battles, insisting: "They were just scuffling to be first into the boozer."

Yet Clough's miracles with Forest turned Bartlett into an international photographer virtually overnight. While he was busily rushing to obtain his first passport, his mischievous mates in the *Evening Post* Photographic Department were preparing him for the ordeal in Athens. John Richardson, big, bold and burly for foot-in-the-door jobs yet the world's biggest hypochondriac when he had time to sit and brood about a sniffle or an ache, warned Trevor B that, unlike the British photographer, Greek "snappers" never risked sitting on the grass behind the goals.

"Why?" asked Trevor B.

"The spiders," replied Richo, in his best doom-laden tone.

So out went Trevor B to buy a ground-sheet to add to his usual working kit. The plane chartered by the Forest Supporters' Club was a propeller job that had to stop and refuel in Zagreb; but the happy party arrived in Athens well in time for the match.

Trevor B noticed a few odd looks from his fellow photographers as he carefully laid-out his ground-sheet beside the goal AEK were to defend and plonked himself in the middle of it. Then he got on with the job of recording the high points of Forest's latest adventure in fantasy land.

His greatest concern occurred when he got back to Athens Airport with the jubilant Forest fans to discover the return flight could not take off at the promised time. The reason given by the airport authorities – not at all embittered to have seen their own heroes trounced by these upstarts from the English provinces – was that the plane had arrived in such a filthy state, they had not been able to find cleaners willing to even venture into the toilets. Eventually, after what seemed an eternity, it occurred that they ought to allow the supporters to fly home before any of them became aggressively frustrated; and so Trevor B's pictures missed only the early editions.

Only after he had been congratulated on a great job did Richo confess that the spiders story was an invention; a wind-up. It was also part of our steep learning curve!

Meanwhile Lawson, travelling in better style with the Forest squad, was able to phone over quotes from Clough for a front page story, headlined 'Give us our due!' Clearly exasperated by experts in the media making Forest second-favourites against the Euro-wise AEK as well as Liverpool, Clough challenged: "Just what have we got to do to get our just desserts? Everybody is so willing to write us off. But we just keep on proving them wrong. Do we have to go 136 games without defeat before people accept that we are a good side? We did English football proud here yet again last night when back home they were writing us off because we were supposed to be not as good as Liverpool. We came to Athens hearing all about AEK scoring four, five and six goals. They got one last night and that was from a dodgy penalty."

Even though a booking in Athens led to a ban for Burns, the return leg at the City Ground was a romp reminiscent of the cavalier manner in which Forest had played to earn promotion to the First Division only three seasons earlier. Forest won 5-1 with goals by Burns' replacement, Needham (12 minutes), Woodcock (35), Anderson (40) and the inevitable Birtles (66 and 72).

By the time of the quarter finals in March, of course, Lawson was out of our team and comments from Clough, Taylor and the Forest players were out of our stories. And we were not welcome on Forest's squad or supporters' flights to the away legs. As if that was not enough to give this novice sports editor a sleepless night or three, there was also a revolt by Forest supporters to write about.

So on Wednesday night 7 March 1979, I was in the ridiculous situation of criticising Forest after they had defeated Grasshopper of Zurich 4-1 in the home leg of their European Cup quarter final. Claudio Sulser, a striker worshipped like a pop star in otherwise conservative Switzerland, had shocked the home crowd as early as the 11th minute by sprinting away from Lloyd, holding off Clark and beating Shilton – something Liverpool had not managed in more than five hours!

Forest responded by regularly missing chances but scoring through Birtles (31 minutes), a penalty by Robertson (47) and, to kill the tie, Gemmill (87) and Lloyd (89). But my report was not as idolatry as might have been expected of a 'home paper'. It began thus:

> What a night! And what a fright Nottingham Forest gave their fans before building a 4-1 lead ... A goal down in 11 minutes – and a brilliant one, too – the Super Reds scored twice in the last three minutes to give themselves a scoreline that was just for Forest and yet harsh on Grasshoppers.
>
> That's a contradiction, yet so was the match. Forest had 30 corners; Grasshoppers had three. Forest had 33 shots; Grasshoppers had five. Yet until Archie Gemmill's left foot and Larry Lloyd's head doubled Forest's score in those last three minutes, it looked as if Grasshoppers had virtually escaped The Siege of the City Ground.

And imagine the mischief in my beady eyes as the front page story mildly compensated us for all of the violence we had endured from flying pickets over the weeks. It went like this...

> Nottingham Forest passed a thin, sombre "picket line" on their way to more sensational European Cup glory last night. It was thrown up by Supporters' Club members who have paid £2.50 each for tickets for the League Cup Final at Wembley on Saturday week but now find they cannot have any. They staged their silent protest outside the main entrance to the City Ground ... And the crowd of 31,949 was about 10,000 less than the capacity of the ground, leaving the club to ponder whether there was a boycott by other disgruntled fans.

The problem was, of course, that Forest's burgeoning fan base had far out-grown its ticket allocation. So even while our story of rebellion was rolling off the presses, Forest secretary Ken Smales and his assistant Paul White were telephoning round the country in search of clubs who had not sold their share. Welcome to the downside of success!

For photographer Trevor Bartlett and me, there was an upside to the ban from the Forest aircraft. The owner of the *Evening Post*, Colonel Forman Hardy, had been persuaded by his son Nicholas to purchase a private jet. Nicholas, in his early 20s, was learning to fly said six-seater. So a jaunt to Zurich would be a wonderful diversion from strikes and freezing weather on 21 March 1979. Whether the pilot, Colin Bond, thought it such fun is open to question. We flew into Zurich around 5pm local time, had a quick snack at the airport, took a taxi to the match … and flew out barely an hour after the final whistle. Poor Pilot Bond never got closer to the action than the runway; he spent his time in Switzerland organising the refuelling of our pocket rocket and making sure we had a return flight plan through the night.

The match was nearly as exciting! Despite telling me in the build-up to the return that his team had no chance, Sulser scored from a penalty to give his highly vocal supporters a glimmer of hope. But Forest snuffed out any danger within five minutes, as my report explained:

> Martin O'Neill, cast into the shadows by the £1m appearance at the City Ground of Trevor Francis, grabbed his share of the European Cup limelight in Zurich last night… His far post poaching came in the 33rd minute, only four minutes after Grasshoppers had taken the lead.

Forest's business-like performance was relaxing compared with our charging around. But our efforts ended with Bartlett's pictures adorning the *Evening Post* from the first edition (which went to the presses at 11am) on Thursday 22 March. The fact that we two Trevors had no sleep for more than 30 hours was irrelevant; adrenalin seemed as endless as Forest's successes.

Come the semi-finals, though, Cologne brought us all down to earth with the help of the Forest pitch. It frequently resembled a cabbage patch, as Clough was wont to point out, and was infuriatingly counter-productive to Forest's style, which involved players moving and passing at speed. Nothing moved faster than the teeming rain on the night of 11 April 1979, when Forest and Cologne played out a pulsating 3-3 draw.

It could have been a lot worse, too; the result – not the weather. Cologne were 2-0 up in the first quarter of the game through Dutch international Roger van Gool and Dieter Müller. Forest fought back with such skill and purpose that Birtles (28 minutes), Bowyer (53) and Robertson (63) put them ahead. Game over? Not a bit of it! One of Japan's first footballing exports to Europe, Yasuhiko Okudera, was sent on as a late substitute and fired off a long shot, more in hope than expectation, with five minutes left and the sides reeling in the sapping conditions like punch-drunk heavyweights. The ball slithered through the increasingly liquefied mud – and squirmed under Shilton's dive. My colleague David Stapleton called it "the worst mistake of his brilliant 18 months with Forest".

By the time the second leg was played on 25 April, thousands of Cologne supporters had already booked their travel, tickets and hotels for the final to be played in Munich on 30 May. Their reasoning was simple: if their heroes could draw 3-3 at the City Ground, victory was a certainty at home.

Oh they of too much faith! My report of the frantic, dramatic second leg started:

> Ian Bowyer, known as 'Bomber' ever since he was hailed among the best young English strikers nearly a decade ago, headed Forest all the way from Cologne to Munich in the 65th minute of last night's nerve-tingling second leg… As goals go, it was simple. 'Bomber' instinctively stooped to nod it in from six yards after John Robertson's left wing corner had been headed on by the irrepressible Garry Birtles. What made it remarkable was that it was the first of only two on-target shots Forest had all through this night of high drama.

And, as if by instinctive magic, Trevor Bartlett provided the photographic evidence of the crucial moment when Bowyer stooped to head the winner as Burns willed it in…

There were shades of the Second World War in the drama. Whereas a Japanese sub had all but sunk Forest at the City Ground, a Lancaster Bomber proved decisive in the return leg. And there were unconfirmed reports that somebody with a Clough-like drawl had observed in the Cologne dressing room area after Forest's epic 1-0 win: "I know now why this lot lost the War. They don't know how to attack." The rumour was never confirmed. Neither, significantly, was it ever categorically denied.

Shilton more than compensated for his first leg error despite suffering a shoulder injury in the first half. As the final seconds ticked away, Cologne defender Harald Konopka fired in a swift, swerving low shot from almost the same spot from which Okudera had struck at the City Ground. Swooping at full stretch to his left, Shilton parried the ball away from the bottom corner of his goal and then, as Cologne feet pounded towards him, dived again to smother the ball before it dribbled out for a corner that would have put the Forest defence under almost intolerable pressure with most of the 61,000 crowd baying for an equaliser to justify their outlay for the Final.

'Wunderbar' as the *Evening Post* heading screamed the next day after Pilot Bond, his eager assistant Nick and we two Trevors had flown in from another 30-hour shift.

7

Final on a budget and a plastic bag

· · · · · · · · · · · · · · · · · · · ·

SUDDENLY THREE times more "lifetime supporters" than Forest had ever seen at the City Ground wanted tickets for the 1979 European Cup Final in the Olympic Stadium, Munich, on 30 May 1979 – the first European Cup tie for which Trevor Francis would be available. The fact that the opponents, the Swedish champions from Malmo, would be the underdogs and would play like a team content to keep down Forest's score was overlooked in the general euphoria.

Just about the only person in Nottingham who did not want to be there was my Editor.

Mr. Snaith's hostility to Clough had not wavered through Forest's run to Munich, retention of the League Cup and runners-up finish in the First Division. On the contrary, dear boy.

In the privacy (some would say 'Ivory Tower') of his spacious office, as more and more space was taken in his paper by preview stories, he asked me in all seriousness: "Do we really have to be at the Final?"

I was speechless. But his wide-eyed expression showed he was not joking. So he went on: "I mean, it's all going to be on television. You can get your report from there."

"It's not quite the same," I began. "And what about pictures?"

"The agencies will be there."

"For goodness sake," I laughed out loud, though I was acutely aware that the age gap made me feel I was cheekily trying to stand up to my Dad. "This is the biggest sporting occasion in the history of this county … in the history of the East Midlands."

"But it's not in your budget," Mr. Snaith said, red face almost purpling. "We're not a bottomless pit, you know."

"No, thankfully it's Nick's budget," I said.

"Are you sure?" Mr. Snaith asked.

"I'll check," I said (meaning: "I'll make sure!") and swept out of his office and headed north to Nick's hideaway on the Executive Corridor. Thankfully his reactions to the notion that we should give the European Cup Final a miss were the same as mine: he froze in disbelief then rocked with laughter. And then set about squaring the finances, enabling me to concentrate on previews, booking tickets, and making contact with friendly Swedes for information exchanges (remember there were no websites to plagiarise in these days).

The next surprise came when we four flew into Munich. We already knew that we would not be able to fly home immediately after the match. Ever since the Manchester United disaster in 1957 (in which several of the legendary Busby Babes were among the 23 to die when British European Airways Flight 609 crashed on its third attempt to take off from the snow- and ice-bound runway) Munich Airport had been closed at night. What I did not realise was that Nick fancied his chances as a photographer and was intent on taking colour pictures of the Final. Now that his budget was financing the fiddlers, he wanted to call the tine.

The snag was that I had a stand ticket for him, not a photographer's pass, and there was no way I was going to be able to change that when we arrived at the Olympic Stadium at 5.30-ish on the evening of the match. Nick was crestfallen. Trevor B, never less than inventively resourceful, went off to snaffle his pass and bib – and returned with confirmation that there was no chance of Nick getting one. But Trevor B did have a cunning plan … a possible solution.

The colour of the official photographers' bibs was very similar to a plastic carrier bag from the British Army Stores that Trevor B happened to have with him (to keep his reels of film dry should it rain). Trevor, once on the pitch with his bib in place, bravely offered to slip the carrier bag over his shoulder and smuggle the official bib to Nick at the front of the main stand.

Amid the general hubbub as the massive stadium filled with 57,500 paying customers and VIPs from all over the world, nobody really noticed Nick slip over the boundary wall with his camera (a tiddler compared with the machines wielded by the professionals) and mingle with the photographers behind one of the goals. One steward kept looking suspiciously at Trevor B, indicating he should put his bib on properly. Each time they made eye contact, Trevor B merely smiled and waved back. As the match rolled on, thankfully the steward lost interest in this improperly dressed photographer.

And after both Trevor B and Nick had snapped pictures of Francis heading the only goal – from a Robertson centre after Bowyer had released him in midfield – Trevor B, all nimble 5ft 4in of him, wriggled through the scrum of photographers to take a wonderful picture of the entire Forest squad with the trophy … and even snatched one of Clough and Taylor saluting the Forest crowd just before the Munich authorities "accidentally" switched off the lights. Another mysterious "accident" befell Clough in the press

conference. As soon as he began to get into full flow, his microphone went dead … another case of German revenge for a War jibe in Cologne?

By the time the press conferences were over, it was around 11.00pm. The plan was to grab a taxi to the city centre Sheraton Hotel that Nick had booked us into; a much plusher affair than editorial expenses would have allowed us. Alas, as we exited the stadium, the taxi ranks were empty. Worse, pilot Bond, who proved an extremely able interpreter, discovered that all the cabs were back in the city centre and would not be venturing out to the Olympic Park again this night. So we began to walk along the side of the autobahn, occasionally having to hurdle crash barriers, to stay on course for our hotel two miles or more distant. I began to beg for one of those efficient German police cars to swoop on us. Instead, and much better, we eventually managed to flag down a stray taxi.

As we hustled through the hotel foyer, I caught sight of a morose Colin Barrett sitting alone in a bar. The swashbuckling goal-scoring hero of the first round against Liverpool had suffered a recurrence of his knee injury in the home leg against Cologne and missed the climax to the great adventure. He could not even join the celebrations because Clough detested seeing limping players around his playing squad at all times – probably as a result of the cruel knee injury that ended his goal-scoring heroics prematurely. So Barrett was condemned to staying in the hotel reserved for players' wives and other close relatives. Instinct told me to pop in and have a word with Barrett, even though I daren't quote him.

But Trevor B kept me on course for our room on the 14th floor by pointing out that it was now past midnight. The phone was ringing between our twin beds as we unlocked the door and entered. To my surprise, it was not the office but a German journalist, Siegfried Drach, with whom I had made contact and exchanged information prior to the Cologne ties.

"I have to say congratulations," he said, "but 1FC Cologne would have defeated Nottingham tonight."

I laughed: "Not on your life, mate! But we will argue tomorrow. I have my report to write now."

As I put the phone down, it rang again. This time it was Ann Hemmingway, the copytaker in the *Evening Post* office in Forman Street tasked with taking my dictated match report plus enough other stories to fill one or more of the broadsheet pages that were to be wrapped around the outside of the *Evening Post* on Thursday 31 May 1979. Not having had a second to begin writing anything, it all had to flow off the top of my head. At one point, I became so hoarse that Trevor B disappeared downstairs to find me a drink. He came back with a bottle of red wine that presently made it harder for me to decipher my notes. But Ann, to her immense credit, had all the Malmo players' names in front of her and never interrupted my flow once until I had finished, around 3.30am. Then she said: "Oh Trevor! You've made it a much better match than it looked on telly." Because the one thing TV cannot transmit into a living room is the tension that fills a stadium on an occasion like this. Not that I had time to philosophise, even if the lovely Ann had had the inclination to listen to me.

Only now did it occur to me that Trevor B was absent. It turned out he had returned to the bar after bringing my bottle of wine and met up with Nick, who insisted on opening a tab for the Forest wives – and injured players like Barrett – to have a celebratory drink on the *Evening Post*. "Very thoughtful," beamed Trevor B, taking advantage of the tab to slake his own thirst. Half an hour after I put the phone down, we were on our way to the airport, picking our way through the massive Departure Hall and sundry corridors, all lined with red and white flags, shirts and scarves; all covering slumped supporters sleeping-off their celebrations like contented newts and awaiting their chartered flights that were to whisk them home later in the day.

The airport reopened at 6am. Our six-seater was the third to take-off, at 6.01 and a smidgen. As we curved up into the bright blue sky in a convoy of executive craft glinting in the bright sunshine, I sat back, comfortable in the knowledge that I had done my work and the lads back in the office would read it so thoroughly that no daft mistakes would sneak through to the readers. Trevor B, on the other hand, perched nervously on the edge of his seat hugging a small canvas bag packed with his films. Cameras in those days did not instantly reveal what pictures had been taken so my mate was concerned he had missed the Francis goal. He thought he'd seen the ball go into the net. His rule was that if the shutter closed at the right moment, he never actually saw the ball cross the line.

There was to be much drama – in truth, more than there had been in the match – before Trevor B discovered what pictures he'd taken. Everything went well with the flight until we began to cross the North Sea. The German sunshine was almost instantly replaced by thick cloud and Trevor B joked: "We must be home already." Alas Pilot Bond flicked open the door to his cockpit to inform us: "There's fog at East Midlands. We may be diverted."

"No!" came a three-man chorus.

"I'll see what I can do," responded Bond.

Health and Safety adherents look away now!

Presently, Bond reopened his door and announced: "We can try landing at East Mids providing none of you have any objections." Of course we hadn't. We had to get those pictures back. Even when we began to descend and the fog swept around us in thick waves, there were no visible concerns … though we Trevors both went uncharacteristically quiet.

"It's down there somewhere," said Bond, trying to laugh, referring to the ground.

It certainly was. The pocket rocket's wheels banged down so hard on the runway that, even though he was securely strapped in his seat, Trevor B swore his head hit the roof. It might have been his film bag; but that was so much a part of him, he would readily bleed for it.

It seemed an age before we boinged down again; but this time the brakes went on and Bond sped us towards the small sheds that were all there was to the East Midlands Airport in 1979. As we disembarked near the perimeter fence, a familiar figure loomed through the fog, shouting and waving. Steve Footitt, who had covered several of Forest's home ties with Trevor B, was there in his motor cycle leathers. Instantly, Trevor B sprinted towards him and lobbed the bagful of films over the fence and into his arms. A motor bike would be much quicker along the narrow road into Nottingham than our car; and there was no question of a security alert being triggered in those innocent days … Bond had already advised the airport of the urgency of our mission.

Not everyone was aware of our drama, however. Once the four of us entered Passport Control, we happened across a lone customs officer sitting back with his feet up on a desk, reading his morning paper. "Eyup, where've you come from?" he smiled.

"Munich," said Bond, who obviously knew the border guard.

"I thought we were still closed," he said.

"Really?" gasped Bond, eyebrows rising to mask the mocking in his posh public school voice.

"Good result, warn't it?"

"Absolutely," said Bond.

"Who'd a-thought it, eh?"

"Exactly," said Bond. "I'd better go and tell them I'm here."

While he went to fill in whatever official papers were necessary, off we trotted, through the near-deserted building, into the airport car park, into Nick's car … and so to Forman Street. We had landed at East Mids at around 9.30am. By 10.40am, when we reached the

Paste-Up Room (where pages were composed in the early days of computerised newspaper production before the entire process could be carried out on-screen), the final touches were being put to the designs by the three wise men who did most of the sub-editing, George Bramley, John Lucy and Ray Yeomans. It is to the credit of the kind of teamwork of which Clough would have been proud that the first edition began printing early that day with the unique front page you see here. (Please forgive the mucky fold down the centre; it's an old original that maybe should have gone for chip paper decades ago but is immeasurably too priceless to discard!)

Just after 11am, up in the Sports Department, while wandering around in a useless daze, I was approached by the Editor. This was a surprise because there was always a Board meeting at 11am on the first Thursday of the month. We rarely saw Mr. Snaith on those days at the afternoon Editorial Conference, never mind in "the workshop" at this time. His face was beetroot as ever and I suddenly feared that he'd spotted something glaring … a horror that we had all missed.

Then Mr. Snaith cleared his throat and spoke: "I've been asked – erm, sent – by the Chairman and the Board to tell you that you've done a fine job."

"Thankyou, Mr. Snaith," I said. "I think we've all done a fine job."

"Mmmm," he murmured, turning on his heel and returning to the Board meeting.

An hour or so later, my ever-supportive wife Gill had arrived to talk at me while I drove the 25 miles home, realising I would be pretty tired having had no sleep since 6am on the previous morning. But my glee turned to horror when we went into the *Post* courtyard.

Gone was the Colditz feel; the pickets had melted away with the end of the League football season. Gone was the morning fog; glorious sunshine blazed down on this celebratory day. Yet the old yard was more like Dunkirk circa 1940. It was filled by vans haphazardly queuing to be laden and, even more worryingly, by the street sellers who were usually stationed in all parts of the city centre at this time yelling out the day's headlines and vying for customers. The presses were totally silent.

"What's gone wrong?" I asked nobody in particular.

"Nothing," replied one of the van drivers. "It's just that everybody's sold out. Newsagents, street sellers, everybody. They're fetching a crew from the canteen to print through dinner time."

In fact, the presses did not stop again until they had printed more than twice the average sale of 150,000 copies on that magical day. It remains a record day's sale for the *Evening Post*. As Mr. Snaith was to observe when the figures were leaked six weeks or so later (for TBF never ever officially announced circulation figures): "Even more than we do for a Royal visit … amazing! After all, it was only a damn football match."

It was my turn to murmur: "Mmmm." As you will see from the picture pages, Trevor B captured all the key moments – bless his British Army Stores carrier bag – and Nick made a winning debut as a sports photographer by putting together a collector's package of postcard-size colour pictures that were snapped up like irresistible sweeties in the coming days.

The front page picture showed the faces of every one of the XI plus a few reserves and trainer Jimmy Gordon. On the back row (from left) were: Viv Anderson, Peter Shilton, reserve goalkeeper Chris Woods, John McGovern, Ian Bowyer, David Needham, Trevor Francis, Frank Clark, John O'Hare, Jimmy Gordon. Front: Larry Lloyd, John Robertson, Tony Woodcock, Kenny Burns and Garry Birtles (you remember him – that bloke whose name was spelt wrong in the autograph souvenir a couple of seasons earlier). It remains a collector's item after all this time!

EURO CUP SPECIAL !! .. EURO CUP SPECIAL !! .. EURO CUP SPECIAL !!

FOREST'S hands — captain John McGovern's, to be exact — are on the European Cup.

REDS' GLORY TOUR

MALMO goalkeeper Jan Moller collects a corner despite pressure from Ian Bowyer (8) and Kenny Burns.

TONY WOODCOCK sprawls over diving goalkeeper Jan Moller, who had bravely foiled his lone run on goal.

GARRY BIRTLES misses a chance — ballooning a short-range shot high over the bar.

The front page story revealed that Clough had threatened to delay the kick-off because his pass would not allow him into the VIP lounge pre-match. He argued with the doormen but they were adamant. He threatened that, in that case, the kick-off would have to be

EURO CUP SPECIAL !! · · EURO CUP SPECIAL !! · · EURO CUP SPECIAL !!

The goal that gave Forest Euro-Cup

Pictures from Munich
by
TREVOR BARTLETT

Above: Tony Woodcock celebrates the goal

John Robertson powers in his second-half shot against the post.

Tony Woodcock's lone run on goal is halted by the diving goalkeeper Jan Møller.

Above: The faces of scoring hero Trevor Francis and goalkeeper Peter Shilton tell the end of match story.

delayed until the accreditation error had been rectified. Stunned, the Germans allowed him in.

Who gave us this story at a time when Clough was still not speaking to us willingly? My lips remain sealed even after all these decades. But looking through Trevor B's picture of the Cup presentation, I'm particularly delighted to notice the new Chairman of Forest, Stuart Dryden, is all smiles from his vantage point in the stand. And, looking afresh through the pictures that were not used at the time, this one illustrates so many of the feelings in Munich that magical night…

Captain McGovern with the trophy, Clark, Lloyd, Birtles and Burns share the air of men who know they've done their job. Behind them, three of the Forest Committee men look on with disbelieving delight: Jimmy Pell (the balding gent above McGovern), Geoffrey Macpherson (to the left of Birtles) and Brian Appleby QC (in the spectacles above Burns). A dream come true? These realists had not even dared dream of such riches!

About six-and-a-half hours after we had landed at East Midlands Airport, Forest flew in (minus Clough, who had resumed his family holiday in Spain). By the time they landed, the sun was blazing, the place was thronged by well-wishers – and sales of the *Evening Post* were soaring. Oh, and this was the report (all 1,722 words of it) that I had dictated off the cuff:

All that glittered was not entirely golden in Munich last night, but as an old Bayern veteran of three European Cup triumphs said: "It is not important to play well in big matches. It is important to win them."

Nottingham Forest were seldom near their best, but their historic victory did set even more records.

They are the first club to win the trophy at the first attempt. Their victory means that England is the first nation to provide three European Champions.

And to put the icing on the cake, Europe's first ever £1 million football match was settled by a brilliant goal from England's first £1m player, Trevor Francis.

The golden goal came in injury time at the end of the first half. Ian Bowyer, replacing the injured Archie Gemmill in every sense in midfield, set John Robertson galloping down the left wing. For the first time in the game, Robertson was not surrounded by at least three Malmo defenders. For the first time in the game, he reached the by-line and his perfectly flighted centre looped over Sweden's international goalkeeper Jan Moller and his defenders for Francis to dive and head into the roof of the net.

It was a goal befitting the occasion in Munich's magnificent Olympic Stadium.

But the match will hardly be remembered as a classic by the football purists among the crowd, most of whom seemed to be wearing the red and white favours of Forest.

The noise was deafening as Forest kicked off and the pattern of the game was soon established. Forest flowed forward and Malmo's tactics alternated between packed defence and a frustrating offside trap.

First to fall into the trap was Garry Birtles within seconds of the kick-off. Viv Anderson, who had a better game as a support attacker than as a defender, sent Birtles in pursuit of a through ball that had Moller racing out of his penalty area to clear – but the linesman's flag saved Malmo early embarrassment.

With Larry Lloyd completely dominant in the air, Malmo's attacks appeared to be more in hope than expectation and Forest's thousands in the stands sat back to await goals that seemed inevitable.

The first big chance was created after ten minutes by Frank Clark who showed no signs of the groin injury which had threatened him making a fairy tale appearance at the summit of European football at the age of 35. His quick through ball enabled Birtles to beat the offside trap and out-run the Swedish defence. And the striker who had scored against all four opponents on the way to the final, looked to have struck again as his brilliant chip cleared the advancing goalkeeper. But the roar of delight choked in thousands of throats as the ball cleared the bar and settled on the roof of the net.

Within 60 seconds they were roaring again. This time Bowyer raced through but Malmo defender Ingemar Erlandsson stuck out a boot to concede a corner. As Robertson floated it over, Moller dropped the ball but midfielder Anders Ljungberg was back to clear as Lloyd challenged strongly.

Another minute on, Malmo had their clearest chance of the match. Kenny Burns, who otherwise did not put a foot wrong all night, ballooned a clearance back towards his own goal to leave striker Jan Olof Kinnvall standing between him and glory. But Shilton stood firm and the attacker merely kicked the ball straight up in the air. The goalkeeper controlled the situation from then on – just as he dominated every other Malmo excursion into the Forest danger area.

Francis, who had a brilliant first half, first made his presence felt with a 40-yard run which ended with him being bundled over. Though the free-kick was half-cleared, John McGovern burst into the penalty area but shot wide.

The temperature of the match – played in the cool of the evening of a blistering day in which the thermometer had reached the mid-80s – rose dramatically after 15 minutes. The busy Bowyer challenged for a high ball in midfield and laid out his opposite number, Magnus Andersson, angered the rest of the Malmo team and earned a swift rebuke from the referee.

This touch of steel spurred Forest – and for a time Francis seemed to take complete control of the more meaningful proceedings. First he beat three men with a stunning display of close control but his low cross sped fractionally behind Tony Woodcock and was scooped away for a corner.

Then Francis freed Anderson down the right and the full back's centre floated over both Birtles and Woodcock; and when Robertson chipped it back, Roland Andersson was happy to concede another corner.

Another high cross by Francis had three Forest players queuing unmarked for a crack at goal but Lloyd's downward header was scrambled away as Birtles hunted for a shooting chance.

Then Ljunberg was spoken to by the referee for a late, late tackle on Francis.

A rare Malmo attack ended with Viv Anderson holding Kinnvall on the edge of the Forest penalty area. Though they were given two chances at creating danger from the indirect free-kick, Malmo merely managed to concede a free-kick themselves – ironically, for offside.

Forest seemed to lose their way in the face of Malmo's offside tactics but almost opened the scoring after 29 minutes. Woodcock again showed superb control in the penalty area to lay on a shot for McGovern. The hard-working captain fired powerfully left-footed, but fractionally beyond Moller's right-hand post.

Then McGovern's determination took him past three men on the right to give Bowyer the chance to fire a shot of similar power low to Moller's right. The tall goalkeeper allowed the ball to squirm free but grabbed it as it rolled slowly towards his line.

Malmo's problems multiplied when their captain for the night, Staffan Tapper, limped off after 34 minutes. They had been forced to start the match without two of their best defenders, both injured in earlier European Cup games, and it was a sign of their desperate lack of experience that Tapper had appeared at all. For he broke a toe in the last minute of a training session last night and Malmo manager Bob Houghton explained later: "We thought there was a good chance that once he taped his foot and got his shoe on, it would get better as the game went on. But it did not work out that way."

Very little that Malmo attempted did work out and soon Francis was tormenting their defence again. Playing almost as an old-fashioned right-winger, he tricked his way past three tackles and crossed to John Robertson. But such was the depth of Malmo's defence that Robertson found himself crowded out by three defenders.

With five minutes to go to half-time, Birtles' flick-on gave Woodcock the chance to speed through the square Malmo defence for the clearest chance of the game. But the England striker pushed the ball too far ahead and the advancing Moller was able to smother it.

And the first half whistle was over-due when Forest struck the decisive blow. Bowyer's pass out of midfield sent Robertson galloping down the left, Francis' head-long dive speared the ball into the net – and the stadium seemed full of red and white banners. The neutrals among the crowd had clearly adopted Forest as their favourites – and a firework lit up the night sky as the "Super Reds" re-emerged for the second half.

But Forest rarely sparkled and first Clark and then Burns needed all their experience to cut out darting runs by Tore Cervin who resembled a Lone Ranger as Malmo hunted for an equaliser.

Then Shilton advanced to foil Cervin with Forest's defence standing, looking for an offside decision.

Robertson, whose contributions to the game were fitful, brought a semblance of class with a 30-yard pass which sent Birtles racing to the line to win a corner. But it came to nothing with Robertson suffering from a lack of space and an abundance of markers – problems which afflicted him for most of the night.

Birtles missed a glorious chance of scoring a second goal for Forest when Woodcock helped on a massive clearance by Shilton. With only Moller to beat from less than 10 yards, Birtles lofted the ball high over the bar.

Robertson went even closer after 63 minutes, lashing a close range shot against Moller's right-hand post after another brilliant run by Francis had the Malmo defence in total disarray.

But Malmo stuck stubbornly to their task, limited though they were in attacking ideas. Cervin won a free-kick on the edge of the Forest penalty area but his striking partner Tommy Hansson capped a quiet game by blasting his shot high over the bar.

On the hour, magnificent skills mixed with determination took Woodcock through the massed defence. He chipped the ball over the goalkeeper but as the crowd rose again in anticipation of a goal, it drifted away past the far post.

And that just about summed-up the second half. Forest came so close to totally over-running Malmo – but were so far from breaking their determination.

For example, Robertson was fouled three times in a minute, took the third free-kick himself and saw the ball skim off Lloyd's head and go narrowly wide again.

Cervin, doing his best to ruffle the composure of the Forest defence, managed to get his head to a left wing corner but could not direct the ball well enough to trouble Shilton. The goalkeeper, did, however, have to rush out to correct (sic) a through ball from Erlandsson, Sweden's Footballer of the Year, as 18-year-old Robert Prytz rushed in unnoticed and unmarked.

Then Anderson got in a vital tackle as Cervin bore in on the otherwise unprotected Shilton.

With seven minutes to go Malmo pulled off the ineffective Hansson and sent on yet another midfielder, Tommy Andersson.

But the last act of the game was left to Forest's Anderson. He raced upfield to support a break by Francis – and was caught offside. It was the 16th time Forest had fallen into the trap – but the crowd were past caring.

Even the German supporters were singing: "We all agree, Nottingham Forest are Magic." (That was copytaker Ann's capital M.) They weren't as magic as they can be. But they had done more than enough to win the Cup.

And, of course, the after-match press conference provided me with my first opportunity to quote Clough … though I made sure I skulked towards the back of the packed room so as not to risk him insisting on me being evicted. As a general rule, I never began a story with quotation marks; but I made an exception on this occasion. I'm sure the discerning reader will appreciate my reason…

'IT WAS A CLASSIC' SAYS CLOUGH

"IT WAS a classic," enthused manager Brian Clough about the goal that brought the European Cup to Nottingham. And he gave all the credit to winger John Robertson.

"It was the first time Robertson got to the by-line in the first half. It was a marvellous cross. Scoring goals is never easy — but Bob could have put that one in," he said, referring to Malmo's manager.

"Oh, I don't know," responded Houghton. "I would have hit the woodwork."

HUMOUR

That was a rare moment of humour in the after-match press conference. Houghton was obviously disappointed with his team's performance. "We were poor and one of the reasons was that all three of our most experienced players were not there tonight."

BRIAN CLOUGH

Houghton added: "Trevor Francis was marvellous in the first half. I am pleased for him because I am sure he had been under a lot of pressure since he moved to Nottingham.

"They have got four attacking players of very high class. Francis in the first half and Robertson in the second did very well but our two central defenders also did well against Birtles and Woodcock."

EXCELLENT

But Houghton summed up his disappointment: "The only thing to do in the European Cup Final is to win it because people do not remember losers.

"But Nottingham Forest are an excellent side and technically much better than us. We needed to have a very good day and to play them on a day when they were not at the top of their form. But they don't have many off days."

BOBBY HOUGHTON

As if that was not enough, there was also the need to carry out a news check with the local police in this era when English supporters were beginning to accumulate a reputation for violence. Thankfully, with no arrests reported, I was able to contribute this almost genteel colour piece, which found its way onto the front page underneath Trevor B's fabulous picture of the team with the trophy…

WHILE Nottingham Forest conquered Europe last night, their fans took over Munich — and turned the staid Bavarian capital into a giant Old Market Square.

Red and white scarves, banners, shirts and even socks smothered the city — and most of Munich was amused rather than outraged.

The 20,000 fans from Nottingham won the hearts of the locals in the beer halls and beer gardens so comprehensively that the vast majority of the 70,000 crowd in the Olympic Stadium cheered Forest on — irrespective of their own nationality.

The man with most troubles in Munich last night — apart from one hotelier who had his premises severely damaged by a small fraction of runaway Reds — was the man who carried off the biggest prize, Brian Clough.

Before the match, Forest's manager was denied access to the VIP lounge at the Stadium.

He argued with the doormen. But they were adamant that he did not have the correct ticket, so he would not be allowed in.

He threatened that, in that case, the start of the match would have to be delayed. Stumed, the Germans allowed him in.

The match started on time, Forest's £1 million signing Trevor Francis scored the only goal — and the first man to congratulate him at the end of the match was

Archie Gemmill, who had been on the substitutes bench

Clough left the field with arms aloft applauding Forest's success and opened his press conference under intense lights by saying "This is like being on trial. The sweat's running off me now more than it was during the match."

As the questions rolled in, the microphones had the cheek to break down on Clough. But he overcame that — and had special words of praise for the Forest fans.

He has never hidden his criticism of low attendances at the City Ground. But he said of last night's 20,000: "They did us proud. We genuinely feel emotion when we get a lot of supporters behind us.

Asked if Forest would now play

the South American club champions for the World Championship he said: "If we were invited, we would love to play. But I would not fancy a trip to Argentina in the middle of our League season.

"I would like to invite them to play one match — probably at Wembley in November. Then I would have a week in Barcelona."

Malmo manager Bob Houghton who has always insisted that Liverpool remain the best team in Europe said: "I think some people are going to be disappointed by Forest's performance tonight. But you don't win the European Cup in one game. "You have to win your own league and beat four other European teams. Forest are worthy champions."

Forest's run to glory in the 1978-79 European Cup

	Liverpool (H) 2-0	Liverpool (A) 0-0	AEK Athens (A) 2-1	AEK Athens (H) 5-1	Grasshopper (H) 4-1	Grasshopper (A) 1-1	Cologne (H) 3-3	Cologne (A) 1-0	Malmo (Munich) 1-0
Shilton	1	1	1	1	1	1	1	1	1
Anderson	2	2	2	2 G	2	2		2	2
Barrett	3 G					3	2		
McGovern	4	4	4 G		4	4	4	4	4
Burns	5	5	5					5	5
Lloyd	6	6	6	6	6 G	6	6	6	6
Bowyer	7	7	7	7			7 G	8 G	8
Gemmill	8	8	8	8	8 G	8	8i		
Birtles	9 G	9	9 G	9GG	9 G	9	9 G	9	9
Woodcock	10	10	10	10 G	10	10	10	10	10
Robertson	11	11	11	11	11 P	11	11 G	11	11
Clark		3	3	3	3		8s	3	3
Needham				5 G	5	5	5		
O'Neill						7	7 G	7	7
O'Hare				4					
Francis									7 G

and how the League Cup was retained in 1978-79

	Oldham Athletic (A) 0-0	Oldham Athletic (H) 4-2	Oxford United 5-0	Everton 3-2	Brighton & HA (H) 3-1	Watford (H) 3-1	Watford 0-0	Southampton (Wembley) 3-2
Shilton	1	1	1	1	1	1	1	1
Anderson	2	2	2 G	2 G	2	2	2	
Barrett	3	3						2
McGovern	4	4	4 G		4 G	4	4	4
Burns	5	5 G	5	5			5	
Lloyd			6	6 G	6	6	6	6
O'Neill	7	7	7 G			7	7	7
Gemmill	8	8	8	8	8		8	8
Birtles			9 G	9	9 G	9GG	9	9GG
Woodcock	10	10 G	10	10 G	10	10	10	10 G
Robertson	11	11 P	11 G	11	11 G	11 G	11	11
Bowyer	9			7	7	8	3	
Needham	6	6 G		3	5	5		5
Clark			3		3	3		3
O'Hare				4				
Elliott		9						

Forest also finished runners-up in the First Division, never quite compensating for that run of six draws in seven matches at the start of the season. Final table for 1978-79:

Pos		P	W	D	L	F	A	Pts
1	Liverpool	42	30	8	4	85	16	68
2	Nottingham Forest	42	21	18	3	61	26	60
3	West Bromwich Albion	42	24	11	7	72	35	59
4	Everton	42	17	17	8	52	40	51
5	Leeds United	42	18	14	10	70	52	50
6	Ipswich Town	42	20	9	13	63	49	49
7	Arsenal	42	17	14	11	61	48	48
8	Aston Villa	42	15	16	11	59	49	46
9	Manchester United	42	15	15	12	60	63	45
10	Coventry City	42	14	16	12	58	68	44
11	Tottenham Hotspur	42	13	15	14	48	61	41
12	Middlesbrough	42	15	10	17	57	50	40
13	Bristol City	42	15	10	17	47	51	40
14	Southampton	42	12	16	14	47	53	40
15	Manchester City	42	13	13	16	58	56	39
16	Norwich City	42	7	23	12	51	57	37
17	Bolton Wanderers	42	12	11	19	54	75	35
18	Wolverhampton Wanderers	42	13	8	21	44	68	34
19	Derby County	42	10	11	21	44	71	31
20	Queens Park Rangers	42	6	13	23	45	73	25
21	Birmingham City	42	6	10	26	37	64	22
22	Chelsea	42	5	10	27	44	92	20

League appearances: 42 each – Shilton, Robertson. 40 – Anderson. 36 each – McGovern, Lloyd, Woodcock. 35 – Birtles. 28 – O'Neill. . 26 – Bowyer. 25 – Burns. 24 – Gemmill. 23 – Needham. 20 – Clark. 19 – Francis. 11 – Barrett. 9 – O'Hare. 4 each – Elliott, Gary Mills. 1 each – Withe, Bryn Gunn.
League scorers: 14 – Birtles. 10 each – O'Neill, Woodcock. 9 – Robertson. 4 – Bowyer. 2 – Needham. 1 each – Anderson, Barrett, Gemmill, Mills.

Weeks after the football season ended, Trevor B was summoned into Mr. Snaith's office. It was such a rare occurrence that he instantly felt he must be in trouble. As soon as he entered and saw Mr. Snaith's pate was blushing, he knew he was in trouble.

"I've received this invoice from the hotel you stayed at in Munich," said the Editorial Director, shoving an A4 sheet across his desk. "How did you manage to consume several hundred pounds worth of alcohol in such a short time?" He sat back in his leather chair, satisfied that he had got at least one of us bang to rights.

Trevor B explained that it was the idea of the Chairman's Son that we treat the players' wives to a celebration drink. Imagine Mr. Snaith's incredulity. He detested Clough. The more Forest enjoyed success, the more publicity he had to allow the damned man. Yet we had actually spent money – money that might now be sucked from his precious

Editorial budget – on encouraging them when all we should have been thinking of was rushing home.

If, that is, what Trevor B had told him was the truth.

So off Mr. Snaith marched along the Executive Corridor, unwittingly doing his rather convincing impersonation of *Dad's Army's* Captain Mainwaring in high dudgeon. And back he came, with a perceptively slower stride and his persistent frog more firmly in his throat, to inform Mr. Bartlett that – um – his explanation had been accepted and – um – the invoice would be paid.

8

Out of the cold I'm Clough's mate!

WEDNESDAY MORNING, 4 October 1979, and Trevor B and myself were in the freezing Swedish city of Oester, receiving an unexpected guided tour of the Vaxjo Football Club's facilities from their chief executive, when Clough and Taylor appeared, heading towards us along a winding, bush-lined path beside the training ground. "It's bloody Frecknall," I heard Taylor chuckle to Clough – and braced myself for the mother and father of gloats from the magical manager who had done his best to make my newspaper, as well as me, disappear over the previous 10 months.

Clough had spent the 24 hours before the second leg of Forest's European Cup first round tie against Oester Vaxjo challenging his own club's committee to sack him because he had run up debts in his transfer dealings. It was his way of entertaining the 'Midland mafia' as we jokingly nicknamed the national newspaper journalists who had travelled on Forest's charter flight to the tie. The description, I hasten to add, was given not because the journalists were at all sinister but because they had become accustomed to hunting in a pack. Indeed, they had all travelled to Sweden on Forest's chartered flight. We two Trevors plus the newest recruit to the Sports Department, an ambitious young reporter called Duncan Hamilton (from the Leicester-based agency of the supportive freelance, Roly Orton) had spent the same 24 hours getting to this modest town of 55,000 souls on the edge of the Arctic Circle by public flights. I had taken Hamilton on because the Sports Department had been stretched to the limit since the departures of Bowles and Lawson; and while the pickets had now disappeared, along with demands for TBF to reinstate the 28, no fully-qualified journalists were willing to risk the wrath of the National Union of Journalists by joining we pariahs of the industry. And Clough had still showed no signs of softening his stance against us. So Hamilton was on a learning curve … indeed, we all were.

Clough had the advantage in every way. He knew the Forest committee dare not contemplate dismissing the management that had brought them trophies beyond their dreams. He was 2-0 up on Vaxjo thanks to two goals by Ian Bowyer in the first leg at the City Ground on 19 September. And, crucially from our point of view, our pocket rocket was broken: the six-seater aircraft that had whisked us from previous European triumphs had problems with its direction-finding. Pilot Bond reported this problem when he aimed for Zurich with our then-Production Director, the cheerful electrician called Charlie Wright who was destined to become Managing Director, a few days earlier and landed somewhere in Austria. So we Trevors had to wend our way to Vaxjo by service flights – from East Midlands Airport to Amsterdam, then to Frankfurt in West Germany and then to Vaxjo.

As fate would have it, a fellow passenger on the final leg of the Tuesday night journey into Vaxjo was Geoffrey Macpherson, a Quaker who had become vice-chairman of Forest when Dryden was promoted to the chair. He was a genial, genuine self-made success of a businessman who epitomised the Football Club Director of the era: he treated the sport as a relief from the harsh realities of life. Which, of course, put him and his ilk at odds with Clough's philosophy that nothing could be more important than the Football Club … hence the Manager's oft-uttered complaint: "Those buggers are playing with my livelihood."

Macpherson had been a friend of the *Post* through the industrial dispute; as pragmatic as Dryden in his acceptance that newspaper and football club needed to work together irrespective of whether they enjoyed the experience. Now I sadly warned Macpherson that, because we would not be able to fly back to East Midlands Airport by service flights until Thursday, there would be no action pictures by Trevor B to go with the report this time.

"Oh, that's a dreadful shame," Macpherson sighed, "because you've done so well in the face of the manager's opposition so far."

Encouraged, I asked Macpherson to spread the word among the Forest hierarchy that the fall in our standards would have nothing to do with Clough continuing to blank us for political reasons. The last thing I wanted was the problem to be exacerbated by inaccurate rumours that the *Evening Post* was escalating its war with the European Champions.

So when we three trudged along the icy streets from our hotel to the homely Vaxjo ground to collect our passes for the match, we were far from as ebullient. The fact that the club office was closed somehow suited our mood. We wandered around until we came across a groundsman who, by sign language, indicated we should pop into the solicitor's office across the road. It turned out the solicitor also ran the football club in his spare time. He had plenty of time that morning, too, despite it being the biggest occasion in the history of the club. He proudly took us on a guided tour of the modest-looking ground with its concrete terraces; and it evoked thoughts for me that an English Third Division club could aspire to the European Cup given the business-like attitude evident here. Why not? I'd graduated from scribbling reports about by village team as a 7, 8 and 9-year-old building his own sports paper with the help of League results gleaned from the old wireless. And Wimbledon were in the process of climbing from non-league football to FA Cup winners in a home that was not much more than a pub ground down Plough Lane. Indeed, it was barely three years since Forest had been fearing another spell in the Third Division. So what dream was impossible?

Under the Vaxjo stands, there were more encouragements for local youngsters willing to work to make their sporting dreams come true: gymnasia and tennis courts, which maybe explain why Sweden succeeds in summer sports despite enduring more winter than most. Then the proud lawyer led us into the park beside the ground … and along came Clough and Taylor. It was as if we two Trevors were chained to the railway line with the nasty steaming train clanking closer and closer; there was no escape.

"Morning, young man," said Clough, ever-present squash racket swinging from his hand.

"Good morning Brian," I smiled, nodding to Taylor, who remained a dutiful step behind, keeping his head down literally as well as metaphorically.

"I understand you've got problems, apart from having an arsehole for a boss," Clough went on.

"We can't get back until tomorrow, so my report'll be in tomorrow night's paper but you'll have to wait until Friday for Trevor's pictures."

"That's a shame for you two."

"Aye, well, the boss's plane's broken so we've got to use service flights."

"So I heard."

There was a silence. I waited for the verbal assault. And not for the last time, he stunned me. He drawled: "Why don't you come back with us?"

I am not sure what, or if, I replied but suddenly Trevor B was tugging on the arm of my overcoat, whispering "Noooooooooooooo!"

"There's plenty of room in our plane. You can sit where my directors should be. And we're going back straight after the match," he persisted quietly, persuasively.

"But we're booked into the hotel here tonight and have seats on planes tomorrow," I managed.

"Hey," Clough became louder; his usual dominant self. "I'm not having any mates of mine stuck in this cold hole another night."

Mates of mine! He hadn't spoken to us civilly for 10 months. He was the focal point of the Socialists' war against the *Evening Post* management. "Noooooooooooooo!" whispered Trevor B again, almost swinging on my sleeve in his efforts to pull me away.

"How could we?" I asked.

"Be in the team bus 10 minutes after the final whistle," said Clough.

"OK," I replied, "thanks very much." I reached out to shake his hand but he was already walking away, to catch up with the training session being organised by Jimmy Gordon.

"Nooooooooooooooo!" said Trevor B again, more audibly this time.

"We'll be all right," I said, trying to shake Trevor B's grip from my sleeve.

"He'll wait till we're over the North Sea and tip us out – he's a megalomaniac, you know," cautioned Trevor B.

"Not with 'the Midland mafia' on board, he can't," I argued.

"He's got them in his pocket – look at what he's done for them today," persisted Trevor B. He had a point. On the flight to Sweden, Clough had taken umbrage that five of "my directors", as he called the elected committee that ran Forest, had stayed home. Interpreting it as a vote of no-confidence in himself and Taylor, with the club staring at a debt of record proportions, he suggested they were being driven out.

Dryden swiftly discounted the theory. The front page lead, written by David Stapleton in the match-day's *Evening Post* screamed the headline: Reds' chief says 'Clough stays'. But Clough's version had made national headlines to justify the trips of the 'Midland mafia'. As Clough had told me in the act of kicking me out of the City Ground: "All life's a game."

Now, it seemed, all life was a circle. We were back in favour. So I persuaded Trevor B we ought to take part in Clough's latest game and watch the training session. It served two purposes. It showed the players that we lepers from the *Evening Post* were back on-side with he who must be obeyed. And it gave me an unforgettable insight into how Clough and Taylor put together the human jigsaw that was their team of unlikely heroes.

Clough had always said: "It never ceases to amaze me that so many people have so much difficulty assembling a good football team. How can they make such a simple job so complex?" What happened next in that frozen Swedish park brought the oft-repeated quote to life…

On the third or maybe fourth occasion the fluency of the kick-about was interrupted by the ball disappearing into a mass of hardy shrubs, Clough raised his squash racket – the signal for trainer Gordon to blow his whistle to halt play. Each time the ball had left the pitch, it was because Archie Gemmill's passes were just too far in front of John Robertson on the left wing.

"Mr. Gemmill," Clough beckoned.

"Yes Boss," responded the little Scotland midfield player who was famous for scoring the best goal of the 1978 World Cup Finals, with a mesmerising slalom-like run through the Dutch defence.

"I bought you to give the ball to Mr. Robertson," drawled Clough.

"Yes Boss," agreed Gemmill, who had by this time trotted to a position barely a yard in front of Clough.

"As you'll have noticed, Mr. Robertson is a rather corpulent young gentleman with short legs that do not move as fast as some others in the club."

"Yes Boss."

"So your job is to pass the ball to Mr. Robertson's feet," Clough continued.

"Yes Boss."

"You're sure you can still do that, aren't you?"

"Yes Boss."

"Good, because if you can't we can easily leave you here and find somebody else who can give Mr. Robertson the ball where he wants it."

"Yes Boss."

"So long as we're clear…"

"Yes Boss."

As the winters rolled on and I began to spend more midweek time at the City Ground, usually in the Jubilee Club waiting for management or players to finish training, I got to know the Clough philosophy and Mr. Robertson rather better.

"His pace is deceptive; he's even slower than he looks," Clough would say with a mischievous glint in his eye. Then he would add seriously: "But he only needs to be lightning over 18 inches." That was enough for the mesmeric Scot's wand-like left foot to make space for an accurate cross past his marker and into the opposition penalty area where the centre forward was expected to meet it, ahead of his marker, at the near post while the second striker made for the far post just in case the ball's elevation was higher. Look at the picture of Francis heading the Cup-winning goal in the Munich final and you can see Birtles had been aiming for the near post, only for the ball to go over his head to the far post, where Francis's speed had beaten Woodcock to it.

Robbo's other forte was taking penalties and free kicks; "set-pieces" as they are known in the game. So Clough frequently excused him from chunks of some training sessions and he would spend the time in the warmth of the Jubilee Club, cadging Benson & Hedges tipped cigarettes off me, talking about anything but newsy football matters. Presently one of the coaching staff would pop his head around the door and say: "Excuse me John. The Gaffer wants to try a few set-pieces."

Robbo would stub out his cigarette and slope off with all the overt enthusiasm of a captured truant, shoulders hunched up to his ears, hands stuffed into the waistband of his tracksuit bottoms.

Special treatment? This, remember, was the man who created the European Cup-winning goal of 1979 against Malmo and who would go on to score the European Cup-winning goal of 1980 against Hamburg … all on a diet of chips, instant food and cadged fags, according to folk lore. And his God had equipped him with all the attributes Clough required of a No.11: an ability to stay close to the touchline, thus stretching the opposition defence by denying the right back the option to move inside to give cover to his central defenders; close control so that he could hold the ball until colleagues were able to move up-field and help mount a coordinated attack; enough positional sense to know when to drift back to assist his left back in defence; and, most important of all, a left foot that could caress a ball onto the head of a centre forward with uncanny accuracy or fire a free-kick like a cannon ball through the slightest gap in a defensive wall.

Half-time in Vaxjo also gave an indication of Clough's control. Francis, scorer of the goal in Munich, £1m footballer, theoretically the most precious commodity in Forest's current financial plight, queued just behind me to get into the public urinal under the Main Stand. He was unable to play because he had returned from his summer stint in the USA with an injury but Clough had broken his embargo on injured players travelling with the team to insist Francis took the opportunity to get to know his team-mates better.

"Why not go in the dressing room, Trevor?" I asked through chattering teeth, emitting a cloud of frozen breath.

"The Boss wouldn't like it."

"Oh?"

"Only the team's allowed in there at half-time."

The need for Clough and his players to concentrate on the job in hand was evident either side of our unexpected conversation. Oester's provincial over-achievers, inspired by a crowd of 14,772 – more than twice their average attendance – took the lead, created another couple of credible chances and generally exploited the difficulties Forest were experiencing in the domestic League at the time.

The 1-1 draw was finally achieved by Tony Woodcock converting a looping centre from the 17-year-old – yes, 17-year-old – Gary Mills, drafted in by Clough to do the job that he felt Gemmill was temporarily incapable of doing. Such was the loyalty created by Clough that, as the years rolled by, Gemmill became not just one of his backroom staff but also his chauffeur between his home and the ground when it was patently obvious the manager would risk exploding a breathalyser should he ever venture into the driving seat of a vehicle.

Such were my doubts in Vaxjo about Clough's offer of a lift home, I had insisted we leave our luggage in the hotel rather than drag it to the ground. Only when we were sitting on the team bus and Clough was obviously ready to keep his word did I mention: "Can we go round by our hotel to pick up the bags?"

"For f***'s sake!" muttered Clough. But he ordered the driver to change course.

"You've got two minutes," shouted Clough, his voice suddenly a dozen octaves higher, as the bus drew to a halt at the hotel entrance. In we raced, up the lift, into our rooms, grabbed the packed bags, down the stairs, back to the bus.

"Good lads," he smiled as we staggered back onto the bus. "Now let's get going. I want to get home and I know you do."

At the airport, he insisted his new friends checked-in for the flight ahead of him. The reason: he knew there would be problems. As the Swedish customs officer who had collected our passports pointed out: "There is no Mr. Frecknall on the manifest. Or Mr. Bartlett. Or Mr. Hamilton."

"How can that happen?" asked Clough, his voice even and quieter than usual, not at all challenging. "I thought you were an efficient nation."

"We are, Mr. Clough," said the officer.

"And yet you lose three of my friends from my passenger list."

"That is not possible."

"Oh, have their names suddenly appeared on the list then?"

"No, Mr. Clough."

"So it is possible."

"Apparently so."

"So how can we sort this out?"

The officer shrugged.

"Where's your boss?"

"At home, Mr. Clough."

"Shall we phone him?"

"It is past 11 o' clock. He will be in bed."

"So shall we wake him up or are you going to let my friends come home with me?"

The customs officer shrugged again and waved us through.

On the chartered plane, Trevor B headed for the back seats. As he put it: "Let's get as far away from him as we can." The "him" in question took the second seat from the front on the right, with Taylor beside him, just as he tended to do on the team bus.

Presently, John Wragg of the *Daily Express* (as it was then titled) slipped into the seat on the opposite side of the gangway to us and grinned: "Fancy seeing you here."

"Fancy," I said.

"I still think he'll wait til we're over the North Sea, open a door and throw us out," said Trevor B.

"If he does, there'll be plenty of us left to write the story," smiled Wraggy. Which did not make Trevor B feel noticeably better. He kept straining his neck to peer over the top of the seats for any movement by Clough.

Sure enough, as soon as the 'fasten seatbelts' light went off, Clough stood and headed inexorably towards us. "Told you," muttered Trevor B. "Bloody told you."

Clough's face was impassive as he ignored all comments from the other journalists and made a bee-line for us. "Move over, Wraggy," he cajoled and sat so that, in effect, he was beside me with only the gangway between us.

"I think it's time you and me began to work together," he said.

"That's brilliant, Brian." I could not hide my smile of relief and delight.

"So Wraggy, if I see any of what I'm about to say in the *Express* before it appears in the *Nottingham Evening Post*, I'll know you cannot be trusted."

John Wragg was – and is – entirely trustworthy. We got our exclusive from Clough ... and got Trevor B's match pictures back from Vaxjo in good time for the next day's *Post*.

The atmosphere between Clough and the *Post* took another giant turn for the better when the manager earned a Citizen of the Month Award, presented by the Nottinghamshire Police in an initiative publicised by the *Evening Post*, after he talked a man out of throwing himself off Trent Bridge in November of 1980.

"I told him he shouldn't have gone to watch that lot on the other side of the river in the first place," Clough frequently joked about the situation in the years to come. But the fact was that it was a massive drama at the time. Clough had been in the passenger seat of his car, being driven home from a night match, when his driver (his accountant) was forced to stop because a throng of people barred the way. Realising something was amiss, Clough leapt from the car and realised two policemen – a sergeant and a constable – were trying to talk a man off the parapet.

The citation said that Clough "spoke continually" to the would-be suicide. He would; he was good at that. More important, though, as he spoke, he edged closer and closer to the man until he could embrace him and make sure he did not leap.

The presentation was made by the county Chief Constable, Mr. Charles McLachlan (on the left of the picture). The beaming chap in the middle is none other than Mr. Snaith…

But, first, there was another European Cup Final to be won…

9

Faithful to the Imprisoned Chairman

• •

IT EVENTUALLY transpired that there was a good reason why Stuart Dryden, the Forest Chairman, had not been in Sweden. He was being investigated by the Post Office authorities over irregularities in his village business. In January 1980 he was found guilty of four charges of dishonestly obtaining money from the Post Office. The prosecution claimed he used the ill-gotten cash to pay the wages of part-time holiday staff. Clough stood by him as firmly as Dryden had supported Clough's sometimes unorthodox, but entirely legal, tactics in recruiting players like Shilton.

Dryden's fellow committee members were not so supportive of their Chairman – though they fudged an opportunity to sack him by cancelling a meeting scheduled for the day of his conviction. Their reason was that Forest were due to be playing at Liverpool that night. The match was postponed because of bad weather but the committeemen did not feel able to meet and risk being accused by Clough of deflecting attention from the big match. But such prevarication most certainly did not increase Clough's admiration of their collective moral fibre. More importantly, though, the scandal did not side-track the squad's pursuit of more silverware.

And the fact that Clough had called a truce with us meant that I could revert to being Sports Editor of the *Evening Post* and Editor of the *Football Post*; and leave Hamilton to cover Forest for us. It was not easy; working with Clough never was for anyone. Hamilton would frequently phone me at night to relate afternoon conversations with Clough so that between us we could work out what was on the record and what was not; what was intended for publication and what might have been said in drink. It is amazing how alcohol could loosen tongues but shrink memories throughout football; the last impression I want to give is that Clough's problems in this respect were unique.

There was a good reason why Hamilton called Clough "his l-l-lordship". He had a stutter, so it was murder for him to say: "C-c-c-clough." Not to mention: "M-m-m-manager." Even "D-d-d-uncan" was a problem for him on the phone. But he could roll the letter 'l' so that the speech impediment was hidden in words like "l-l-lordship".

To their credit, Clough and Taylor took pity on the little chap – he stood about 5-foot 3-inches and, beneath his fringe of blond hair looked more like a choirboy than an inquisitor – especially when he was trying to get team news. This is how one conversation went early in Hamilton's days with us, on a Friday after Viv Anderson and had been away playing for England and John Robertson had been with Scotland for midweek internationals…

Hamilton: "Have you g-g-g…"

Taylor: "Got a team?"

Hamilton: "Y-y-y."

Clough: "What do you think? Both my right back and left winger have come back with knocks."

Hamilton: "Well, as you c-c-c-an imagine, I c-c-c-ouldn't be r-r-r."

Taylor: "Right back."

Hamilton: "B-b-b-ut I'm a g-g-g."

Taylor: "Good left winger."

Clough (moving to pat him on the head): "Good lad. But don't tell your f***ing bosses."

It was just one of the straight-faced reminders that politics and trade unionism were still not far from the surface as Forest marched on to their third successive League Cup Final and their second European Cup Final – pausing only to defeat the Spanish giants of Barcelona over two legs to add the Super Cup to their dream-like collection of trophies that should never have been within reach of a club based in the provinces and usually rooted in the second or third tier of English football.

Clough made sure that the Super Cup trip to Spain happened in early February because "we all deserve a bit of sun on our backs." My "f***ing bosses", as he was eternally happy to call them, decided the trip should be a special treat for we two Trevors, for the way we had handled the previous winter's trials and tribulations.

The pocket rocket was rolled out to wing us plus our wives, Gill Frecknall and Sandra Bartlett, to the sunshine leg; and Nick Forman Hardy made sure we were treated like VIPs for three days. Indeed, to this day, both Gill and Sandra possess extremely expensive Coco Chanel handbags purchased for them by the delightful Mrs. Forman Hardy as a souvenir of the era.

In the Press Box, the experienced Stapleton (whose father Albert had covered Notts County for decades) and the newcomer Hamilton settled into tracking Forest's day-to-day progress. Daft as it sounds now, it was almost inevitable that Forest would return home with the trophy.

It was equally inevitable that, even though I sat in the comfort of the Main Stand with Gill, Sandra and Mr. and Mrs. Forman Hardy, I wrote the report for the *Evening Post* of 6 February 1980. It began like this…

> Nottingham Forest last night confirmed what we have been saying since May – that they are the club champions of Europe. And they did it the hard way in the second leg of the Super Cup against Cup Winners Cup holders Barcelona.
>
> Before 100,000 fanatical, whistling, jeering Spaniards packed into the breath-taking Barcelona stadium rather like ants on cliff-faces, our Super Reds managed to:
>
> - Concede a penalty, thus surrendering the 1-0 lead eked out of the first leg in the much more mundane – and muddy – surroundings of the City Ground last week;
> - Lose Trevor Francis, the £1m goal-scoring hero of the European Cup Final, with a leg injury;
> - Miss a penalty themselves (though there seemed little doubt that the Spanish goalkeeper moved before John Robertson actually took the kick);
> - Triumph 2-1 on aggregate thanks to a goal set up by Larry Lloyd and scored by his defensive mate, Kenny Burns.

Needless to say, Trevor Bartlett provided the spectacular photographic proof of the Forest winner, which came from a corner kick by Robertson. It is reproduced here, showing Lloyd taking a tumble (far right) after leaping above the Barcelona goalkeeper, Artola, who can only watch Burns soar to head into the empty net. What it doesn't show

is that only four people in a certain section of the Main Stand stood and cheered the goal: Mr. and Mrs. Forman Hardy and Mesdames Bartlett and Frecknall.

The dedicated David Stapleton did the ferreting for the previews and the after-match quotes, eliciting the news that Francis would be out for some time because his leg wound had required several stitches. Bartlett's picture of him limping off also vividly illustrated how the home fans' incessant whistling affected our wounded hero …

Despite such setbacks, it seemed a foregone conclusion that Forest would retain the League Cup after they saw-off the arch-rivals from Liverpool in the semi-finals thanks to Robertson penalties in each leg. Alas at Wembley, Shilton and David Needham made a hash of a routine defensive situation, leaving Andy Gray (in his pre-Sky Television incarnation) to tap-in the only goal of the Final and earn Wolves an unexpected, unlikely and undeserved victory.

European Cup performances were also less fluent than the previous season but effective enough as Forest got past Arges Pitesti (2-0 at home, 2-1 in Romania), Dynamo Berlin (a catastrophic 0-1 at home, 3-1 in East Germany) and, most spectacularly of all in the semi-finals, Ajax (2-0 at home, 0-1 in Amsterdam).

All of which earned Forest a trip to Real Madrid's legendary Bernabeu Stadium for the Final against Hamburg – fired by England captain Kevin Keegan – on Wednesday 28 May.

No prizes for guessing who were the favourites. Forest had set a record by going 14 games without defeat in the European Cup, beating the previous longest run by Real Madrid. Hamburg had defeated Real 5-1 in West Germany to overturn a 0-2 first leg defeat in Spain in an epic semi-final.

Keegan described the Final as "a dream come true." I got more than I dreamed of when our pocket rocket landed in Madrid to cover the match. Who should we join in the queue to get through Customs than the Hamburg squad. Using the kind of footwork that made John Robertson lightning over 18 inches, I manoeuvred myself to within whispering distance of the England icon, who was surprised to be standing amid Germans in a Spanish airport and suddenly hearing: "Hello Mr. Keegan."

He turned, startled, and I introduced myself. "Oh, hello," he smiled. By the time we'd had our passports checked and Keegan escaped onto the Hamburg team bus, I had enough for a preview story! The final itself turned into a nightmare for the genial Keegan when he was clattered, with the ball far away and all officials' eyes focussed elsewhere, in the opening seconds. To this day, the identity of the Forest player involved in the, er, collision remains a secret. Neither has there ever been confirmation – or, for that matter, denial – of a rumour that there was a bonus on offer to the first player to slow Keegan. What's said in the dressing room stays in the dressing room and ever more shall be so.

The drama of that night, so far as I was concerned, came about 90 minutes earlier, as I walked past the VIP entrances on my way to the Media Tribune. Above the multi-lingual hubbub, I heard a Nottinghamian shout of: "Trevor! Trevor! Trevor Frecknall!"

Peering around, I eventually espied Dryden, fresh from his clash with the law. Lucky he was as tall as a lighthouse, otherwise I'd never have spotted him from his disadvantaged point on the wrong side of a barred gate. While some disciplinarians would say it was fitting he was behind the bars, his real problem was that he had served his time, had made his way out to Madrid under his own steam but did not have a match ticket.

"I'm sure the manager could come up with one if you could get word to him," he said, clearly mistaking me for a miracle worker.

"I'll see what I can do, Stuart," I promised, trying to sound as sincere as he was confident but failing miserably. OK, Trevor B got onto the pitch-side in Munich 12 months earlier using a store's carrier bag as a photographer's bib; but that did not mean I could blag my way into the Madrid dressing rooms while Clough was preparing his troops.

However, I did manage to squeeze into the VIP area and seek out the utterly trustworthy and honourable Geoffrey Macpherson, who in turn managed to contact I-know-not-who … with the result that a ticket was whisked to Dryden and he sat and watched his beloved club make a little more history thanks to a searing low drive by Robertson and some unflagging defending that bordered on the heroic.

So off we Trevors flew again, along with Stapleton and Hamilton, on the pocket rocket back to East Midlands Airport to carry the news and pictures back home. But at least the time pressure was off this time; we were able to fly through the night. It was tempting to say that all this success was getting boring! Why, we even had quotes from Clough, Taylor and sundry players alongside the match report thanks to fine after-match work by Stapleton and Hamilton.

This was the top half of the Evening Post front page looked on Thursday 29 May 1980 after our over-night flight from Spain…

Clough made a rare appearance without his green jersey at the managers' post-match Press Conference, insisted upon by UEFA. He wore a Forest tracksuit top; most likely because he had just signed a new contract, which meant he had received a pay rise. The *Evening Post* had that story exclusively for our previews on the day of the match. As we walked back from the team's hotel in Madrid with the story in my notebook, a thunderstorm exploded on the city centre. The huge avenues ran like canals for maybe half an hour. Another 30 minutes on, they were steaming as the sun blazed down. Sure signs that we were in for drama!

Taylor had spent the weeks between the semi and final doing what he did best: spying. Clough spent the days immediately before the final doing what he did best: telling each player exactly what his job is. After the 1-0 win, Clough provided another flood – a massive gush of praise for his players and his mate Taylor. This is what he said:

> "Absolutely fantastic! Everyone played like a hero. We had application, tenacity, dedication and pride. You name a good quality and we showed it in every department.

"We did everything right. We were forced to defend and did it magnificently. Granted, there were some anxious moments but I don't think we were lucky. All good teams do have an element of luck, though it's crazy to say we were fortunate to have won.

"Our style, remember, is to go forward. That's something Hamburg would not allow us to do. So we adapted and came through quite brilliantly.

"The side battled and covered and ran themselves out. This victory comes close to being one of the highlights of my career. It's a night I'll never forget.

"I was a bit choked at the end. Peter and I walked down the tunnel after the whistle with the crowd noise still in the background. There was nobody else in the dressing room and it gave us time to take in the victory. It was an emotional, satisfying moment for us both after the season's slog."

Afterwards, Clough went back onto the pitch to applaud the mass of Forest fans who had made their way to Madrid … only for the stadium officials to leave him in the dark by switching off the floodlights. "To be fair," he said, "I don't think they knew I was going back out. But even without their help, I was glowing so much with pride and pleasure they could have seen me in Barcelona."

Sadly from Trevor Bartlett's point of view, Forest had rushed to one of the darkest corners of the pitch to pose with the trophy immediately after the presentation. So his souvenir picture was not quite of the quality of its mate that he'd taken in Munich 12

months earlier. The Forest team was: Shilton, Anderson, Lloyd, Burns, Frank Gray (Bryn Gunn substitute, 85 minutes); O'Neill, Bowyer, McGovern, Gary Mills (O'Hare substitute, 68 minutes), Robertson; Birtles.

In the back row (from left) are: reserve goalkeeper Chris Woods, McGovern, reserve defender David Needham, O'Neill, Gunn, Mills, Shilton, O'Hare, Robertson (under supporter's hat). Front: Gray, Lloyd, Birtles and Burns.

One of the many pictures that showed how delighted the players were, in this age before deadpan expressions and clichéd comments were *de rigueur*, was this one of Robertson, the scorer in Madrid and goal-maker in Munich, with Lloyd, the brick wall in every match…

They may look a tad like Laurel and Hardy, but they never played like jokers.

We at the *Post* also had the luxury of having Clough, Taylor and the Forest players to talk to for articles in the *'Forest Champions of Europe'* 64-page colour magazine that we produced in August 1980 to preview the new season. 64 pages! No shortage of advertisers willing to pay through the nose this time! And the feature headlines oozed optimism…

- "We want to win the lot" – Clough himself in typically modest mood.
- "We'll frighten the lives out of 'em" – captain John McGovern.
- "Ian (Wallace) will give us a flyer" – Larry Lloyd on the new striker from Coventry City.
- "In praise of Ponte" – Frank Clark on Raimondo, a Swiss import from Grasshopper.

Twelve months earlier, the leading features for 'Forest Kings of Europe' – another 64-pager funded by advertising – had come from anywhere but the City Ground because we were still barred from talking with any Forest player…

- Bill Shankly, the legendary Liverpool manager, on the likelihood of an all-British final.
- Jock Stein, the first GB manager to win the European Cup, insisting Forest had been "brilliant" and not lucky.
- Sir Alf Ramsey, England's World Cup-winning manager in 1966, explaining why Forest were unlikely to become as consistently successful as Liverpool.

Imagine managers of the quality of Shankly and Stein happily chatting on the telephone to a cold calling journalist they'd never met before from a provincial paper miles away from their spheres of influence! Our contemporaries would never get past first base of the club press office receptionist now.

As for England's World Cup-winning manager of 1966, I'd hi-jacked Sir Alf in the tiny Nottinghamshire village of Bunny. He was opening the annual village fete at the invitation of former Forest goalkeeper Alan Hill, who also did some invaluable scouting work for Clough but agreed with the Dryden/Taylor view that the club needed the *Evening Post's* publicity despite the Gaffer's political hostility. As we sat in the village hostelry, the Rancliffe Arms, Sir Alf reasoned: "Forest won the European Cup because they had method. They had a plan in that each player knew what was expected of him and each did his job with excellent efficiency. No, I don't expect them to be as consistently successful as Liverpool. They don't have the background … the foundations." Even a great man like Sir Alf seemed to have got it wrong as Forest basked in the glory of retaining the European Cup with this sequence of results.

Forest's run to glory in the 1979-80 European Cup

	Oester Vaxjo (H) 2-0	Oester Vaxjo 1-1	Arges Pitesti (H) 2-0	Arges Pitesti 2-1	Dynamo Berlin (H) 0-1	Dynamo Berlin 3-1	Ajax Amsterdam (H) 2-0	Ajax Amsterdam 0-1	Hamburg (Madrid) 1-0
Shilton	1	1	1	1	1	1	1	1	1
Anderson	2	2	2	2		2	2	2	2
Frank Gray	3	3	3	3	3	3	3	3	3
McGovern	4	4	4	4	4	4	4	4	4
Lloyd	5	5	5	5	5	5	5	5	5
Burns	6	6	6	6	6		6	6	6
Needham						6			
O'Neill	7	7			7	7	7	7	7
Bowyer	8 G G		8	8 G		8		8	8
Birtles	9	9	9 G	9 G	9	9	9	9	9
Woodcock	10	10 G	10 G	10					
Robertson	11	11	11	11	11	11 P	11 P	11	11 G
Francis					10	10 G G	10 G	10	
Bryn Gunn					2				
O'Hare				7					
Mills		8	7						10
Stan Bowles					8		8		

However, Sir Alf was proved right come the 1980-81 European Cup. Forest went out in the first round, defeated 1-0 in each leg by the Bulgarian champions, CSKA Sofia … and Liverpool went on to reclaim the treasured trophy with a 1-0 victory over Real Madrid in the Final in Paris.

There was, however, one winner among the Forest party in Sofia – my photographer mate Trevor Bartlett. Now that we were mates with Clough, he had flown out with the Forest squad alongside Duncan Hamilton and David Stapleton. I stayed home to do my office job. After the match, my intrepid trio went back to the team hotel with the squad and Bartlett, one of the most sociable people I've ever met, decided to broaden his experience by visiting a casino for the first time in his life.

He purchased a handful of chips and lost all but one of them instantly on a backgammon table. As he set off towards the exit in search of the more familiar surroundings of a bar, he was drawn towards the only vacant chair around a roulette wheel. Sitting down amid sundry Bulgarian Army officers and serious-looking gentlemen wearing dark suits and matching frowns, he slipped his lone chip onto a number. All these years later, he thinks it was 34. The wheel was spun. The dice seemed to bob in and out of every nook and cranny more than once before finally coming to rest – in 34. He knew in that moment exactly how Trevor Francis and John Robertson had felt when their European Cup-winning goals nestled in the nets of the packed stadia in Munich and Madrid.

Bartlett's joy at scooping the jackpot was complete when one of the spectators around the table, Peter Shilton, gasped: "Wow, mate! How did you do that?" Shilton's penchant for gambling was legendary in Nottingham; not quite as admired as his goalkeeping, but of considerable interest in the days before even the world's best footballers were far from millionaires.

So Bartlett's small frame seemed to expand with the heady success of the moment and he mentioned something like: "Aah! You've got to have the magic formula."

Both laughed and, in his euphoria, Bartlett did not notice the eyes of the men in suits narrowing as he collected his winnings. But once something like 1,700 US dollars had been reluctantly counted into his hands, his impish humour led him to opine that he could now afford to buy the entire hotel in this rather drab Communist country. After a celebratory drink in the bar – accompanied by many admiring comments from Forest players and coaches – Bartlett wended his way to the lifts and his bedroom. He did not think too deeply about the man in dark suit who accompanied him; after all, the Berlin Wall was still firmly in place, casting shadows of suspicion whenever East and West met, even in sporting arenas.

But when the same man in dark suit was lurking outside his bedroom next morning, Bartlett knew his situation was a little more sinister than routine. Indeed, as the lift descended, the man asked him how he had managed to win the house jackpot, leaving him in no doubt that the hosts were convinced he had cheated them. Recognising that he would never get out of the country with the cash, he gave it to the only untouchable in the squad: Brian Clough.

His caution was justified at the airport when his shadow, the man in dark suit, asked him for the money. "I haven't got it," he said, struggling to keep a straight face.

"Who has it?" asked the surly shadow.

Bartlett pointed to Clough, asking: "Do you fancy frisking him?"

With the massed ranks of the Midlands mafia of media men now aware of what was happening, Bartlett was allowed through check-in and onto the plane, where sceptics assured him he might as well have left the cash in Bulgaria … "You'll never see it again, mate," they assured him.

They were wrong. Clough handed it over in time for Bartlett to take wife Sandra and their two sons on a surprise holiday to Spain. And the incident forged such a bond of trust between the pair that for years thereafter, Bartlett was Clough's photographer of choice whenever a special picture opportunity arose.

This even stretched to a fortnight-long pre-season preparation camp in Sweden a few years later. I had little trouble persuading the new Editorial Director, Barrie Williams, that it would be an ideal opportunity for Hamilton to get to know the new players Clough had shipped in from around Europe (mainly the Netherlands). But Bartlett was equally confident that there was no way the Photographic Department budget would stretch to flights for him; and told Clough as much one lunchtime at the City Ground.

Clough instantly picked up the phone to call Williams. Informed he was out at lunch, he left a message asking Williams to call him back. When they finally made contact, Clough started with: "I wish I had a job with three-hour lunches on expenses…" Having thus got Williams on the defensive, Clough then stunned the eves-dropping Bartlett by saying: "I understand your photographic budget won't stretch far enough to pay for your Mr. Bartlett to come with me to Sweden pre-season, so I'll pay for him. I take it that's OK?" It was an offer Williams could not refuse.

And then came a pre-season in Holland. Travel was courtesy Townsend Thoresen. Bartlett drove his little Ford Fiesta to Harwich, and took the ferry to the Hook of Holland. It was only when he was ready to return that he realised why Clough had not wanted him to fly. The manager wanted him to take "some goods" home for him.

The "goods" turned out to be three trees. Each of them was 6 feet high. Each was, of course, illegal. Not wanting to risk the *Post* being banned again, Bartlett agreed on condition that Clough wrote a covering letter for him to show Customs at Harwich. Clough obliged, stuffed the note in an envelope, helped Bartlett fold the branches of the trees round and round in the back seat – and waved him off.

Bartlett's reception at Harwich was predictable. "You can't import them, sir," said the first Customs officer to set eyes on the mass of foliage that had taken on a life of its own around the driver.

"I know," said Bartlett.

"So why are they in your car, sir?"

"Because Brian Clough asked me to bring them over for him."

"Oh really." The Customs officer was, as if by magic, joined by three colleagues.

"Yes. He's given me a covering note for you to read." Fishing in his pocket, Bartlett plucked out the envelope and handed it over. He hadn't read it. For all he knew, Clough could have written: "Arrest this man. He's a maniac and an imposter." Plainly he had not because the Customs officer passed it around his colleagues. They went into whispered conference. And after an hour they wished him a safe journey!

Long before he reached his home on the outskirts of Nottingham, Clough was on the phone to his wife, Sandra, asking about his trees. "For some reason Cloughie loved trees," Bartlett recollects. "He never said why. But wherever we were, he'd often break off conversations to point out some tree or another."

And when these three were duly delivered by Bartlett to the Clough household, they were given places of honour in his arbour.

10

Batting-off catastrophes his way

AFTER THE final whistle blew on Forest's reign in Europe with their defeat at the hands of CSKA, one of their ticket holders in the back row of the Main Stand stood up, turned round to me, pushed his face towards mine and said: "I told you the bubble would burst." He had, too. Almost two years to the night earlier, amid the euphoria of the 2-0 victory over Liverpool that had started the great European adventure. Through all of the triumphs that followed, I'd forgotten his pessimism; and he had remained ever-present but silent. Yet now, somehow, he seemed to represent the view of a considerable number of men who called themselves Forest loyalists, having followed the club through thin and thinner since their 1959 FA Cup triumph. They had frequently complained about the expense of tickets for these extra matches; and now it was almost as if they were going to be relieved – almost happier – with a strictly domestic diet.

With this lack of ambition among some of the support matching the shortage of finances in the club's bank account, by all that's logical, Hamilton should have covered the end of the Clough phenomenon in quick-time. The magical manager suffered blow after blow that would have floored a mere mortal and, come to that, most megalomaniacs…

The knock-out was almost delivered by Peter Taylor. Clough's most trusted ally retired with health problems and then not only returned to League management at Forest's hated rivals, Derby County, but lured Clough's talisman match-winner John Robertson down the A52 to join him. "When he sat in his office and told me he wanted to get out of the game, I cried," Clough confessed.

When Taylor made the most sensational comeback since Lazarus, Clough raged that Taylor was a "rattlesnake" and, to his eventual great regret, never spoke to his old mate again.

The European Cup-winning squad was broken-up, partly by Clough realising that players of modest ability can be inspired to perform above their norm for only a limited period but also because the undreamed-of stream of trophies had not generated a big enough cash flow to satisfy the bankers. So at the height of their successes, Forest had to shrink their wage bill to survive.

Despite the financial restrictions, Forest went amazingly close to adding the 1984 UEFA Cup to their unexpected collection of European silverware. They swept past Vorwarts from Frankfurt 3-0 on aggregate, PSV Eindhoven of The Netherlands 3-1, Glasgow Celtic 2-1 and Sturm Graz of Austria 2-1 to earn a semi-final against Anderlecht, the perennial champions of Belgium.

Ace photographer Trevor Bartlett well remembers the away tie against Celtic. The first leg had ended in a goalless draw at the City Ground so the Scots were all set for a glory night against the best manager never to lead the 'Auld Enemy'. Bartlett's initial battle was to persuade Clough to allow him to take pictures for the *Evening Post's* match preview. "F*** off and let me get on with my job," was the under-pressure manager's first reaction a couple of days before the tie as management, players and media settled into a lovely hotel beside one of Ayrshire's most famous golf courses. It so happened that Motor-mouth was with his wife Barbara at the time. It was a rare occasion for Barbara to be "at work" with him. She was usually busy with her own jobs at a school in Derby and as matriarch of the family. She was so thorough at it that Clough was moved to utter, more than once: "Women run everything, you know. The only decision I've taken in my house in the last 20 years is recognise Angola as an independent state."

Whether the quiet and considerate Barbara had a word with her impulsive husband by the Scottish seaside, Bartlett never found out. But he was surprised to be summoned to Clough's presence a little later to be told: "We're all going for a walk into town in the morning, if you want to come along with your camera…"

This little pre-match exercise fitted in perfectly with one of Clough's basic rules of man-management: "You need to get players relaxed because in any profession you do better when you're not afraid."

As management and players strolled, Bartlett clicked his pictures. And when they reached the town, Clough asked him to repay the favour by finding a suitable hostelry in which the Forest party could relax. Bartlett approached an elderly local who was only too pleased to guide them to "the best place for miles around" – and join them in the Best Room. Indeed, so at home did the gentleman begin to feel that, before long, he was telling Clough what team to select for the following night's match.

Not wishing to be rude … for he did not want to generate more antagonism among the locals than already existed … Clough eventually struggled through the throng to tell Bartlett: "If you don't get your new friend out of here, you'll never live to get those f***ing pictures to Nottingham." Not being one of the diplomatic corps, Bartlett swiftly led the somewhat bemused Scot out of the door.

"So how are you going to get your pictures to Nottingham?" Clough asked him on the stroll back to the team hotel.

"By train from Glasgow," said Bartlett.

"And how are you going to get to Glasgow?"

"By taxi, I suppose."

"Hang on." Clough strolled to the hotel reception and explained to the helpful staff: "My friend from the *Nottingham Evening Post* needs to get an urgent parcel on a train from Glasgow to his paper. I don't suppose you could arrange transport for him, could you?"

"Of course, Mr. Clough!"

So bright and early on match-day morning, John Richardson was able to pop into the Parcels Office at Nottingham Midland Station and collect films containing enough pictures to illustrate half-a-dozen big matches, never mind this one that Forest had already lost in the minds of many of their home supporters.

Forest won the match, of course, too. And nobody in football doubts that they should have reached the final, against Tottenham Hotspur. They won the City Ground leg of their semi-final against Anderlecht well enough, 2-0. The official UEFA website states this about the return leg: "The English team conceded a dubious penalty and had a goal disallowed as they crashed 3-0 in Brussels to lose out 3-2 on aggregate. Anderlecht would later be found guilty for their part in the bribery scandal, and banned for a year from European competition."

We wuz robbed! Another referring decision puzzles Ian Bowyer
in the tie against Anderlecht.

The Anderlecht chairman confessed, years later, that the referee had been paid £27,000 prior to the second leg. For £27,000 Clough could have bought one-and-a-half players from non-League and turned them into European-standard footballers! Not that he ever saw the irony.[3]

Years before the confession, Clough was adamant: "It was a crooked match and he was a crooked referee. That was a cup we could and should have won."

He was less willing to acknowledge his own biggest short-coming when it came to team-building. Clough, once a centre forward who scored 204 goals in 224 games for Middlesbrough and 63 in 74 for Sunderland before his cruel knee injury, had enough problems filling Forest's No.9 shirt to fill a chapter in a football annual.

He almost resigned when the money-men insisted he sell Garry Birtles to Manchester United to reduce the overdraft on what became known as The Brian Clough Stand. Only a promise he had made to his wife in the wake of his departure from Derby County kept him at the City Ground. "I told her I'd never resign from a job again and leave us wondering where my next wage packet was coming from," he frequently recalled.

Trevor Francis suffered a career-threatening knee injury and Clough excelled in persuading Manchester City to gamble £1 million on him. It did not turn the Maine Road squad into European Champions. Clough tried a variety of speedy, skilful, goal-scoring players without ever fully replacing the unique Francis.

He signed Peter Ward from Brighton and Hove Albion and Ian Wallace from Coventry City, both prolific scorers before their arrivals at the City Ground, but rather quickly came to the conclusion that neither of them had the necessary muscle to give the other crucial room in front of goal as Peter Withe and Birtles had for Tony Woodcock.

Simultaneously, the *Post's* new-boy Hamilton soon made an impact by using lengthy and somewhat obscure words early in his reports. For example, the first time Clough opted for a mini strike force of Wallace and Ward, in a 2-1 victory over Leeds United on 22 October 1980, Hamilton assured his *Evening Post* readers the following night that the "... new striking tandem did enough to suggest that, despite their lack of inches, they possess the tenacity and temerity." He went on to praise "the Scot's alacrity for work."

To the frustration of this Sports Editor, who shared Wallace's affliction of having ginger hair, the little Scot managed only 36 goals in 134 Forest matches between 1980 and 1984 (compared with 58 in 130 for Coventry City) before moving on to Brest in France. Cynics would say the only thing he won with Forest was an accolade for Trevor Bartlett...

As the story on 27 February 1981 reported, Bartlett's picture of Wallace horizontal as he headed home his goal against Leeds won him a place at a Royal Photographic Society exhibition in London. The provinces were heavily out-numbered by national newspaper

---

[3] Tottenham won the 1984 UEFA Cup Final 4-3 in a penalty shoot-out after both legs against Anderlecht had finished 1-1. Instead of leading his team into the matches, Clough commented for ITV.

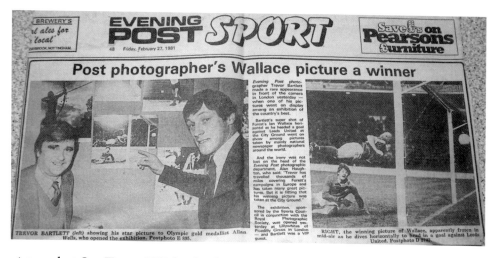

Post photographer's Wallace picture a winner

Evening Post photographer Trevor Bartlett made a rare appearance in front of the camera in London yesterday — when one of his pictures went on display among an exhibition of the country's best.

Bartlett's super shot of Forest's Ian Wallace horizontal as he headed a goal against Leeds United at the City Ground went on show among pictures taken by mainly national newspaper photographers around the world.

And the irony was not lost on the head of the Evening Post photographic department, Alan Haughton, who said: "Trevor has travelled thousands of miles covering Forest's campaigns in Europe and has taken many great pictures. But it is fitting that his winning picture was taken at the City Ground."

The exhibition, sponsored by the Sports Council in conjunction with the Royal Photographic Society, was opened yesterday at Lillywhites of Piccadilly Circus in London — and Bartlett was a VIP guest.

TREVOR BARTLETT (left) showing his star picture to Olympic gold medallist Allan Wells, who opened the exhibition. Postphoto E 895.

RIGHT, the winning picture of Wallace, apparently frozen in mid-air as he dives horizontally to head in a goal against Leeds United. Postphoto D 3763.

pictures but Our Trev, a VIP for the day, caught the reigning Olympic 100m champion Allan Wells for a souvenir picture of his own.

Back home, the no-nonsense Trent Enders, as swift of wit as they were accustomed to sports reporters' bland clichés, quickly christened our new boy Duncan 'Hamilton Academical'. Clough broke off his pretence that "I never read your Tory rag" to observe in obvious awe: "Some of his words are bigger than him." And Mr. Snaith's successor as Editorial Director, Barrie Williams, asked me to "have a word with him". I obeyed, albeit reluctantly because I always felt that reporters should have free rein to express themselves; and, almost inevitably, the episode led to an obviously less-confident Duncan calling me even more often at home to ask whether he could use specific words/phrases.

At this time, rumours of "bungs" in football were rife. The word was that "everybody's at it". The fact was that nobody knew who or what was really triggering the deals in these days before the invention of agents as "middle-men"; and the authorities were no more inclined to delve into the clubs' accounts than they are now. So the whispers prospered; some to epic proportions.

One such tale was that Clough decided that Wallace, signed for £1.25 million in July 1980, would rediscover his scoring touch only if he could line-up alongside a tall, strong centre forward like Mick Ferguson. After all, the pair had scored 38 goals as a pair in season 1977-78. The problem in 1980-81 was that Ferguson was still at Coventry, who were themselves an ambitious top-tier club at the time; those Ferguson-Wallace goals had lifted them to seventh place in 1977-78. So, rumour had it, Forest folk talked to another First Division club's folk (in these days before agents invaded the game) about how much compensation should be slipped into the brown envelope of legend to ease a tall, strong centre forward to the City Ground for an up-front fee of £500,000 without alienating the long friendship between the decision-makers at each club. A sum was determined and, rumour had it, was neatly folded into the fabled brown envelope that, rumour had it, always changed hands in such deals. The parcel was placed in the hands of two trusty

Forest lieutenants and, rumour had it, they drove from the City Ground, out towards the East Midlands Airport, then south along the M1 to the Leicester Forest East Service Area. There they parked at approximately 6.45pm one cold and misty winter night, rumour had it, awaiting the arrival of two of the selling club's representatives who would take charge of the envelope. Alas, rumour had it, the appointed meeting time ticked by with no sign of the selling club's men. These being the days before mobile phones were glued to the ears of every mover and shaker, rumour had it, The Forest Duo were at a loss as to what to do next. Fearing the consequences if the move stalled, rumour had it, they sat tight for another hour or more … until the windows of their saloon had misted-up and they began to attract the attention of travellers who had walked past them earlier, fed and watered themselves, and were now about to continue their journey. Eventually and reluctantly, rumour had it, having become the rather embarrassed targets of autograph-hunters, The Forest Duo drove away from the car park, motored the short distance to the M1-M69 junction, swung round the roundabout and took the M1 north back towards Nottingham. As they passed the exit from the north-bound Leicester Forest East Service Area, rumour had it, they were almost side-swiped by a car that approached them from the inside and then followed them, flashing its headlights. Angry enough at their failure to pass the envelope that would have posted a tall, strong centre forward as if by magic to the City Ground, rumour had it, the Forest driver floored the accelerator and sped off. Their pursuer, rumour had it, gave up the chase at the Loughborough junction. Only on the following morning, after a series of telephonic communications, rumour had it, was it discovered that while The Forest Duo had waited in the south-bound car park of the service area, the selling club's folk had been waiting in the north-bound car park. By amazing coincidence, rumour had it, the selling club's folk had left their park at the precise moment The Forest Duo had sped past. Recognising them, rumour had it, the selling club's folk had tried to attract their attention. Forest came *that* close, rumour had it, to signing a tall, strong strike partner for Ian Wallace.

Only once over the coming years did I become sufficiently brave (in drink) to ask Clough if that story was at all close to the truth. He smiled, poured us both another drink, and merely said: "I keep hearing that all sorts of clever people are investigating the books of football clubs in search of financial irregularities. From what I hear about the way football clubs keep financial records, I shall be long gone before even the smartest investigators come up with anything that makes sense, either way. And before you ask if that's on the record, keep your notebook in your pocket, drink up, sober up and f*** off home."

Instead of the tall, strong centre forward first targeted, Forest got Justinus Soni Fashanu.

One of the mantras upon which Clough built his enormous on-field successes was: "It only takes a second to score a goal." And that was all it took to persuade him he must have the muscular striker known to all as Justin Fashanu. He watched on BBC Television's *Match of the Day* Fashanu score The Goal of the 1979-80 season. He turned like a 6ft 4in ballerina and volleyed a goal from just outside the penalty box for Norwich City against Liverpool's supposed defence of all-stars. And that was it.

Clough was smitten; happier to make Fashanu the first £1 million black footballer in the Football League than he had been to make Francis the first £1 million footballer in the Football League. Indeed, as the years rolled by, Clough frequently insisted he paid £1 under a million for Francis on the grounds that "his head was too full of his own importance already". He never made that claim about Fashanu.

Alas, the Fash strike of genius turned out to be a flash in the pan. Worse, in Clough's mind, Fashanu turned out to be homosexual. Quite how Clough was not aware of this before he completed the signing was a mystery … unless, of course, in this era before political correctness got anywhere near football, all of Clough's staff took it for granted that he must have heard the rumours. It is more likely that the desperation to sign a big partner for Wallace led to corners being cut in the background check that Peter Taylor would normally have carried out as a matter of routine.

So it came as a hammer blow to Clough when a Sunday red top tabloid blazed the news that the big lad had been visiting gay clubs. Fashanu was barred from the City Ground … "I'm not having him in the first team and I certainly daren't have him around my apprentices," Clough asserted.

For good measure, Clough brought in security men to ensure Fashanu did not even get into the training ground – and off-loaded him across the river to Notts County. Which is where I came in while Hamilton produced the stories from the mayhem that was the City Ground. To my utter astonishment, I received a phone call from Jack Dunnett to inform me I held the key to the move going through.

Dunnett explained that he had agreed a fee [around £150,000] with "the selling club" (Notts County's Chairman was the President of the Football League but could not bring himself to string together the words "Nottingham" and "Forest"). Using the gift of the gab that comes naturally to a barrister and Member of Parliament, he had even persuaded Fashanu to take a cut in his salary. But Fashanu's lowest demand was still somewhat higher than the oldest club in the Football League could afford.

Clearly his financial needs and priorities were different from those of Notts County's then manager, Jimmy Sirrel, who lifted them from the near the re-election zone of Division Four in November 1969 to the rarefied atmosphere of the First Division [as the Premier League was then called] in May 1981. When Sirrel moved from a trainer's job at Brentford to manage Notts, Dunnett explained they had "no money for transfers and little for wages." Some six weeks later, around Christmas-time, Sirrel made a somewhat sheepish visit to the office of the club secretary, Dennis Marshall, a wonderful servant of the club through decades of its trials and tribulations in the lower reaches of the League. "Are you alone?" Sirrel asked furtively. "Yes, Jimmy – what can I do for you?" Sirrel, acting not at all like the bony little bruiser who'd learnt to survive in the toughest area of Glasgow as a child, shuffled and hesitated to such an extent that Marshall thought he was going to resign.

What the gruff manager wanted, though, came as an even bigger surprise to Marshall. "D'ye think I can have me wages this week?" Sirrel asked. "Of course, Jimmy," Marshall almost exploded with relief. "It's just that the savings have gone and Mammy needs to go shopping for the bairns." To explain: "Mammy" was what Sirrel always called his matronly wife, Cathy. "The bairns" were their two children plus innumerable apprentices and trialists who were lodging with them so that they didn't feel homesick during the festive season. Even while Sirrel was mumbling his apologetic explanation for wanting a week's wages after six weeks of living on his meagre savings, Marshall was delving in a shoebox in his office safe – and coming up with a handful of wage packets, which he handed over with a heartfelt: "Happy Christmas, Jimmy!" "Aye," Sirrel responded, "it will be if we get a result tomorrow." What a unique football man! And to make his achievements with Notts County even more special, the rise through the four Divisions of the English League format of the time was completed under the same chairman (Dunnett) with the same captain (Don Masson, who played for Scotland in the 1978 World Cup Finals) and the same trainer (Jack Wheeler) … though the addition of Howard Wilkinson as assistant manager had refined the club's final push into the top Division. They even had the gall to celebrate their arrival by defeating the new League Champions, Aston Villa, 1-0 at Villa Park in their first match back in the top flight for 55 years.

And now, in December 1982, Dunnett made it sound as if it was down to me to extend Notts' stay in the top flight. He explained that, if I could take on Fashanu as a columnist, it would help lift his income towards the level to which he aspired. "I could only afford £40 a week," I said. "That'll be most acceptable, I'm sure – thank you very much," replied Dunnett, putting the phone down. I called the Meadow Lane office. Marshall answered, as he frequently did – though gone now were the days when he would joke that the faithful few supporters only phoned during adverse weather to check whether matches were still on and he'd respond with: "Yes – and we won't start until you get here."

Now my question was: "Have you really signed a million-pound footballer?"

His reply, backed by his trademark chuckle, was: "To be precise, I think *we* have signed Justin Fashanu. Do you want to talk to the manager about it?"

I did.

Sirrel didn't.

He had heard himself described as "the manager who never says anything" by Terry Bowles – the *Evening Post* striker who was now compiler of his club's programme, among other things – and he was happy to live down to the description whenever he smelled controversy … and he smelled controversy as soon as he found himself talking to a reporter. On this particular occasion, he didn't fancy talking to his friend Trevor either. So I talked to Dunnett again and got the story … and the weekly column.

Only when I made my first visit to Fashanu's flat did I wonder at Forest's failure to discover his lifestyle before they signed him. The place was in The Park, the poshest part of Nottingham beneath the ancient Castle, surrounded by leafy boulevards and enough tennis courts to host an international tournament every summer; 22 Tennis Mews to be precise. It was 9.30am on a Thursday morning. The door was answered by a handsome, muscled young man who introduced himself as "Justin's masseur". He was in pristine, tight-fitting white vest and tracksuit bottoms. The hand he extended to shake mine was silky soft; not at all the grasp to which I was accustomed. He led me up the curving staircase – and there was Fashanu reclining on his back in just his white underpants on the masseur's table, his muscled body glistening with whatever oils masseurs use.

And that was where he remained, enjoying his massage, while I asked the questions to help me ghost-write his first article as an *Evening Post* columnist. It was a somewhat exotic chore to which I became accustomed over the next few months, though I must confess that Fashanu was about as cerebral as a columnist as he was effective as a striker: he scored 20 goals in 64 appearances to help Notts remain in the top flight for three years before moving to Brighton and Hove Albion in the summer of 1985 for a reported £115,000.

At all times in his dealings with me, Fashanu was what my late mother would have called "a really nice boy". Always polite, quietly spoken, well-mannered; precisely what you would expect of the son of a Nigerian barrister living in England. All had not been idyllic, though. Justin's childhood was rudely interrupted by his parents breaking-up. He and his brother John (who found footballing fame with the ultra-macho team that represented Wimbledon in this era) found themselves in a Doctor Barnado's Home. When Justin was six, they were fostered out to a loving couple in Norfolk; and, to someone like me also brought up in a loving rural atmosphere, it seems that he spent the rest of his life expecting the best of people. Alas, he committed suicide in May 1998 after more controversy surrounding his sexuality.

Never mind, Brian, as the macho football world would react. Lay back and think of England...

Clough committed one form of suicide – some say thrice over – either side of his Fashanu debacle. He was indisputably the best manager England never had; he proved over and over – and over – again that there was nobody better at getting 110 per cent out of players considered by other good judges to be no more than moderate. Alas, he killed off his own chances of being appointed to the task with a regularity that became as monotonous as the national team's failure to add to the World Cup triumph orchestrated by Sir Alf Ramsey in 1966. In 1977, by which time he and Taylor had led Derby County to an unlikely League Championship and been robbed of a European Cup Final appearance by appalling refereeing in the semi-final, Clough the motor-mouth was the people's choice to boss England. The job went to Ron Greenwood, the quiet and philosophical manager of West Ham United. Clough's outraged reaction to being invited to an interview by the FA International Committee swung it. How dare anyone question him? But, as ever, he came up with a memorable quote or two for the national newspaper reporters. Discussing his worth while the FA men were living up to their acronym and, er,

Fumbling About, he proffered: "I wouldn't say I was the best manager in the business …
but I was in the top one."

And after he had been overlooked: "I'm sure the England selectors thought if they took
me on and gave me the job, then I would want to run the show. They were shrewd because
that is exactly what I would have done." By 1982, Greenwood was adjudged a failure. But
this time the FA opted for Bobby Robson, who had done for Ipswich almost what Clough
had done for Forest (won the League and the UEFA, rather than European, Cup). Robson
proved himself as single-minded – and ruthless – as Clough by instantly dropping the
England captain, Kevin Keegan. Supporters of Newcastle United responded by spitting on
Robson the next time he watched a match in his home city. England lost only one of 28
qualifying matches under Robson but when that lone defeat, to Denmark, led to them
failing to qualify for the 1984 European Championships, he instantly offered to resign and
hand the reins to Clough. Imagine the speed with which the FA red tape strangled that
notion!

And so there was no escape for Clough from the City Ground. No cash for him to
continue cavalier signings such as Shilton and Francis.

No inspirational assistant Peter Taylor; though it cannot be emphasised enough that
a down-to-earth and utterly loyal character called Ron Fenton greatly decelerated
Clough's tendency to self-destruct.

No real chance of another League title. There were so many transfers in and out in the
first half of the 1980s, it was a shame the Committee could not have afforded to fit swing
doors to save the old double-doors almost wearing out their hinges.

No real prospect of further European glory because the team was too unsettled. But
no chance that Clough would settle for a quiet life in mid-table.

And therefore no chance of us at the *Evening Post* having anything like a quiet winter.
No wonder Hamilton began to feel the heat to such an extent that he asked for a break
from the day-to-day trauma of providing a back page lead story.

When I returned to the Forest beat, Clough had learnt to *look* benign as he sat at his
desk in his green jersey and flat cap, listening to records by his favourite singer, Frank
Sinatra. Long-players went on for hours and he appeared to know and savour every note.
But he remained so utterly unpredictable that, from all the lyrics he loved, the only phrase
that fitted him was *"I Did It My Way"*.

11

Back to the day job with Psycho

● ● ● ● ● ● ● ● ● ● ● ● ● ● ● ● ● ●

HAVING YEARNED to be a sports reporter since I was at primary school – and not grown into the type of cowardly boss who would delegate the most difficult job to even the most eager of employees – I returned to the daily grind at the City Ground with mixed feelings.

Which was entirely fitting because Clough's mood swings were becoming more and more erratic. Initially I felt this was because of his frustrations: no matter how he shuffled his pack of players, irrespective of where he found his next signing (he was a pioneer at importing players from Switzerland, the Netherlands and Iceland in the 1980s), he went for the best part of a decade without getting his hands on a trophy.

But as time went on and he relied on folk such as Archie Gemmill (by now his reserve team coach) and his accountant (a shadowy figure so tight-lipped and secretive that I cannot recall his name) to drive him between his Derbyshire home and the City Ground, I began to realise that he was struggling ever more with the drink demon that had dogged him virtually since injury ended his playing career prematurely.

The only time the accountant impacted on me was as a waiter. It happened on 19 March (though I cannot be sure of the year). I had promised Gill a wedding anniversary treat (a trip into the Derbyshire Peaks). Clough decided he must see me, in his office, that very morning. To kill two birds with one stone, I took Gill along and she chatted with secretary Carol while we did the business. When we emerged, Clough nodded towards the women and whispered: "Who's that young lady?"

"Carol," I said, straight-faced.

"Behave!" he growled.

"My wife," I acknowledged.

"What's she doing here?"

"It's our wedding anniversary."

"I wouldn't have kept you so long if I'd known she was here."

"That's all right. We're off out now."

"Blow me!" he strode over to Gill, grabbed her hands, pulled her to her feet, gave her a kiss on the cheek. "Sorry I've been keeping him away from you a fair bit lately. But as you realise, we've been fairly busy. How long have you been wed, sweetheart?"

"For as long as you've had Nigel," Gill said.

"Since '66?" he asked. We nodded. "In that case, your treat's on me. You deserve something special, sticking this bloke for so long! Get yourselves to my local and whatever you want for lunch is on me."

"I can't do that, Brian."

"Of course you can – now, er, get off!"

So off we went to the Kedleston Hotel, a quite awesome Georgian Country House Hotel situated in the village of Quarndon, four miles from Derby City Centre. The Grade II listed building was designed and built by Robert Adam in 1761 as a coaching inn to house visitors to the nearby Kedleston Hall; and now we were met at the entrance by Clough's smiling Accountant, who (silently, as was his wont) led us to a table beside a window with panoramic views of the Dales resplendent in their springtime rebirth. He then proceeded to serve us: the best Sauvignon Blanc in the house; a three-course meal; coffee. And having settled the bill, he waved us off on our travels to one of our favourite walks, from Edale to Castleton and back.

Next time I saw Clough, I thanked him profusely. "It was the least I could do," he insisted. "And why did you leave a tip? When I told you it was my treat, I meant it was my treat."

All this at a time when the "Midlands media mafia" were, by and large, ignoring him – partly because they decided he had become too cantankerous by turning up late, or not at all, for appointments; partly because they were confident that John Lawson would provide them with any news he wanted them to have; and partly because *The Sun*, in the shape of its chief columnist John Sadler, would get the big exclusives. That was fine for Clough and his personal bank balance in the era before managers were expected to have formal media conferences at regular intervals. It was a development that brought smiles of contempt to the faces of my "f***ing bosses"; they interpreted his choice of tabloid as an admission that his Socialists had lost the war against newspaper modernisation. It was not so convenient for Hamilton or me. Especially when his rages at not winning silverware led him to berate any player who uttered a comment that he considered to be out of place.

Steve Chettle, a sturdy, genuine and utterly honest local lad who had won England Under-21 honours as a centre back, was a spectacular sufferer in this respect when Forest reached the FA Cup semi-finals, and were inevitably drawn against Liverpool, in 1988. As was customary, all the players agreed to charge for exclusive interviews, pool all of the cash into a central fund and share it out among themselves at the end of the Cup run. Most of the articles were what is known in the newspaper trade as "human interest": harmless enough: tales of how they had drifted into football and stardom; where they would be now if it hadn't been for the scout who spotted their football talent, etc.

And it seemed trivial to Chettle, a youngster about to face the immensely experienced threats of Ian Rush and John Aldridge, when his interviewer asked him what he ate for breakfast on match days.

He fumbled for an answer before mentioning poached eggs.

"On toast?" asked the reporter casually.

"Sometimes," replied the player.

So imagine his surprise when Saturday's back page lead carried headings asserting that the young, relatively unknown Chettle was set to go to work on an egg and have Liverpool's lethal striking duo on toast.

Worse, imagine Clough's reaction! "You've just done their manager's job for him," Clough raged. "He won't need to motivate his strikers now will he?"

Chettle's plea that he never said anything so inflammatory did nothing to console the Manager.

He ranted: "But you gave that f***ing journalist the chance to say it for you. There's only one way to stay safe from the cunning bastards – say nowt to them."

This from a manager whose oxygen had been publicity, as much as vodka had become his fuel!

Such was Clough's unpredictability that even the strongest minds in his team suffered crises of confidence from time to time.

Stuart Pearce, for example. He had joined Forest from Coventry City in 1985 as the makeweight in a £300,000 deal that also took centre back Ian Butterworth to the City Ground. Pearce was aged 23 and had been a full-time professional for only two years. Before that, he had played for part-time professionals Wealdstone and worked as an electrician in his native West London.

He was so uncertain about his move to the East Midlands that, even while he was making his first few appearances for Forest and wowing the supporters with his ferocious but fair tackling, he was advertising his services in the match programmes as a skilled (but anonymous) electrician.

The identity of the "sparks" in the advertisement on the centre pages, just above where the name of the Forest left back appeared, only became apparent when one of Clough's greatest friends, ever loyal to the club's financial backers, phoned the number in the mysterious advert. He wondered why the workman could not pop round to give a quote on a job until "sometime after 2pm" – but all became clear when Pearce turned up with his training gear mingled with his tools in the boot of his car.

Why did he do it? Because he wasn't sure he was going to make it at such a high level. Why did he not include his name in the ad? Because he didn't want his opponents – or,

more crucially, his Manager – to think he lacked confidence. *Post* photographer Steve Mitchell persuaded him to pose for this picture … using sparklers to create the impression of an electric connection:

Lacked confidence!?! This same Stuart Pearce went on to play 401 matches for Forest over the next 12 years, most of them as "The Captain," as Clough called him; even more as "Psycho" as the imaginative Trent Enders lovingly nicknamed him. He is widely regarded as the best left back the club ever had; and many would add that he is the most inspirational character ever to play for them. That thought, voiced off-field, would bring a blush to the cheek of the modest Pearce, who rarely gave opponents a glimpse of any chink in his armour.

What shocked Clough most about him, though, was something that even the master manager did not spot for a season or two. And then after one match, he suddenly mentioned in an unusually conspiratorial whisper: "The Captain doesn't wear pants."

"You what?" I asked, wondering how that fitted into an after-match analysis as much as whether I had heard him right.

"He goes … what do you call it?"

"Commando," said a smiling Ron Fenton, as helpful as Peter Taylor ever was at filling the gaps in the conversations. I remained speechless; mainly because the *Evening Post* was not the kind of publication to make news of such a revelation for fear of over-exciting the grannies in the suburbs at teatime and all I really wanted was a line for Monday night's back page. "That's braver than his tackles," persisted Clough, straight-faced, open-mouthed, genuinely in awe. I laughed, though I don't think he had intended the *double entendre* involving tackle(s). "Me … I'd be terrified of the damage the zip might do," he added, shuddering and shaking his head.

"And he goes horse riding with that wife of his," Clough went on, by which time his eyes were wide and almost watering as he imagined the pitfalls that could befall his brave Captain.

"Still, Brian," I sought to steer him back to football, "not many strikers catch him with his pants down…" That fell on stony ground, too.

An exception came in a Saturday afternoon match at West Ham United towards the end of 1987, when Pearce was beginning to establish a place in the England defence. Forest were leading 3-2 and the final seconds were ticking away when, instead of using his muscled scythe of a left leg to welly the ball out of Upton Park and halfway up East London, he tried a delicate chip to a midfield colleague. The pass was totally unexpected by either the midfielder or anyone else connected with Forest: players, supporters or management. Worse, the Hammers pounced on the loose ball, took advantage of the rest of the Forest defence being off-guard and sneaked an equaliser they did not deserve.

Clough remained tight-lipped. He merely sent The Captain out to talk to me before he went off to join with England squad. *What's The Boss said, Stuart?* "That if I do the same at Wembley, I needn't come back to Nottingham. He'll give me away. That I'm a defender and I'd better concentrate on f***ing defending."

Pearce played a blinder at Wembley the following Wednesday night and became so important to Forest that Clough wheeled out all of his backroom staff for a celebration picture when The Captain signed a two-year extension to his contract in 1989 …

Captain's salute: Pearce with Clough, assistant manager Ron Fenton and first team coach Liam O'Kane when he extended his contract in 1989.

Pearce also went on to become Forest's most-capped outfield player with 78 appearances for the country he loved with a passion that remained undiminished when he became a crucial part of the management squad under Sven Goran Eriksson and Fabio Capello.

A similar character, Kenny Burns, was another "hard man" who never lost his respect for Clough. After playing in the centre of Forest's defence during their most historic adventures – the Division One title in 1978, European Cup triumphs in 1979 and 1980 – he went on to play League football for Leeds United, Derby County, Notts County and Danish club Elfsborg before taking to non-League football with Ilkeston Town.

One wet and misty Saturday night, it so happened that the team coaches carrying Forest and Ilkeston back home along the M1 from matches in the north were parked in the southbound service area known as Woolley Edge in Yorkshire.

The Forest coach had been brought to an unexpected halt by Clough needing to relieve himself of some of the vodka he had consumed *en route*. One of his stipulations was that there be no toilet on the team coach because one had backed-up at one of his previous clubs and there was no way he was going to risk repeating that messy experience. So those of us sufficiently privileged to travel with the team had to cross their legs, unless they were The Boss. On the rare occasions he could not "hold on to it", the coach driver, Albert, would drift into the darkest recess of the next service area, and The Gaffer would stumble out, escorted by one of his staff.

On this occasion, the deed done, Clough was shuffling from behind the coach towards the coach door when a ghost-like figure drifted past. Quick as a flash despite the lack of light around us and the abundance of vodka consumed, Clough drawled: "Good evening, Mr. Burns."

"They're not for me, Boss," responded Mr. Burns, who was revealed to be holding out two bags of fast-food chips and burgers as Albert put his headlights on.

"I'll believe you," Clough chuckled, adding as he mounted the steps back into the coach: "And I don't care anyway now."

As Clough settled back into his seat and the bus swung back onto the M1, even he was astonished by the incident … "I never dreamt my influence was so long-lasting," he mused as he drifted back to sleep.

He had always insisted: "It's absolute nonsense to suggest that players lived in fear of me. They knew where they stood with me. There is a difference." But that incident showed innocent me how rigidly he ruled his players and how intensely he was respected. If a strong-minded character like Burns could be so instinctively servile four or five years after he last played for Clough, one wonders how many of the lesser types ever managed to get to sleep. Or maybe that helps to explain why there was such a rapid turn-over.

To balance this subservience, though, one young player's mother caused a sensation at about this time by hitting Clough with her handbag. Or, to be precise, she would have caused a sensation if the story had not been suppressed at her request lest it hindered her son's progress. I feel safe to end the secrecy now…

The player was Darren Wassall, a likeable and articulate young man who had made his way through the A-team and established himself in the Reserves, though there was no way he was going to become a first team regular while the immaculate Des Walker had breath in his lithe body to maintain his reputation as the fastest central defender on the planet.

Wassall had suffered a nasty injury in a reserve match: an opponent's stud had left a hole the diameter of a 20p piece in the palm of one of his hands. Clough never liked injured players being anywhere near the changing rooms when the fit members of the squad were either preparing to go out training or relaxing after their work-outs. Having heard him scream "Don't limp" at a number of wounded heroes, I tended to the belief that such sights reminded him of his knee tragedy as a young man; but the faithful Fenton always insisted it was because The Gaffer did not want the fit players to see "anything negative".

Be that as it may, Wassall turned up for treatment one morning while the players were out training. That was fine. Not so good was the fact that the physiotherapist, Graeme Lyas, feared the wound was not healing as it should. So he asked Wassall to await a doctor's visit. Sadly, Clough got back to the dressing room area before the doc.

"Why aren't you training?" he asked Wassall.

"Because of this, Boss," said the player, holding up his raw hand.

"I'm worried it's infected," Lyas chipped in.

"It's not now," said Clough, gripping Wassall's wrist and spitting into the palm of his hand. "That's cleaned it," added Clough, marching on down the corridor.

A night or two later, after a match, Clough emerged from the double doors through which he'd kicked me several years earlier, expecting to have no more than autograph books thrust at him, as usual.

So imagine his surprise when a sizeable handbag whacked him beside the head. He reeled back against the door as his attacker said: "And don't you dare spit on my son again!"

Mrs. Josephine Wassall is the protective mother's name. Small, bespectacled, a secretary by trade; she was as feisty as Clough's own PA, Carol Parker. Mrs. Wassall worked for the governing bodies of British athletics for many years and, when I became a colleague in the late 1990s, we both wished such spirit existed among more people in our new, much more politically-correct environment. "After you, Claude," is not the attitude that will create a new pair of Ovetts and Coes, for example.

After her sensational assault, her next move after a sleepless night was to phone Clough the following morning to apologise. What a brave woman! "No need, pet," he replied. "I deserved it. We're level now, right?" And Darren himself was allowed to recover at nature's own pace.

By the time Jo Wassall and I became workmates at UK Athletics a dozen years or so later, her son Darren had moved on quite regularly, too. After making 27 first team appearances for Forest, he had spells at Hereford United, Bury, Derby County, Manchester City and Birmingham City before he moved into non-League football in 2000 – at Burton Albion. There, the manager he linked-up was with none other than Nigel Clough. And when Nigel became the manager of Derby County, Wassall moved with him as one of the coaches in the Rams' Academy. So neither the spit spat – nor the hand-bagging – had any lasting effects. Except, perhaps, to bring two ultra-sports-minded families closer together.

12

Is the non-shaver strong enough?

· ·

TO GET myself out of the office in the winters when Hamilton was faithfully covering Forest, I had often reported on A-team matches on a Saturday morning. These were basically the League clubs' futures on parade; the 18-year-old apprentices striving might and main to turn their childhood dreams into adult reality on the pitch much as I had done on the touchline.

Mansfield Town played on a windswept, exposed school playing field in the village of Edwinstowe where, I discovered, the groundsman was Johnny Franks, who had been the left arm opening bowler for the Nottinghamshire Schools Under-15 cricket team in which I played in 1960. He got as far as an interview at Trent Bridge for a place in their County Championship squad but, outrageously, was turned down when the Committee realised he stuttered. So imagine his pride when his son Paul earned a place in the county team in 1996.

Notts County had several homes for their games in the Midland Intermediate League; and Jimmy Sirrel always said that the hardest job in management was to sit down with a teenager at the end of his apprenticeship, look him in the eye and say: "Sorry, son…" The manager-who-never-says-anything explained: "It's like giving that boy a death sentence. All he's ever wanted is to be a footballer. And you're killing his ambition."

And, though he never said as much, Clough definitely shared that sentiment. Steve Stone is proof of that.

Despite his undoubted hangovers and his mantra that he wanted to control everything at the club "from the laundry lady onwards", if Forest's first team were playing at home on a Saturday afternoon and the A-team were performing on the training ground in the morning, Clough would appear with his golden Labrador Del Boy at his heel to watch the teenagers. Even the parents proudly watching their off-spring would virtually stand to attention as The Boss patrolled the touchline, quietly watching what was happening on the field.

Alas, he hardly saw Stone kick a ball as an apprentice. Born in 1971 in Scotland (at a place called Knockentiber) but brought up in the North-East of England, Stone broke a leg before he had settled into the apprentices' routine: train in the morning, lunch in the Jubilee Club (the supporters' bar) so that an eye could be kept on their diet, tidy-up after the professionals in the afternoon, live in club-owned terraced houses that backed on to the Bridgford Road end of the City Ground. He was sent home to recover but was horrified to discover the bone knitted together "green", which meant it was bowed. So it had to be deliberately broken by a surgeon, leaving the teenager worrying (a) whether it would "straighten out this time" and (b) whether he would still have the blistering pace that had first earned him the coveted place at Forest. He stayed in Nottingham this time so that the surgeon could keep a close eye on him.

Little by little, I got to know him in the middle of the 1988-89 winter when he and the established right winger of the time, Gary Crosby, were both going through an unusual exercise to restore leg muscles after serious injuries. Crosby, who had been plucked for £15,000 from the obscurity of the Beazer Homes League[4] at Grantham when he had become resigned to football taking second place to his job as a joiner, had suffered a serious injury to his knee in a League match against Coventry City in mid-November 1988; as good as a death knell to his football ambitions so far as Clough's experiences were concerned.

Post-Christmas, they were taking it in turns pushing Crosby's saloon car up a gentle slope in a narrow *cul de sac* beside the Jubilee Club. One pushed, the other sat and steered. Then the other pushed while his mate steered. Every now and then, Physiotherapist Lyas would emerge and check on them. The one thing Lyas never heard was a complaint. Despite being surrounded on three sides by high brick walls, all those two men saw each day through their sweat-stung eyes was the prospect of playing again…

I talked to them quite frequently during their rest periods, out of admiration for their determination as well as a desire to write a story about them. But they were adamant that they would never speak to me again if I did. And they would certainly never pose for a picture of them shoving the car.

The reason? "The Gaffer doesn't like to read about his injured players."

Once or twice over the weeks, I tested this assertion. Invariably at the end of any audience he granted, Clough would ask: "Anything else before I get on with my work?" So I asked if he had any idea when Crosby would be back – and mentioned "that determined young lad recuperating with him."

---

[4] The Beazer Homes League (formerly the Southern League) was one step below Football League status in the era when there was no automatic promotion up into the League.

Clough's eyes would darken but he never actually blanked me on the subject; merely said a variety on the theme: "When I know, I'll let you know."

And sure enough, towards the conclusion of the 1988-89 season, he said towards the end of a conversation about the team he had selected for the following day: "Oh and I know how you like a little story for a Saturday ... I'm giving young Stone a professional contract. I've no idea whether he's worth it. But as you've kept telling me, he deserves to have a chance. And my coaches, whose opinions I value much more than yours, tell me he deserves another chance. He's certainly not had a chance while he's been an apprentice down here. So we'll see how he gets on over the next 12 months."

"That's brilliant, Brian," I said.

"Wrong!" he snapped. "It'll only be brilliant if he makes it. If he doesn't, then he's wasted another year of his life and I've notched up another bad decision."

"It's never a waste when you're chasing your dream, is it?" I responded.

"Steady on, young man! It's my job to come up with the one-liners. But that's a good one – stop laughing and make a note of it. Now f*** off and let me get on with my work."

"There's nothing else then?"

"Hey, you're being greedy now! F*** off."

I was out of the office corridor and into the public foyer before I heard him shout: "Oh aye – hang on!"

I turned and, to my surprise, he led me into his office; "the inner sanctum" as it was reverentially called by all. He sat me down, fetched me a Scotch and ginger, poured himself a vodka (a task he usually asked Carol to carry out) and sat at his desk, still wearing his trademark flat cap.

"I'm also going to give a year to young Scot Gemmill," he almost whispered.

"Right," I said, getting out my notebook again.

"Not because his father works for me. Make a note of that. That little bugger [Archie] is after my job but he'll never get it, I'll make sure of that."

He was smiling now, his cheeks glowing from the fresh Trentside air and the return of his innate mischief.

"Can I use that?" I smiled.

"Better not," he said. "But young Gemmill has done enough to suggest he might be able to make it. I just worry about whether he's strong enough."

"He's not prone to injuries, is he?"

"It's not that." Clough's voice became little more than a conspiratorial whisper even though we were alone and he had closed the door. "He's still a bairn. He's 18 but he's not shaving yet. Hardly got a whisker on his face or his body. He's still a boy and this is a man's game. But he's got all the other qualities you look for in a young footballer so I'm giving him a year. He and young Stone get on well so hopefully they'll egg each other on – and not make me look like a sentimental old fool. Now – drink up and f*** off and make what you can of that."

Except, of course, it wasn't a question of what I could make of the story but what Steve Stone and Scot Gemmill *did* make of Clough's double gamble.

Both became international stars. Just two more who owed Clough for giving them extra time to make their dreams come true ... and this at a time when the master-manager was supposedly on the downward spiral.

Stone, his speed undiminished by his injuries and his strength improved by those hours spent pushing Crosby's car, played in 229 matches for Forest in the decade from 1989, mostly in the right wing position previously occupied by such luminaries as Martin O'Neill and Trevor Francis. He made nine appearances for England and was part of their squad at Euro 96.

Young Gemmill – he'll always be "Young Gemmill" because of the pioneering trail blazed by his combative father – played 245 games for Forest during the 1990s and won 26 caps for Scotland. He then followed his father into coaching so successfully that he was employed by the Scottish FA to improve their Under-19 team.

What a shame a similar future did not await Gary Charles, who had begun to make his name in the very match against Coventry in which Crosby was badly injured. He was 18, a slightly-built but fleet-footed full back born in Newham in East London ... and he made a sensational debut, way out of his favoured position, on the left wing for an injury-ravaged team.

Even more amazingly, Clough had been persuaded to take the Wednesday night gamble by what he had seen in a Derby Sunday League match four days earlier. Clough's older son Simon, who ran a newsagent's shop half-a-mile from Forest's ground in West Bridgford by day, enjoyed his Sundays organising a team of locals. Brian, as was his paternal wont, encouraged the Forest apprentices – and any slightly older players living in the club's lodgings at the time – to watch these matches. There were two reasons for this: if he could see them, he knew they were not getting into mischief; and it helped him show them how he expected them to behave.

On this particular Sunday in November 1988, Simon was a player light. Brian suggested he use one of the Forest lads. There was a brief discussion about the legality of it all; but the unanimous verdict – i.e., Brian's – was that "that lot" (meaning the opposition) "won't know he's a ringer because they've never seen him before and it'll probably be years before they clap eyes on him again. He'll blend in with your bunch of scallywags."

To his utter astonishment, the master-manager saw enough in the ensuing 90 minutes on a wind-swept park pitch to select Charles for the match against Coventry. Charles responded by scoring one goal, creating havoc – and generating enough publicity for poor Simon's club to face allegations that they had indeed fielded an unsigned, unregistered player; a County Football Association's equivalent of a hanging offence.

The world seemed to be at Charles's feet, even though he had some stern competition from full backs like Brian Laws and Stuart Pearce before he could begin to think of a career in the top flight at Forest.

But from November 1988, every time Forest had a match in or near the East End of London, Clough would get Albert to drive the bus through the estate in Newham where Charles grew up. Albert would slow down – partly because of the traffic, partly at the behest of Clough – while the manager peered out at the towering concrete blocks of flats and marvel: "How on earth did that boy learn to play football here? Where on earth did he find any grass for a start?"

I tried asking Charles many more than once. His consistent answer was to shrug and ignore all suggestions that we should do a picture-story about where he took the first steps in a career that led to two England caps and eight years with Forest.

Aside from a brush with the law arising from a crash involving a car he was driving around the time he made his initial breakthrough, his progress was satisfactory enough for him to march out proudly in the Nottingham Forest team that faced Tottenham Hotspur in the 1991 FA Cup Final. Charles was the hapless player who was almost cut in half (accidentally, of course) by a tackle from the super-hyped Paul Gascoigne. Sadly, Charles also took a similar route to "Gazza" to oblivion. After only 56 first team games in those eight years at Forest, he had spells at Derby County, Aston Villa, Benfica, West Ham United and Birmingham City without fulfilling the potential Clough had spotted on that park pitch … and, as he struggled to come to terms with life outside football, he had so many alcohol-related problems that he served a couple of prison terms.

Stone, young Gemmill and Charles vividly illustrate what a lottery football will always be for star-struck talents.

13

Wonderful Wembley Wednesday nights

BY THE time I began to cover Forest's daily affairs again (attending home and away reserve, as well as first team, matches to do the job properly), they were providing an amazing number of members of England squads selected by Bobby Robson, a manager who was rarely less than helpful to the media but struggled to remember names. In other words, he was a complete contrast to the man most supporters would have chosen for the job, my 'mate' Clough.

Forest have provided England with 38 players since the club was founded in 1865; it is a startling fact that 15 of them won caps during The Clough Era. They are Viv Anderson, Garry Birtles, Gary Charles, Nigel Clough, Stan Collymore, Colin Cooper, Peter Davenport, Trevor Francis, Steve Hodge, Larry Lloyd, Stuart Pearce, Steve Stone, Des Walker, Neil Webb and Tony Woodcock.

There were so many that the *Evening Post* hierarchy agreed that we should depart from the tradition of relying on Press Association reports of international matches and attend in person. As the other members of the Sports Department all had busy schedules now that we were filling four, rather than two, pages per night, it was only fair that I should go. And there was one particular international match at the old Wembley Stadium that encapsulated all of the elements that made such visits so memorable.

It was England's 1-0 victory over Denmark in a friendly (if there ever is such a thing in football) in September 1988; the first match after the squad had (surprise, surprise) failed spectacularly – or, rather, miserably – to match the country's expectations in that summer's European Championships. The team had lost 1-0 to the Republic of Ireland, 3-1 to the Netherlands, the eventual champions, and 3-1 to the Soviet Union to finish bottom of the first round group.

So imagine the splutters of outrage from the London-based football reporters when no fewer than four of Clough's men were called up by Robson. After all, what had these provincials won in the past few years? And imagine my parochial delight when Webb scored the only goal of the game and I got back to the office at about 3am on the Thursday morning, lit a cigarette while my computer terminal was booting-up and began my report:

> Nottingham has given our national sport a lot over the years … the oldest League club in the world, shin pads, crossbars, a side that won the European Cup a couple of times…
>
> It gave a little more at Wembley last night: four of the 13 who helped restore some of the pride mislaid in the European Championships finals and, more important in the short term, who doused the insensitive, hysterical criticism of their selections.
>
> Neil Webb, Stuart Pearce, Steve Hodge and substitute Des Walker all played their parts in beating Denmark 1-0 – and in drawing the sting of the men of the National press who almost insisted on a London-based XI to take the field.
>
> Webb was England's man of the match. Indeed, he was *the* man of the match, make no mistake about that irrespective of what you might read elsewhere today about captain Bryan Robson leading his men out of the wilderness. Robson was a left-sided bit-player while Webb ran (and ran and ran) the show from centre stage.
>
> It was Webb who won the midfield battle of strength with Liverpool's Jan Molby. "How are you, Dynamite?" asked the big Dane's club manager, Kenny Dalglish, in the Banqueting Suite after the match. 'Dynamite' shook his head glumly, unable to find words – much as he had been unable to undermine Webb's impact.

And that was just the start of me rubbing it in on behalf of the Foresters. These were the days before statistics were routinely compiled; indeed, this was an age before computers, not to mention computer nerds, were routinely available. So I had sat in the Wembley Press Box, overlooking the Royal Box, and constructed my own detailed panel to explain exactly how the Forest Four had fared on the hallowed turf…

15/9/1988

FACTS

THIS is how Forest's 'fab four' contributed statistically to England's 1-0 win over Denmark.

● NEIL WEBB made 36 accurate passes to team-mates and four that found the opposition. He won six tackles and lost four. He won three heading duels and lost one. He scored the lone goal and had one other shot, off-target.

● STUART PEARCE at left back won 13 tackles and lost three (including two free-kicks conceded). He won two heading duels and lost two. He made 28 accurate passes — half of them probing, forward passes as opposed to 'safe' ones across the back line — and made four inaccurate passes.

● STEVE HODGE on the left side of midfield won 16 tackles and lost five (including two free-kicks conceded). He made eight accurate passes and one inaccurate, plus a swerving cross that forced Danish goalkeeper Troels Rasmussen to scramble full length to hold.

● DES WALKER in the centre of defence for the last 26 minutes, won seven tackles and lost one, won his only heading duel, and made ten accurate passes and two inaccurate 'passes' — both long clearances up-field.

The titbit in the report about Dalglish and 'Dynamite' Molby came from my habit of roaming around the corridors of Wembley after the matches and the set-piece media conferences. As ever, I could have done with two of me: one to do the formal stuff with the management, one to stake-out the dressing room area and catch the players. Not having a big enough staff to afford two on a night match, I had to trust my judgement (and luck) and simply be grateful that I always had an excellent photographer to illustrate whatever I wrote. Trevor Bartlett was the keenest of the originals; and by the late 1980s he was being pushed by the equally eager Steve Mitchell and Richard Denning, a local lad who had graduated from being dark room assistant to a status that led to him illustrating the England v Denmark report with some fantastic exclusive pictures.

For me, it was a rare night when sheer enjoyment took over comprehensively from the usual strait-laced clichés that we had come to expect from our heroes.

Manager Robson set the tone by making the national media wait 30 minutes for his appearance. How they fretted! Deadlines were ticking away. Ploys of how to set him up with a pre-arranged series of questions had to be re-thought given the urgency of the hour. And when he finally strode in, he had all guns firing.

"The criticism has been vicious," he said of the inquests into Euro 1988 and the selection of this team. "This was our answer. We are still together even if there are so many people against us. I told the players to stand up and be counted and that's exactly what they did. It was a performance of character that gives us fresh hope." His script could have been written by Clough. And what followed was right out of The Clough Guide To Controlling Situations. He got up and marched out, leaving 'the national mafia' to scramble after him to try and catch him along the corridors.

I left them to it and went in search of the Forest Four. As I neared the dressing room area, the eerie silence – and absence of black-suited marshals – told me I was too late … until I heard one set of approaching footsteps … They turned out to belong to Des Walker, a 22-year-old from the East End of London who had already become a legend among Nottingham Forest's most vocal supporters, the Trent Enders, who would sing this assurance to rivals: "You'll never beat Des Walker …" Fancy fate allowing me to catch him tonight of all nights! Such was the central defender's sullen, secretive nature, I had almost resigned myself to never being able to interview Walker. But this night was different. He had made his England debut, as substitute for Tony Adams, the Arsenal captain. Gone was his habitual sulk. He was so elated, it was as if he was a lad again enjoying the kick-abouts on Hackney Marshes. As we walked up the Wembley tunnel – yes, I walked up the Wembley tunnel alongside the great Des Walker – there was no facade of a professional footballer uttering clichés to a journalist going through the motions of "getting a line for a follow-up". We were two kids fulfilling all our childhood dreams.

And the usually tight-lipped Walker was almost skipping with joy as we skirted the pitch, made our way beneath the old Royal Box and eventually found our way up to the Banqueting Suite where he was to enjoy the after-match hospitality.

I didn't use all his gushing phrases in the following day's *Evening Post* because I knew he would be terribly embarrassed for his mates to read his thoughts, genuine and heart-warming as they were. For example, I didn't mention that he'd taken me up the famous Tunnel because: "I just want to step on the Wembley pitch once more tonight." These were the quotes that appeared in print:

POSTPHOTO R6384/12

VERDICT on the BIG MATCH

15/9/1988

WEBB THE DAREDEVIL

by TREVOR FRECKNALL

Picture: RICHARD DENNING

● Who's a clever boy than? Stuart Pearce (right) shares a joke with his Forest colleague and England goalscorer Neil Webb last night.
POSTPHOTO R6384/3

Super show by Sout

DES WALKER clutched his first full England shirt, covered by the autographs of his international team-mates, and said:

"That's the first time I've felt on top of the world in a pre-match kick-about.

"The nearest I've been to Wembley before is for a Michael Jackson concert. I didn't even play in the centenary tournament here last season because I was injured.

"Before I went on, I was nervous. It was 1-0, a very tight game, and you think of all the things that can go wrong.

"But once I got out there, I was okay. Terry Butcher is a great talker — a stalwart in every sense — and I can honestly say I never felt at all uneasy."

STEVE HODGE, his lip still swollen after successive accidental kicks in training with Forest last Friday and in the match at Everton 24-hours later, managed a broad smile after his first international for 14 months:

"It was hard. It's always hard at this level.

"I never thought, after I missed the European Championships, that I would be back so soon.

But with Waddle and Barnes being injured, I thought there might be a chance."

Was he affected by the low attendance persuading the Wembley authorities to close the stands opposite the Royal Box?

"It doesn't matter, does it? All that matters is playing for England — and in a winning side."

STUART PEARCE — polite and pleasant off the field as he is forthright, even fearsome, on it — declined to comment.

"Nothing personal," he said to me.

"But I understand the Forest captain takes the view that the national newspapers have said so much about England in the last few days that the players' most eloquent response was the victory. If so, he's got a point.

Pearce's tight-lipped refusal to talk did not dilute his enjoyment of the victory, as you will see from "Gordi" Denning's fabulous picture of the Forest captain with match-winner Neil Webb that led the *Post's* back page on that Thursday…

And to cap it all, as I went to find "Gordi" in the Press Room after completing my foraging for interviews, I met Robson marching along a corridor.

"Well done, Boss," I said as we passed.

"You've got a busy night, Nottingham," he smiled. "Didn't your boys perform?!"

By the time I set off from the office to drive home at about 4am on that Thursday, I was exhausted yet elated. Clough always said: "It's not the football that tires you out. It's the travelling back and forth." I never disagreed. And I always reminded him that I couldn't really start work until he had stopped playing. The first time I did so, he thought about it for long moments and then drawled: "So that's why you look so much older than me." For the Denmark match, I'd driven to Wembley on the Wednesday afternoon, set off on the return journey around midnight after gathering all those post-match quotes, spent the 120 miles or so discussing with "Gordi" how we were going to parcel-up our goodies for the *Evening Post* and the following Saturday's *Football Post*; and then typed my reports in the dead of night while "Gordi" developed his pictures. So on my trip from the office to home in the Trentside village of North Muskham just north of Newark, I was able to reflect that – to use one of Clough's favourite phrases – I'd done myself, the players and the readers proud in that I had managed to tell the story basically through the thoughts of the people who made it, i.e., the players and the manager.

I was brought down to earth the following lunchtime. It was Friday, of course; and I always hung around outside the Jubilee Club to catch Neil Webb so that I could 'ghost' his column for the following night's *Football Post* while also hoping to grab the team selection from Clough or, more usually, Fenton.

Walker was first out of the dressing rooms. He marched straight up to me, jabbed me in the chest and said: "Never do that to me again."

"Do what?" I was genuinely taken aback by his aggression.

"Quote me," he said.

"Why?" I asked, finding myself laughing nervously.

"You've made me look like a star-struck prat."

"Rubbish," I laughed, "I've made you sound like a footballer who's proud to play for his country."

"Well, you won't get another chance," he persisted. "I'll never talk to you again." And off he stalked, flooring the accelerator of his car so swiftly that he literally smoked out of the car park.

By this time, Webb had joined me. "That's Des," he shrugged. "We've all been winding him up cos he's never shown any emotion before." Walker never did again, either, through the 59 appearances he made for England over the next six years – most notably alongside Terry Butcher and Mark Wright during the run to the 1990 World Cup semi-finals, when Bobby Robson's team was knocked out by Germany on penalties. This remains England's best World Cup performance since Ramsey's wingless wonders won the Jules Rimet Trophy in 1966 … not that any lucky journalist managed to get Walker's innermost thoughts about the achievement. He didn't even join the age of the cliché. He simply kept his mouth shut.

14

Clough imprisons Newcastle United

BRIAN CLOUGH was incandescent as he climbed aboard the team bus to travel home from the shrine known as St. James's Park, Newcastle, on 29 October 1988. Forest had defeated their hosts, Newcastle United, 1-0 in the First Division. The goal had been scored by his latest gamble in a striking position, Lee Chapman; but there was no sign of satisfaction. What had infuriated Clough was the feebleness of the home team that afternoon.

"Those players are an absolute f***ing disgrace," he asserted as the Forest bus slowly edged away.

"Look at those poor buggers," he nodded out of the window, where thousands of glum supporters were still hanging around, their shoulders hunched, their despair clear for all to see.

"This is not just a football club to them. This is their life-blood. And those f***ing players who were out there today are shrivelling it up. They've got no idea."

He paused. He sighed. He waved a commiserating hand to a group of fans who recognised him as Albert crawled along the packed streets. He had played for Middlesbrough and Sunderland and yet was hailed by their biggest enemies at Newcastle. And long minutes later, when Albert eased the bus onto the A1M, Clough half-turned his head towards the seats occupied by Lawson and myself.

"Did either of you have your notebooks open by any chance as we left the ground?" he asked.

"No," said Lawson.

"Yes, Brian," said I.

"Can I have a look at it?" he asked, quietly and casually, reaching a hand towards the gap between the twin seats.

"Of course, Brian."

"Good lad."

Presently the book re-appeared, via Ron Fenton in the seat beside Clough. Not surprisingly it was minus a page of red-hot, emotive quotes.

"The Gaffer never comments on the opposition," said Fenton quietly.

"I should have remembered," I replied.

About 13 months earlier, I had been on the fringe of a 'Midland mafia' chat with Clough just after Newcastle had made a contentious signing to replace England international striker Peter Beardsley. Instead of going for a proven British goal-scorer, they became the first club to introduce a Brazilian to the Football League. He had been christened Lima da Silva, one of 11 children, and had begun his working life in a salt mine until someone spotted he could play football rather well. Now he was known as Mirandinha.

"How do you think Mirandinha will get along on Tyneside?" Clough was asked.

"He'll be fine for a week or two," Clough said. "But I'm not so sure how accustomed he is to being knee-deep in snow with the wind blowing straight up his jacksy from the Arctic Circle. Does it snow on Copacabana beach? Well, it'll sure as hell snow – and sleet and hail – on this little bit of Brazil in the coming months."

Oh, how we laughed. Clough didn't. "Hey – I'm being serious," he said, finger wagging. "And I'm also off the record because I've no intention of doing the Newcastle manager's job for him and winding that f***ing Brazilian up for when he plays against me."

Proving that Clough was as successful as a soothsayer as he was as a star-maker, Mirandinha made only fitful positive contributions. Newcastle finished bottom of the First Division in 1988-89. Mirandinha moved back to warmer climes.

Months later, Clough took revenge – on behalf of the Tyneside hordes left desolate by the shortcomings of their heroes and, equally, on behalf of the Newcastle United manager at the time, Jim Smith.

The pair went back a long way. Smith had been the manager of Birmingham City when Clough bought Trevor Francis for Nottingham Forest. Both were steeped in football, overtly unforgiving of know-nothing directors, well aware that their futures were in the hands of players whose wages and contracts were making them less faithful by the season … and as for those meddling agents who were beginning to realise football was the latest big-money market for them to move into…

So after a Central League[5] match at the City Ground, won by Forest Reserves even though Smith had fielded most of his first team, Clough invited his old mate into the Chairman's Room for a drink.

"I can't stop, Brian – I'm travelling with the team," said Smith.

---

[5] The Central League was a competition for the reserve teams of all Football League clubs in the North and Midlands.

Long-term pals: Jim Smith and Clough.

"Hey – don't you mean they're travelling with you?" Clough drawled. I laughed. He scowled. Smith said nowt. Clough took his time pouring drinks for all three of us plus, I think, Archie Gemmill, the highly successful Forest Reserves' coach; and toasted our continued health.

"Where are they now then?" Clough asked of the Newcastle squad.

"On the bus," said Smith, taking a large gulp.

"Do you think your driver deserves a drink?" Clough asked, and was out of the door and down the corridor without awaiting a response.

Gemmill and Smith made somewhat uneasy small-talk while I sipped my Scotch and ginger and strained an ear down the corridor, where Clough was talking with his secretary, Carol, and the Newcastle driver was expressing his gratitude. The driver was clearly astounded to be treated like royalty by none other than Brian Clough; Carol merely took it in her neat and tidy stride.

"Right then," said Clough on his return to the Chairman's Room. "Your driver's having a cuppa and a bite to eat and your players are on the bus so let's relax for a while."

"The bloody players will be in the bar by now," said Smith.

"Not unless they can pick locks," Clough drawled.

He'd locked them in the bus! And there they stayed "for as long as they embarrassed you tonight, Jim" – 90 minutes plus a 10-minute interval – by which time the windows had misted up and those who had broken into a sweat during the match were doubtless shivering with cold.

There was no such discomfort in the Chairman's Room. Clough and Smith got on so well and chatted so easily that I reckon they would have yarned on through the night. But there came a moment when Carol discreetly knocked on the door and said: "Sorry to interrupt, but the driver's worried he'll be out of hours if he doesn't get going soon."

"Good," said Clough, reaching for a refill. "Let the buggers walk home!"

"Well, I'm in no condition to walk home," chuckled Smith, clambering to his feet and collecting his driver.

Shaking hands, he assured Clough: "You've done me a power of good – as always!"

"And do yourself a favour," shouted Clough to his departing friend. "Keep reminding them buggers who's in charge."

Smith stuck it at St. James's Park until March 1991, by which time it was clear Newcastle were not going to earn promotion from Division II and there was no sign of an end to a power struggle in the boardroom.

Asked why he was resigning, Smith shook his head sadly and simply said: "They're unmanageable."

15

Sorry we chinned your fist Brian

· ·

THE 14TH YEAR of Brian Clough's reign at the City Ground was the most traumatic. He was fined a record amount by the Football Association for thumping two Nottingham Forest supporters in January 1989. He rebelled against the timing of the freeing of Nelson Mandela in February. He led the club to another little piece of history: when they won the League Cup and the Full Members' Cup, they became the first to secure two major trophies in the same season. And he watched in disbelief as 96 Liverpool supporters died on the terraces of Hillsborough in the early minutes of an FA Cup semi-final. It was enough to turn anyone to drink!

The thumping of supporters came at the end of Forest's 5-2 victory over Queen's Park Rangers in the quarter finals of the League Cup on Wednesday night, 18 January. It had been such a wonderful performance that the London club's fans among the crowd of 24,065 were reduced to chanting, long before the end: "We want a riot." They didn't mean it; or, in this lawless era, maybe they did; whatever, it did not materialise. It was merely their way of saying that an abandonment was all that could save their hapless heroes, who incidentally were managed at the time by Trevor Francis. But it could have been different if they had been faced by a stampeding horde of Forest supporters gloatingly charging across the pitch towards their corner of the terracing at the end of the thrashing.

The Forest faithful were so elated by the performance that, at the final whistle, several decided to race onto the pitch to congratulate *their* heroes. The progress of two such supporters from the Main Stand towards the touchline took them across the route Clough was quick-marching from his seat in the dug-out to the tunnel that led to the changing rooms. His first instinctive hook caught an ear. His second bounced off a cheek and almost stopped a young invader in his tracks. There were cheers up in the Press Box

(a) because it was typical of The Gaffer and (b) because he had given them a bigger story than a crushing win over his most expensive disciple. Even better, ITV cameras caught it all.

Before he set off home, Clough made no fewer than three offers to resign. The Forest directors, for whom he had so little time, instantly unified in support of him. The club Chairman, Maurice Roworth, an accountant who was a worthy successor to Stuart Dryden as a Clough supporter, was adamant: "What the fans did was the equivalent of trespass, and that is an offence. What the manager did was right. We support him 100 per cent. It was an example of how he cares for this club's property and for football."

The support was not confined in-house at a time when the majority of folk in the country believed that football hooligans were being given far too much leeway; "special treatment" that would not have been granted to rioting pickets, for example.

The Nottinghamshire Constabulary's Assistant Chief Constable, Mr. Edward Griffiths, promised that Clough would be interviewed. Simultaneously, his colleague in charge of policing the match, Chief Superintendent Michael Holford, told the *Evening Post* it was unlikely any charges would be made. And in case he felt people might consider he was still sitting on the fence, he added that none of the alleged victims had lodged complaints. Only irate TV viewers had called for action against Clough. Other callers had praised the manager … "One even suggested he deserved a medal," said Holford to as many of the media as would listen.

And we at the *Evening Post* had no qualms about supporting Clough. Kid-glove treatment of ill-behaved supporters had achieved nothing through the four years since football-related violence had supposedly reached its nadir with the deaths of 39 Juventus supporters and the injuries to more than 600 others before the kick-off of the 1985 European Cup Final against Liverpool in the Heysel Stadium, Brussels. This tragedy had resulted in English clubs being banned indefinitely from European competitions, a judgment that infuriated disciplinarians such as Clough who felt it dreadfully unfair that innocents should be punished so severely.

In addition, the anti-Clough editor Mr. Snaith had retired and been replaced by a younger man more attuned to modern tastes, Barrie Williams. Think Jack Regan of *The Sweeney* with a nightly Opinion column at his disposal and you've got the *Evening Post* Editorial Director who bustled up the corridor from the Guest Room that night, overcoat flapping with every rapid stride, to instruct: "The Pro-Clough campaign starts here, mate." I never told him he'd been beaten to the start by Chairman Roworth and Chief Superintendent Holford. But, not for the first time, the *Evening Post* found itself in an opposing corner to most of the rest of the media who set out to urge the FA to crucify Clough. And it made a change from squaring-up politically.

By the time of the next match, three days later, we had found two of the supporters who had felt the greatest force of Clough's clobbering; and they agreed to apologise for trespassing on his pitch. They duly turned up at the Forest offices before the match against

Aston Villa: clean-cut, well-dressed Mark Wheeler (18) and Paul Richardson (17) from Bingham, a small market town about 10 miles east of Nottingham.

Both made articulate, reasoned apologies, as you can see from the picture-story that appeared in the *Football Post* only a few hours later ...

POSTPHOTO T586

CLOUGHIE 'IS OUR HERO'

TWO more of Nottingham Forest's pitch invaders apologised to manager Brian Clough this afternoon.

Mark Wheeler, 16, and his 17-year-old mate Paul Richardson, both from Bingham, made their peace with the manager before the match with Aston Villa.

Paul said: " We have been thinking about it ever since Wednesday night and ... well, he is our hero."

Mark said: "We wanted to congratulate Lee Chapman on his four goals. Brian was wrong to hit us but we were wrong to go on to the pitch.

"We have both made statements to the police saying we are sorry and we apologise to Forest."

Their move follows apologies yesterday by two other supporters who felt Clough's wrath for running on to

the pitch after Forest 5-2 win over Queen's Park Rangers in the Little-woods Cup quarter final.

Forest have so far received 254 letters from the public after Clough's reaction to the invasion was shown repeatedly on television.

A club official said this afternoon that 234 of the messages favoured Clough and 20 were against his actions.

There was, of course, one group for whom Clough was not a hero. The Football Association had been embarrassed by him with tedious frequency. His ever-populist views – no more cerebral than plain commonsense to the majority of football followers – were as much thorns in their sensitive underbellies as his frequently-voiced criticism of their tendency to play safe in the choice of international team manager. So one can imagine the gleeful hand-rubbing that went on inside their Lancaster Gate headquarters in London as every news bulletin carried footage of the "assaults" from the Wednesday night until Saturday, when the speculation was how many fans Clough would "clip" by way of an *en*

And there was an alternative picture for the *Evening Post*
to use with a follow-up story on the Monday.

"... and racing down the wing, a quick clip round the ear, swerving round a defender, another clip round the ear and yes! — a stunning left hook to the chin!"

core. The *Evening Post* was not the only newspaper to try and bring a smile to the scenario via Jak's cartoon...

And just in case our 120,000 or so daily buyers had not yet fully got the message, the front page splash on Saturday 21 January contained Clough's considered appraisal of what he had done...

My full story read:

Manager Brian Clough said "sorry" to his Nottingham Forest players before they faced Aston Villa this afternoon – then kissed and made-up with two of the fans he hustled off the pitch on Wednesday night.

The incident after the Littlewoods[6] Cup quarter-final against QPR totally over-

So sorry —Clough

Apology to team

MANAGER Brian Clough said "sorry" to his Nottingham Forest players before they faced Aston Villa this afternoon — then kissed and made-up with two of the fans he hustled off the pitch on Wednesday night.

The incident after the Littlewoods Cup quarter-final against QPR totally over-shadowed Forest's 5-2 victory, their sixth in 19 days.

And Clough recognised the fact during his team talk to the players, whose hectic spell of two matches a week continues on Tuesday when they travel to Ipswich Town in the quarter-finals of the Simod Cup.

"The players and my apologies more than anybody else," said the manager after the meeting with them behind locked gates and doors at the City Ground.

"I am concerned they have not got the praise they deserve for what they have done this week.

"The incident overshadowed their achievements in winning at Tottenham and their beating QPR in the Littlewoods Cup."

But the incident was in the spotlight when Clough met councillor supporters James McGowan, 25, and 20-year-old Sean O'Hara in the guest room at the City Ground.

Clough quietly explained to them that what he did was regrettable, but that he was concerned about how QPR fans would react to wrong Forest supporters running on the pitch towards them.

by TREVOR FRECKNALL

"we were right out of order," said McGowan, who lives in Clifton. "My mum's disowned me."

"Dad's disowned me," said O'Hara, from Bestwood Park. "We came to apologise because we have supported Nottingham Forest all our lives and, don't want to do anything to harm the club."

Clough accepted their apology in the traditional manner of a man from the north-east. He planted a big kiss on each of their cheeks.

Backing

A club official said that two of the calls had been from school head teachers. And a retired policeman had also rung in, giving backing to Clough.

Of the early letters on the subject to arrive at the City Ground, 89 supported the manager's action and 11 were against.

"People are getting in touch with us from all over the country," added the spokesman. "I've taken calls from as far apart as Chester and Newcastle, from people asking me to tell the manager they believe he was right."

> *B Brian Clough, apologised to his players then made-up to two contrite fans who had run on the pitch.*

---

[6] Littlewoods were the sponsors of the League Cup at the time.

shadowed Forest's 5-2 victory, their sixth in 19 days. And Clough recognised the fact during his team talk to the players, whose hectic spell of two matches a week continues on Tuesday when they travel to Ipswich Town in the quarter-finals of the Simod[7] Cup.

"The players need my apologies more than anybody else," said the manager after his meeting with them, behind locked gates and doors at the City Ground. "I am concerned they have not got the praise they deserve for what they have done this week.

"The incident detracted from their achievements in winning at Tottenham [in the League] and then beating QPR in the Littlewoods Cup."

But the incident was in the spotlight when Clough met contrite supporters James McGowan, 25, and 20-year-old Sean O'Hara in the guest room at the City Ground.

Clough quietly explained to them that what he did was regrettable, but that he was concerned how QPR fans would react to seeing Forest supporters running on the pitch towards them.

"We were right out of order," said McGowan, who lives in Clifton [the housing estate in the south-east of Nottingham in which Forest's England defender Viv Anderson was reared]. "My Mum's disowned me."

"Dad's disowned me," said O'Hara, from Bestwood Park [an estate in the north-west of Nottingham]. "We came to apologise because we have supported Forest all our lives and don't want to do anything to harm the club."

Clough accepted their apology in the traditional manner of a man from the North-East. He proffered his cheek so they could kiss it.

And public support grew for the manager in telephone calls and letters to the City Ground. A club official said that two of the supportive calls had come from school head teachers. And a retired policeman had also rung to give backing to Clough.

Of the early letters on the subject to arrive at the City Ground, 49 supported the manager's action and 11 were against. "People are getting in touch with us from all over the country," said the spokesman. "I've taken calls from as far apart as Clacton and Newcastle, from people asking me to tell the manager they believe he was right."

One fact was omitted from the story. On the long walk down the main corridor from the entrance to the Guest Room, assistant manager Ron Fenton suddenly grabbed one of the supporters by the shoulder.

---

[7] Simod were the sponsors of the Full Members Cup, introduced after the Heysel Stadium Disaster to provide First and Second Division clubs with an extra midweek competition.

"What's up?" asked the startled fan.

"You're wearing an ear-ring," said Fenton.

"Warrabout it?"

"If you don't take it off now, The Gaffer will do it for you in there – and he might well tear your ear off when he does it."

The fan laughed! "Oh aye. I see what yer mean." Slipping the stud into his pocket, he mooched into the Guest Room, grinning at the thought of meeting his biggest hero in the whole world.

"Take your hands out of your pockets, young man," Clough growled, by way of a greeting. But otherwise, the – er – reconciliation went as well as could be expected. And there was another good story for Monday's paper…

● Brian Clough, surrounded by some of his young players, faces the City Ground crowd before the Villa match

It was headed 'Thanks a million!' and beneath the pictures of Clough surrounded by players on his way to the dug-out, Stuart Pearce firing a trademark free-kick and being congratulated on the second of Forest's four goals, the story read…

> Brian Clough today thanked the *two* Nottingham Forest teams which ended one of his most traumatic weeks in management in impeccable, winning style.
>
> His tributes went to:
>
> The players who trounced Aston Villa 4-0 at the City Ground on Saturday to extend their winning run to seven matches in 22 days; and
>
> The backroom staff who stuck to the club's routine amid the controversy that enveloped Clough after his treatment of invading fans on Wednesday night.
>
> Surrounded by assistant manager Ron Fenton, coaches Liam O'Kane and Archie Gemmill, plus Alan Hill and Alan Clarke who look after the young players, Clough said: "The team was superb against Villa. But I didn't do it. I wasn't here. The coaching staff did it for me. It was important that we got a result with the turmoil that the club had been in for the past three days…."
>
> And Clough revealed that he disrupted his post-match routine to congratulate 19-year-old Terry Wilson on his performance against Aston Villa and their 'Rambo' striker, 21-goal Alan McInally, who managed only one (off-target) shot.
>
> "I got out of the bath to come back into the dressing room and tell him he was incredible," said Clough.
>
> And the manager joked:"We've got a quiet week now. The first team are at Ipswich tomorrow night in the Simod Cup quarter-finals; the reserves at Newcastle United on Wednesday, seeking to stay top of the Central League; the under-18s entertain Stoke City in the Purity Midland Intermediate League on Saturday morning; and there's the small matter of the FA Cup fourth round tie at the City Ground against Leeds United on Saturday afternoon."
>
> Serious again, Clough went on: "Liam got it right when he said we don't even have time to enjoy winning well. We don't even have time to sit down and enjoy it."
>
> And he included the under-18s' contribution in his praise. They twice came from behind to draw 3-3 at Derby County on Saturday morning.
>
> "The spirit in this club is bursting out of us," he said.
>
> By now, Forest have received 394 letters about the Clough incident. All but 36 support the manager.

And to prove the point about spirit, he insisted we all had another drink. Or two. There was good news, bad news for Clough on 27 January.

The Director of Public Prosecutions, Allan Green QC, announced that Clough would not be prosecuted. He had become involved personally, it was explained, because of the "sensitive nature of the inquiry".

Before anyone had a chance to consider whether "sensitive" was the right adjective to use in conjunction with a scuffle on a football pitch in front of a television audience of millions, Clough got the bad news he expected from the FA. They charged him with bringing the game into disrepute.

While most of the national newspapers relished the threat to Clough's future, our campaign on his behalf continued apace.

Chairman Roworth came up with a classic line when I asked him, in the wake of the FA charge, if he was still behind Clough. "No," he snapped. "I'm beside him." Roworth added: "He has always been an ambassador for discipline – not only in football but in life in general – and his motives after the Rangers match were good ones."

The local brewery that was sponsoring Forest, Shipstones, announced a £500,000 deal to extend their backing to 1992. Big money in the days before the Premier League transformed the fortunes of the top few.

Judgment Day was 9 February. On the eve of the visit by the FA's three-man tribunal, I was given the *Evening Post's* main news feature page to set the scene. I summed-up:

> If the FA Commission does throw the book at "the people's champion",
>   the public reaction will be of fury.
> If it doesn't the tacky tabloids will resharpen their knives.
> The three wise men from the FA really cannot win.
> And they probably know it.

It did not deter them from savouring their pound of flesh. Clough was fined £5,000 – more than anyone else in the history of Football Association disciplinary charges of any kind – and banned from the touchline of all Football League grounds for the rest of the season.

The news emerged just in time for our biggest-selling edition, the 2pm one, on Thursday 9 February.

As I wrote this story, I seriously felt that the follow-up would be Clough walking away from the job and the entire sport…

> The Nottingham Forest manager Brian Clough was fined £5,000 by the FA
> this afternoon after being found guilty of bringing the game into disrepute.
>   It took the disciplinary commission nearly four hours to reach their verdict
> at the City Ground.
>   The 53-year-old Forest manager was also banned from the touch-line at all
> League grounds until the end of the season.

CLOUGH IS BANNED

— and £5,000 fine for Forest boss

THE NOTTINGHAM FOREST manager Mr

But Mr Clough will be able to be on the Wembley touchline should the team reach one of the three cup competitions they could still win.

matches at Wembley and would not stop Mr Clough coaching youngsters on park pitches.

Edw — dou on fut

MPs WERE r Edwina Cur future after he formance befo Commons Cor
One leading ber of the cor ueating the in eggs rowed behaviour as and "very sad' Ann Winter for Congle "Edwina Curr edly frosty. walled every acted like a gr Mrs Winter felt Mrs Currie that she had r future.
Doubts over future came a

But Mr. Clough will be able to be on the Wembley touchline should the team reach one of the three cup competitions they could still win.

The record fine and ban come after an incident after a Littlewoods Cup game against Queen's Park Rangers when millions of TV viewers saw him strike out at fans invading the pitch.

They were celebrating Forest's 5-2 win in the quarter-final.

Nottinghamshire police said there was insufficient evidence to bring a prosecution against Mr. Clough and the four fans involved later went to the ground to apologise.

Neither the referee nor the linesmen mentioned the incident in their official report to the FA.

FA chief executive-designate Graham Kelly said the ban did not apply to matches at Wembley and would not stop Mr. Clough coaching youngsters on park pitches.

He said Mr. Clough had told the commission he would not appeal against the sentence.

The commission also ordered Forest to print warning notices in the club programme and display them around the ground for the next three home games.

They were also ordered to improve segregation of home and away fans at the City Ground.

After the decision, Mr. Clough left the ground without comment.

It is believed the commission took into account more than 750 letters of support for the beleaguered manager, the League's longest-serving, who has had an exemplary record.

Next morning bright and early, I was on the phone to Chairman Roworth. He assured me there was no point rushing to the City Ground because: "I've told him to leave it to his staff this morning and spend time with Barbara." The theory was that Clough's utterly level-headed wife would persuade him against walking away, but only after a long verbal battle.

But the biggest consistency about Clough throughout his career was his capacity to do the unexpected; and he surprised everyone – especially me. He arrived at the ground at his usual time … and chose me as his medium to let the world know he had drawn a line under the whole episode.

Not that I was aware of that as I drove to the City Ground. I felt nearly as much trepidation as I had almost a decade earlier; when he kicked me out and banned me at our first meeting. Now it was 9.30am and I had an hour and 15 minutes to get a front page lead story for the first edition. From long before my arrival as Sports Editor, Clough had been well aware of all our edition times … 10.45am for the first edition and 'regional' pages to the towns of Newark and Grantham plus rural Lincolnshire and east Nottinghamshire; 12 noon for the Mansfield and North Notts edition; 1pm for the heavily populated areas of South Nottinghamshire into North Leicestershire and South-East Derbyshire; 2pm for the biggest-selling edition in the conurbation of Nottingham; and 3.30pm for the Late Extra to pick-up one-off sales to folk leaving shops, factories and offices.

Despite all our support of him, I gave myself only a slim chance of updating the holding story we had about "Nottingham and the football world waiting to hear whether Brian Clough was going to work on" after the punishment. It had been in all the national papers, on every radio station, on television news bulletins hourly. We needed something new!

My heart sank when I entered Pavilion Road, which leads from Trent Bridge to the club car park. As in the days immediately after the incident, the City Ground was in fortress mode. All of the match-day marshals had been summoned – and willingly answered the call though it meant many losing money from their full-time employers. They guarded all of the entrances, which were locked. The huge iron gates at the main entrance of the car park were closed and chained; and thronged by a mass of supporters bearing banners in support of Clough and reporters armed with notebooks they hoped to fill with contentious material.

I got out of my car and edged through the crowd. As soon as one of the bibbed marshals spotted me, he became enormously animated. Instinctively, I wondered about shrinking back. My mind filled with memories of being called a scab by strikers and pickets and I'll be honest; I panicked. But the man persisted and I edged up to the wrought iron gates. "You can come in," the marshal shouted above the hubbub.

The gate opened a slight notch, the crowd surged forward but only I was allowed through. I was escorted across the park, into the office corridor – and then into the Chairman's Room. There, Roworth "marked my card" – code at the time for giving me a story without wanting to be identified as the source – about the supporters wanting to pay. Then he drifted away while I went to the public phone in the foyer of the Jubilee Club to dictate my story to the office: no mobile phones, let alone lap-tops and emails, in those days!

The follow-up story, for the early editions on Friday 10 February, made yet another front page lead …

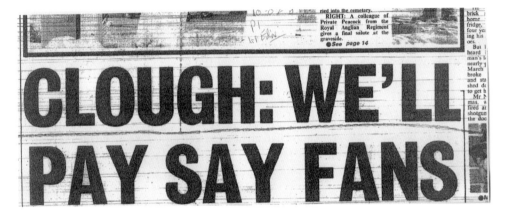

The story read:

> Nottingham Forest fans today started ringing the City Ground offering to pay Brian Clough's £5,000 FA fine.
>
> The fine – with a ban from the touchlines of all League grounds until the end of the season – was … the biggest punishment ever handed out in English football.
>
> Today the club urged Mr. Clough to reconsider his decision not to appeal against the verdict …
>
> He has never queried officials' decisions during his lifetime as a player and manager – and was praised as "a beacon" by the Referees' and Linesmen's Association in a letter to the commission.
>
> But it is understood the touchline ban was sufficiently devastating to persuade him to contemplate resignation – for the fourth time – over the incident.

And then it was hold-your-breath time. Coming off the phone, I glanced at my watch. It was just before 11am. Even as I wondered what to do next, feeling like a spy in a war zone, the door to the dressing rooms opened and, half an hour later than usual, the first team squad filed out but, instead of strolling towards the training ground, stood and formed a kind of guard of honour. To my astonishment, and trepidation, Clough walked out, grabbed my right lapel and led me along the line of solemn-looking players. More than one whispered: "Been good to know you" or words to that effect. He took me into the changing rooms area (where I had never been allowed before), turned right towards the Guest Room, right again up the long corridor towards the exit.

'Oh no! Not again,' I thought. 'Don't just throw me out today!' Just when I thought he was going to kick me through the doors, he swung left and then left again – and we were in his office. He kind of dropped me in a chair and went behind the desk to his own seat.

"So," he drawled, "what do you want to know?"

"What's it like to be the biggest criminal in the history of football, Brian?"

"You what?" he asked, almost whispered.

"That fine's the biggest the FA have ever given anyone …"

He took a deep breath. He looked intently into my eyes. And instead of saying "F*** them all – I'm off" – as I fully expected him to do – he said in his most assertive voice:

"The FA have done me proud." And, slapping the palms of his hands on his desk, he stood so briskly that I thought he was going to bid me goodbye now. Instead, he fumbled among a pile of correspondence on the far left corner of his desk and came up with the letter that Roworth had mentioned from the Referees' and Linesmen's Association. "I was absolutely astonished to get this," he said, sliding it in front of me.

"Well, you've never given them any trouble, have you?" I coaxed. He didn't respond; simply sat down again, staring out at me over his spectacles, his face absolutely expressionless.

"So what are you going to do next?" I ventured, holding his gaze but revealing my nerves by fiddling with my notebook.

"I've got a team to pick for tomorrow," he said. And with that, he unclasped his hands, leaned forward and picked up his phone. "Get the *Evening Post* please, Mrs. Parker," he said evenly to his secretary. "Copy, isn't it?" he added, looking at me. Speechless, I nodded.

"15 paragraphs – no more," he told me, handing me the phone.

"Hello, Copy" chirped one of the lovely lady typists, as I got the handset to my ear.

"It's Trevor Frecknall here …."

"Oh thank God for that – they're going spare here thinking he's thrown you in the Trent." A quick glance across the desk suggested that, if Clough had heard that, he was ready to ignore it.

Not for the first time, I dictated a report off the top of my head. And it was like covering a match at The Den, Millwall's old ground in the East End of London, with the home supporters hanging on to every word and suggesting I ought to have a few of their scarves stuffed in my mouth if I muttered anything that displeased them. Clough's right hand hovered close to the phone, ready to cut me off at the first sign that I'd over-stepped the mark in articulating his mood.

As soon as I reached the specified number of paragraphs – I hadn't been counting but he obviously had – Clough gently cut me off, then astonished me again by saying: "I suppose you want a picture to go with that."

I couldn't believe my luck. He gestured that I should phone the office again. They couldn't believe their luck. They sent the burliest foot-in-the-door photographer on the staff, John Richardson. Clough sent out a message to the gatemen that "My friend Mr. Richardson from the *Evening Post* is popping in for coffee" and, within about 15 minutes, 'Richo' materialised, blinking and baffled.

By then, I was halfway through my 'breakfast' – and feeling slightly tipsy. For Clough had begun the wait for the photographer by saying: "I think we've both earned a drink."

Secretary Carol materialised with a vodka for him and the biggest Scotch with the least ginger I had ever attempted, especially on an empty stomach so early in the morning.

Clough prepared for the photograph by slipping on his trademark flat cap and putting a tracksuit top over his green sweater. Swapping the vodka glass for a coffee cup, he smiled slightly at the sight of Richo fumbling his equipment in his haste to get the picture – sorry, The Picture – and added to the big man's embarrassment by saying: "Come on, man – I've got a training session to get to."

Click, click went Richo's camera. "Was I smiling?" asked Clough. We both said we thought not. "But are you certain?" he drawled. "I don't want to be seen smiling. Better take another."

Click, click went Richo's camera again. "Hey – I said one more," he growled, rising from his chair. "Thanks very much Mr. Clough," said Richo, gathering his camera case in his huge arms and carrying it out into the corridor to re-pack.

Was there a slight twinkle in Clough's eye? You be the judge. And, while you're at it, figure out why he's given us a thumbs-up. Maybe because all life's a game…

"Drink up," Clough told me. "And if I hear any of that story on radio or the television before I read it in your f***ing paper, I'll know you can't be trusted."

With that, he was gone – off through the back gate from the ground, down by the Trent to the training ground – pausing only to usher Richo out of the office block.

I lit a cigarette – far from the first I'd had on this unbelievable morning – and said something like: "What do you think to that, Carol?"

"I think you ought to play safe and stay here until The Gaffer's seen his story in the *Evening Post*," she smiled. So I did … though I never tried Scotch and ginger for breakfast again. And still felt a little heady when I got back to the office in late afternoon to write my stuff for the *Football Post*.

The picture-story made a fabulous front page for the *Evening Post* main edition … and the more I look at Richo's picture, the more certain I am that there's a hint of a smile on that cherubic face.

Here's what I'd dictated. Call it sycophantic if you like. I call it one of the most memorable exclusive stories of my 45-year career as a journalist:

DAY AFTER...AND THERE'S NO BITTERNESS

Clough — FA did me proud

Brian Clough got back to doing what he does best today – managing his football team.

And his top priority was picking the team for tomorrow's game at the City Ground, ironically against Queen's Park Rangers.

It was after the Littlewoods Cup match against Rangers that Mr. Clough repelled a pitch invasion using methods which led to the most severe FA sentence ever handed out.

He was fined £5,000 and suspended from the touchlines of every League ground from February 23 until the end of the season by an FA disciplinary commission for bringing the game into disrepute.

But there was no bitterness from Mr. Clough as he spoke to *the Post* in his office today. He told us: "The FA did me proud.

"I was wrong to do what I did and they took what action they had to take. I am sorry I let them down. I had never let them down in my life."

And he added: "The police did me even more proud." [Clough nodded approval when I dictated that.]

This was a reference to an article in the *Police Review* of February 3 in which a writer examined "the actions of Britain's most popular manager from a legal standpoint and not as though it was Custer's last stand."

The article said: "Thank God there are the Cloughies of this world who will not stand idly by and see standards eroded.

"The backbone seems to have been removed from so many members of society and nowadays far too many people are willing to stand by, watching the wrong-doer and then harangue those who are prepared to challenge lawlessness.

"I would much rather defend the case against Brian Clough than prosecute it."

Mr. Clough made it perfectly clear that he is remaining as manager of Forest: "I play QPR tomorrow, Barnsley on Monday, Bristol City on Wednesday and I have Watford next Sunday.

"That's my job. And I have got training in the meantime. [At this point, Clough himself chipped-in with the next sentence…] On top of that I have to talk to journalists and go to Board meetings. [That was the only time he smiled throughout the proceedings.]

"Now, I've got a team to prepare for tomorrow."

Only now have I re-read it and realised that (a) I never used the word "Nottingham" as in "Nottingham Forest" and (b) he short-changed me on the promise of 15 paragraphs. But not for the first or last time, one of Clough's favourite phrases sustained me through the rest of my working day: "What a game, eh?"

16

Striking problems but success returns

· ·

Daft as it sounds, it is possible to argue that the Forest squad of 1988-90 was even more resilient than the one that won the European Cup twice. I know, I know … line them up against each other, and the 1979-80 mob looks immeasurably superior … But was it?

1978-80 squad	*1988-90 squad*
Peter Shilton. Footballer of the Year 1978. Goalkeeper for all Forest successes 1977-82 except the 1978 League Cup. Won 125 England caps 1970-90; and Clough always argued it should have been many more. Was generally acknowledged as the best goalkepper in the world during his prime.	**Steve Sutton.** Signed for Forest from school in 1977 thinking he had a better chance in Division 2 than with Clough's top-flight Derby, who he had supported as a schoolboy. Had to await departures of Shilton and Dutch internationals Hans van Breukelen and Hans Segers before becoming first-choice.
Chris Woods. Lincolnshire-born goal-keeper. Came through the Forest apprentice scheme from 1975. Played only 6 League games for Forest but made name in 1977-78 League Cup-winning team with Shilton Cup-tied. As career blossomed at QPR, Norwich and Glasgow Rangers, won 43 England caps 1985-93.	**Mark Crossley.** Barnsley-born goal-keeper came through Forest apprentice scheme. Big, brave and agile, he made a blinding League debut v Liverpool 1988 aged 19. Played over 300 Forest games (in which he became the only 'keeper ever to save a penalty taken by South-ampton's Matt Le Tissier) and won 8 Wales caps.

Viv Anderson. Local born right back nicknamed "Spider" because his legs seemed telescopic when he tackled, came through the Forest ranks to make 328 appearances (15 goals) for Reds 1974-84 before moving on to Arsenal, Manchester United, Sheffield Wednesday, Barnsley and Middlesbrough. Was the first black player selected for England: 30 appearances 1978-88.

Steve Chettle. Local born, tall and powerful, signed pro forms for Forest in 1986, captained England Under-21s in his 12th match for them. Made League debut v Chelsea in 1987 and became a regular at either right back or centre half, though he was predominantly left-footed. He played in 527 matches for Forest in the next dozen years, finishing up as the club captain.

Frank Clark. Aged 31 when he joined Forest for free from Newcastle United. Stepped in at left back when Barrett was injured, won 1979 Euro Cup medal and made 117 League appearances. He was always Clough's first choice to be Forest's next manager; and led the club back to the top flight in his first season, 1993-84. By the time he left the City Ground in December 1996, Forest under him had played 178, won 73, drawn 58 and lost 47.

Brian Laws. Aged 26 when he joined Forest for £120,000 from Middlesbrough (121 apps) having made his name with Division Three Burnley (154 apps 1979-82). Had a typical Clough welcome: ""I've never seen you play. I'm going on the recommendation of Ronnie Fenton. So if you're crap, Ronnie signed you. If you're good, I signed you." He won two Wembley finals with Forest and then moved into management.

Frank Gray. 81 appearances for Forest 1979-81 after moving from Leeds United. 32 Scotland caps 1978-83.

Gary Charles. Had his promising career as a full back ruined in tackle by Paul Gascoigne in 1991 FA Cup Final.

Larry Lloyd. Mountainous centre half and crucial part of the "spine" of Forest 1978-81 (148 appearances, 8 goals) after spells with Bristol Rovers, Liverpool and Coventry City. 4 England caps 1971-80.

Colin Foster. Played less than 80 games in the centre of Forest's defence (1987-89) and was a big winner with the bank manager. He cost Forest £50,000 from Orient and moved for £750,000 to West Ham.

Kenny Burns. Cost Forest £155,000 from Birmingham City, repaid them handsomely 1977-81 with 137 appearances as a brick wall of a central defender (and scored 13 goals, including the European Super Cup winner in Barcelona). Won 20 Scotland caps 1974-81. Moved on to Leeds United in 1981 and Derby County in 1984.

Des Walker. Born in North London, he came through Forest's apprentice ranks, signed pro in 1985 aged 18 and became one of England's best, and certainly fastest, central defenders. Played over 300 matches for Forest and 59 internationals for England. Only 5ft 11in, but few argued with the chant of the Forest faithful: "You'll never beat Des Walker."

John McGovern. Clough's captain and midfield ball-winner at Hartlepool 1965-68, Derby County 1968-74, Leeds United 1974 and Forest 1974-82 (253 League appearances). Won every trophy bar FA Cup, just like Clough, who valued his destructive role: "His job is to win the ball and give it to those who can use it. When he's at his best, you never notice him." Won Scotland Under-23 honours.	**Steve Hodge.** Local-born, spanned both Cup-winning eras. Joined Forest 1980, played almost 150 games; sold to Aston Villa for £450,000 in 1985; moved to Spurs 1986; back to Forest for £575,000 in 1988. Won 24 England caps; came home with Argentine shirt worn by Diego Maradona when he scored his infamous "hand of God" goal in the 1986 World Cup Finals in Mexico.
Martin O'Neill. Made 285 appearances, mainly as speedy and tricky right winger (48 goals) for Forest 1971-81. 84 Northern Ireland caps (8 goals) 1871-84. The most successful manager, by far, so far, of Clough's many "disciples". Indeed, long before O'Neill's successes with Aston Villa, Clough reckoned: "If he'd been English or Swedish, he'd have walked into the England job." There is, of course, time yet…	**Gary Crosby.** Was aged 23 when Forest paid £15,000 just before Christmas 1987 to take him from Grantham on the recommendation of the non-League club's astute manager, Martin O'Neill. Played 152 League games for Forest either side of a long injury lay-off that did nothing to dilute his fearlessness despite his frail appearance. Became one of Nigel Clough's backroom staff at Burton Albion and Derby County.
Archie Gemmill. Dynamic midfielder made 261 appearances for Clough at Derby County 1970-77 and 58 at Forest 1977-79 before moving to Birmingham. Returned to coaching roles at Forest 1984 until Clough retired. Earned 43 Scotland caps 1971-81 (8 goals including best of the 1978 World Cup Finals).	**Neil Webb.** Joined Forest from Portsmouth for £250,000 in 1985. Over the next four years, played a massive creative part in all of Forest's successes, contributed 47 goals in 146 matches) and became a regular midfielder for England (26 caps). Chose to move to Manchester United in 1989 (£1.5 million).
Garry Birtles. Signed for £2,000 from non-League Long Eaton United to replace Peter Withe (who made 75 appearances and scored 28 goals 1976-78 before being sold to Newcastle United) as "The Centre Forward" as Clough called them. Scored in European Cup opener v	**Nigel Clough.** Born on 19 March 1966 (two days before his Dad's birthday), signed pro forms for Forest in July 1985 and reigned as 'The Centre Forward' longer than most, until 1993, when he moved to Liverpool for £2.75 million. Scored more than 100 goals for Forest in

Liverpool to become instant hero. 32 goals in 87 Forest appearances before club's poor financial situation forced his sale for £1.25 million to Manchester United (11 goals in 58 appearances 1980-82). 3 England caps 1980.

301 League appearances and won 14 full England caps to go with the 15 he collected at Under-21 level. Proving his fearlessness, he followed Dad as the Derby County manager in 2009 after impressing at Burton Albion.

Tony Woodcock. Local born, had loan spells at Mansfield Town and Lincoln City before scoring 36 goals in 129 Forest appearances 1973-79. Went on to prosper at FC Cologne and Arsenal before settling to management in Germany. Won 42 England caps (16 goals) 1978-86. He and Birtles were the duo who, above all others, inspired a generation of non-League players in the environs of Nottingham to believe League stardom with Forest awaited them if they deserved it.

Garry Parker. Oxford-born midfielder, cost Forest £260,000 from Hull City in 1988, when he was 23. Scored on his Forest debut in a 1-1 draw v Aston Villa. Initially made his mark on the left wing, particularly when Forest beat his first club, Luton, in the League Cup; then ran almost the length of Wembley to score one of his pair in the Simod Cup v Everton – thus proving it was amazing what Clough could do with "a man who's pace is deceptive. He's a lot slower than he looks." Shades of Robbo!

John Robertson. Made Forest's 1979 European Cup-winning goal 1979, scored their winner in 1980. 385 appearances (scoring 81 and creating many more with his accurate crosses from the left) 1970-83 then joined Peter Taylor at Derby (72 appearances, 3 goals, 1983-85). 28 Scotland caps (8 goals) 1978-83. Went on to form a Clough/Taylor type of managerial partnership with O'Neill.

Brian Rice. A Glaswegian winger signed from Hibernian for £175,000 in 1985, aged 22, he made it clear he wanted to play in the centre of midfield when his contract came up for renewal in 1989. Clough kept him on a weekly contract until Rice relented three months later. As soon as he'd signed a new long-term deal, Clough dropped him. Played just over 100 times for Forest in 6 years.

David Needham. Central defender reared by Notts County (1966-77) where he attracted attention as an apprentice by arriving at training driven by his mother in a Rolls-Royce. Sold to QPR for £90,000 in summer of 1977, he moved to Forest for £140,000 six months later and was cover for Burns and Lloyd until 1982. Earned 6 England B caps.

Lee Chapman. A Clough rarity: a successful striking gamble. Cost £40,000 from French Division Two club Niort in 1988 when most thought he was over the hill after scoring 112 goals in 320 League games for Stoke, Arsenal, Sunderland and Sheffield Wednesday. Twice a Forest Wembley winner before moving to Leeds for £400,000 in 1990.

Ian Bowyer. 564 appearances in Forest's midfield (96 goals including the priceless 1979 European Cup semi-final win in Cologne) in two spells 1973-81 and 1981-87 either side of a brief spell at Sunderland.	**Tommy Gaynor.** Limerick-born, joined Forest from Doncaster Rovers for £25,000 aged 24 in 1989. Seized first team chance when Nigel Clough was injured that Christmas and was in the two Wembley successes.
John O'Hare. Bought for £20,000 by Clough from Sunderland, the Scottish striker repaid him at Derby County (65 goals in 248 appearances), Leeds for 44 days (1 in 7) and Forest (14 in 101), often as a substitute.	**Franz Carr.** Lightning fast right winger bought by Forest only three days after he signed pro forms at Blackburn, aged 18, in 1984. Made 131 appearances (17 goals) before moving to Newcastle in 1991.
Gary Mills. Aged only 18 when he became a European Cup-winner against Hamburg in 1980. Never fulfilled his 'Boy Wonder' expectations and left in 1982 after 58 appearances (8 goals). Later managed Notts County, 2004.	**Phillip Starbuck.** Local-born striker looked set to emulate Birtles/Woodcock when he scored on his League debut v Newcastle and home debut v Liverpool around Christmas 1986 aged 18. But never became a regular.
Stan Bowles. Made 19 appearances (2 goals) for Forest 1980-81 after making his name as a maverick goals-maker with QPR. Renowned for his gambling, was frequently tracked to sundry greyhound stadia by Peter Taylor and moved to Leyton Orient.	**Terry Wilson.** Born in Broxburn, Scotland, joined Forest as a scrawny 16-year-old from school in 1985. Made his midfield debut v Southampton in 1987. Proved so adaptable, he also became a reliable central defender. Made over 100 appearances for Forest.
Charlie George. Another 'glamour boy' signing, Made his name with Arsenal (133 appearances, 31 goals) 1968-75 and Southampton (44 appearances, 11 goals) 1978-81. Played twice on loan with Forest 1980 before Clough decided: "No thanks." He went off to Hong Kong for a brief spell.	**Nigel Jemson.** Striker joined Forest from Preston for £150,000 in 1988, aged 19. Was so confident, Clough said: "He's the only player I know with a bigger head than mine." Scored Wembley winner against Oldham but never became a regular. Moved to Sheffield Wednesday for £800,000 in 1991.

Imagine these XIs facing each other when the players were in their Forest prime:

Late Seventies Euro-stars   *Late Eighties Wembley wonders*

	Clark	Robertson			Hodge	Laws	
Shilton	Burns	Bowyer	Woodcock	Chapman	Webb	Walker	Sutton
(Woods)	Lloyd	McGovern	Birtles	Clough	Wilson	Chettle	(Crossley)
	Anderson	O'Neill			Parker	Pearce	

Back in the real world, the appearance in the lists of Birtles, Woodcock, O'Hare, George … Nigel Clough, Chapman, Gaynor, Starbuck and Jemson means this is as good a time as ever to catalogue the relentless search for strikers that gave Clough more torment than he had filling any other two positions during his reign at the City Ground. The shape of his team never really changed: 4-4-2 with one of the strikers tasked with being first to the crosses at the near-post and the other being on hand at the far post on the off-chance that the ball travelled that far.

When he arrived at Forest, he inherited Barry Butlin, who scored 20 goals in 88 matches, and a thrice-capped Scot, Neil Martin, who scored 28 in 119 games for Forest between 1970 and 1975. Martin swiftly gave way to O'Hare, whose value to the Clough system far out-weighed his ratio of 14 goals in 101 matches.

Even the faithful O'Hare had to give way to the irresistible partnership of Peter Withe (28 in 75) and Tony Woodcock (36 in 129 after 'wake-up' loan spells at Lincoln City and Doncaster Rovers), who provided most of the firepower than won Forest the 1978 League title.

When Withe was sold to Newcastle United early in the 1978-79 season, Clough expected another graduate from Forest's apprentice scheme, Stephen Elliott, to become Woodcock's partner. But Elliott was given only four matches before Clough sold him to Preston North End and, in something akin to desperation, turned to a local lad who had been in the shadows for a couple of seasons since making his debut on the wing.

The player in question was Garry Birtles. He had cost Clough £2,000 from Long Eaton United, a Midland League club part-way to Derby along the A52 (now named in honour of Clough). Only after Birtles had become a local hero by scoring in the European Cup first round win over Liverpool did Clough confess that, on the day he had gone to spy on Birtles, "the half-time Bovril was better than him". Birtles went on to score 32 in 87 games and collect medals for fun before moving to Manchester United for £1.25 million.

With Woodcock now at FC Cologne in Germany, Clough struggled to find a successful new partnership. Peter Ward from Brighton and Hove Albion managed 7 goals in 33 appearances between 1980 and 1983. Ian Wallace from Coventry City topped the club's scorers for two seasons in a stay that yielded 36 goals in 134 games. Justin Fashanu contributed 3 in 32 during his brief stay. And Trevor Christie played 20 games in 1985 without bringing back the trophy-winning days.

The nearest Clough got to a saviour of a striker during this hellish half-decade emerged from the dockyards of Merseyside. Cammell Laird FC were persuaded to part with 21-year-old Peter Davenport for the price of a new set of shirts and shorts. He made his debut on May Day 1982. Fitting, said the critics. "May Day" was a seafarer's distress call; and Clough was sinking from the high standards he had set himself. Davenport responded by topping the club's scoring lists in 1983-84 and 1984-85; and totalled 54 in 118 – a fabulous strike rate given the club's general struggles. He was so valued that Clough almost resigned rather than sell him. But the accountants had the final word: Davenport went to Manchester United on 12 March 1986 for £750,000.

The better news was that Birtles had returned from Old Trafford and contributed another 38 goals in 125 games from 1982-86. And by the time he moved on, across the Trent to Notts County, another youngster from the Midland League was beginning to make his name as "My Centre Forward".

Nigel Clough had been signed from Heanor Town, aged 18, on 15 September 1984. Before the whispers about "favouritism" had died down, he made his debut on Boxing Day against Ipswich Town. For the seven seasons from 1986, he made the No.9 shirt his own, totalling 101 goals in 311 matches alongside a variety of partners, some of whom were Paul Wilkinson (8 in 43 after being bought from Everton), Phil Starbuck (2 in 36), fellow ex-apprentice Lee Glover (9 in 76 in between numerous loan spells elsewhere), Lee Chapman (27 in 31 after being bought for £40,000 from French Division II club Niort and before moving on to Leeds United for £400,000), Tommy Gaynor (10 in 57, many of them on the wing), Nigel Jemson (13 in 47) and David Currie (1 in 8 between joining from Barnsley and being shipped on as Oldham Athletic's record buy at £460,000).

The best of the buys was the one who seemed least likely to succeed. Chapman, tall and swift, had never quite fulfilled his potential in England; had married an actress (Lesley Ash, most recently of *Holby City* fame) long before WAGS were in fashion; had disappeared into the French Second Division; and looked like a perennial university student with his foppish fair hair falling over one eye. His arrival prompted Clough to say: "If it works, I signed him. If it doesn't, Fenton did."

Poor Chapman never got the credit he deserved in his short but successful spell at the City Ground. Even on the night he scored four goals, he was up-staged; it was that fateful Cup tie against QPR that ended with supporters running into Clough's fists.

17

Change seats and get us winning!

．．．．．．．．．．．．．．．．．．．．．．．

THE REASONS for my praise of the 1988-90 squad begin with the fact that they overcame a dreadful start to the 1988-89 season. By the time they lost 0-2 to Manchester United at Old Trafford on Boxing Day, they had won only 4 League matches, drawn 10 and lost 4, including a 1-4 home trouncing inflicted by Arsenal in a televised match. If Allan Hansen had been a pundit at that time rather than a pillar of Liverpool's defence, he would surely have assured the world and Clough: "You can win nothin' with kids."

Clough himself observed: "Our team is so young, every game away is like a school outing. Our biggest problem isn't injury. It's acne." But he remained faithful to them; to do otherwise would have been an admission that he had been wrong. It was, however, a huge gamble: those who were not terribly young were dreadfully inexperienced at the highest levels.

Instead of diving into the transfer market, Clough called a summit of all of his coaching staff to analyse what they were doing differently from other seasons. He volunteered the fact that he was trying to stay off the alcohol but called on them to think deeply about anything else that might have changed.

Each coach in turn went through his routine and promised nothing had altered since the previous season. The physio, too, assured that he wasn't trying any new routines. Gemmill pledged that the reserves and teenagers were going through the paces that had always been demanded of apprentices. O'Kane did not need to testify about the first teamers; Clough knew all about them from his ventures to the training ground with his faithful pet dog, Del Boy. So the search widened…

The sponsored cars given to the coaches by a local dealer came under suspicion. Their registration letters were NFL. Could that stand secretly for Nottingham Forest Losers?

This theory was dismissed over post-match drinks one Saturday night; there was no way the coaches were going to contemplate losing this, their first, perk!

Then I became the focus of attention as I sat on the leather couch beside the door, quietly savouring my Scotch and ginger. "Have you switched seats in the Press Box?" Clough asked. I blinked; he explained that he'd heard I had – revealing that he'd even questioned marshals of key areas around the ground in his quest to get the team out of its rut. In fact, I had moved in one seat from the end of the front row in order to stop my left elbow being nudged by everyone trudging up and down the gangway. "Will you kindly move back to where you sat when we were winning games?" he asked. I laughed but stopped short of retorting: "Where? Outside in the car park where you kicked me?" He didn't so much as smile. Neither did Ron Fenton, Liam O'Kane, Archie Gemmill, Alan Hill...

"OK then – I'll move," I said, suddenly feeling even more isolated than I normally felt on these occasions.

"Good lad," he drawled. "Let's have another and then get off home to our families."

"Is this on the record, Brian?" I asked.

"No, young man," he said evenly. "This is internal club business." Damn! A great story I couldn't tell. And it got better. Spookily, Forest went on to win 15 of their next 18 matches. And I never got so much as a Man of the Match nomination.

For his part, Clough defied and deceived the admirably supportive Barbara by starting to drink again. She thought he was sticking to his new fitness regime with a bottle or two of diluted orange juice as he sat watching the television on his rare evenings at home. She even became worried when he occasionally stumbled as he rose to his feet and sometimes struggled to climb the stairs. She confided in some friends at the City Ground that she was concerned he might be suffering from the onset of something like a muscle-wasting illness. So imagine her emotions when she discovered the truth. He had gone back to alcohol; and his orange juice was nine-tenths vodka. So there was no wonder he was unsteady on his feet by bedtime.

Only a fool would say the transformation in results was caused by Clough returning to vodka or me moving one seat along in the Press Box. But there is no doubt that Forest's fortunes turned after that strange summit meeting.

Neither was the success brought about by inspired team selection. On the contrary, it was sparked by a Boxing Day injury to Nigel Clough – "The Centre Forward" as his dad called him – during the 2-0 loss at Manchester United. For the next match, against Sheffield Wednesday at Hillsborough on New Year's Eve, Clough drafted in 26-year-old Irishman Tommy Gaynor, who had had a largely undistinguished eight-match run earlier in the season (though he had bullied hapless Chester City in the League (Littlewoods) Cup. He responded with the first goal in a 3-0 victory over Wednesday and then found the net in each of the next three matches before himself being put out of action by an injury.

The manager knew for certain at this point that his luck had changed; Gaynor's pain saved him making an awkward selection decision. For by this time, Clough Junior was fit again, and I was far from the only journalist wondering whether Dad would keep Son out of the starting XI. As it was, Nigel was able to return, the team stayed on its roll and did not drop a point until QPR held them 0-0 on February 11 in the game that followed the mayhem of the FA disciplinary commission's punishment of the Manager.

Even his banishment from the touchline and to the stands did not stop the successes – Forest flowed to seven more wins in the next 10 matches – before he suffered an interesting afternoon of banter sitting among the home supporters in the main stand of Wimbledon's ground at Plough Lane, which surely will remain forever the only top-flight ground ever to be situated in a pub back garden. Fittingly in the minds of some, it was April Fool's Day and Forest made it his least-favourite afternoon by losing 1-4 to the immensely physical team whose long-ball style had been memorably criticised by Clough with the analysis: "If the Good Lord had intended football to be played in the sky, He would have put grass on the clouds."

However this setback was sandwiched by two 2-0 home wins in the League, over Manchester United and Norwich City, that served to set them up nicely for an unprecedented spell of two Cup Finals and an FA Cup semi-final within three weeks.

Not even a careful planner called Brian Clough could prepare fully for what was to come, though: two Cup triumphs either side of the deaths of 96 supporters in British football's biggest ever tragedy.

The League (Littlewoods) Cup Final on 9 April 1989 was pretty routine, though its build-up enabled the *Evening Post* to evoke many memories of the 1959 FA Cup Final, in which Forest had defeated Luton Town. The Nottinghamians had not enjoyed as much as a sniff of a club day out at Wembley in those three decades until Clough had begun to weave his magic; and now he was at it again, master-minding a triumph over the holders of the trophy, who had defeated Arsenal, the short-odds favourites, 3-2 with something of an epic performance in the 1988 Final…

After the drama of the two-leg semi-final against lowly Bristol City – especially 120 minutes on a pudding of an Ashton Gate pitch in a downpour almost as intense as a cyclone whipping up the Severn Estuary – the Final was almost anti-climax, certainly routine for this journalist.

Although Luton took the lead with a header by Ray Harford, Forest won 3-1 with two goals by Nigel Clough (one a penalty after Steve Hodge was sent sprawling) and one by Neil Webb with Clough sitting, expressionless all afternoon, on the bench that passed for a dug-out at the old Wembley. This was the full Forest team: Sutton, Laws, Pearce, Walker, Wilson, Hodge, Gaynor, Webb, Clough, Chapman, Parker. On page 157 is the cover of the *Evening Post's* 8-page Picture Special to commemorate the occasion…

It ought to be added, with some emphasis, that the League Cup was a much more important competition in the minds of the leading managers in this era than it became in

Neil Webb slips his goal past Les Sealey in Forest's 3-1 win over Luton Town.

the 2000s. Clough was not the only perceptive boss to use it as a means to keep his first team squad in a two-games-a-week mindset in preparation for the end of the UEFA ban on English clubs taking part in European competitions. So it is interesting to see the attendances, not to mention the results of Forest's ties on the way to the 1989 Final:

Date	Opposition	Venue	Result	Scorers	Attendance
Sep 28	Chester City	Home	6 – 0	Clough 2, Pearce, Webb, Hodge, Gaynor	11,958
Oct 12	Chester City	Away	4 – 0	Gaynor 3, Crosby	4,747
Nov 02	Coventry City	Home	3 – 2	Foster, Hodge, Clough	21.201
Nov 30	Leicester City	Away	0 – 0		26.704
Dec 14	Leicester City	Home	2 – 1	Clough, Chapman	26,676
Jan 18	QPR	Home	5 – 2	Chapman 4, Clough pen	24,065
Feb 15	Bristol City	Home	1 – 1	Pender og	30,016
Feb 26	Bristol City	Away	1 – 0 aet	Parker	28,084
April 9	Luton Town	Wembley	3 – 1	Clough 2 (1 pen), Webb	76,130

LITTLEWOODS CUP FINAL SPECIAL

FOREST'S TRIUMPH IN PICTURES

We've won the cup!

Super Reds' day of glory

THE Littlewoods Cup is Forest's — and just look at the joy on the faces of Terry Wilson (that's not really a Scottish cap he's wearing), striker Lee Chapman, sub Lee Glover (peeping out from behind his memento), goalmaker Tommy Gaynor, former Luton midfielder Garry Parker, sub Steve Chettle, tireless Steve Hodge, goalkeeper Steve Sutton and, beneath the hat, captain Stuart Pearce.

● Below: Man of the Match Nigel Clough celebrates one of his two goals in Forest's 3-1 win.

● More great pictures of a great day for Forest — and their fans — inside this *Evening Post* picture special.

The success put Forest in the perfect frame of mind for the following Saturday's FA Cup semi-final against perennial foes Liverpool at Hillsborough. They had beaten the Merseysiders 2-1 at the City Ground in a League match back in November, when they were in the doldrums. Now they were in much better form, their confidence was sky high and nothing, not even mighty Liverpool, could stop them pursuing the only trophy to elude their manager during his career. Or so they thought…

18

Hillsborough, British football's biggest horror

Advertising boards become make-shift stretchers in the horror of the Hillsborough disaster.

FOR THE *Nottingham Evening Post* the 1989 FA Cup semi-final between Liverpool and Nottingham Forest was to be notable for yet another technological breakthrough. Thanks to the battles against the Luddites of the printing industry – and the Scargill supporters of the picket lines – a decade and more earlier, we were now acknowledged to be the most advanced newspaper in Europe. There were still outposts of resistance to this modernisation; and none was more intransigent than the Socialist Independent Republic of South Yorkshire, as we called Scargill Country (out of respect for the power wielded by the chief of the National Union of Mineworkers, I hasten to add). There was no way that the freelance journalist who owned the telephone lines in the Hillsborough Press Box would allow any representative of the *Nottingham Evening Post* or *Football Post* to use one of his instruments of communication. So for the past several seasons, our reporter (me, Stapleton or Hamilton) had had to take with us a 'copy runner' who would dash out of the stadium armed with the reporter's notes from time to time, find a public telephone and call the office with the running reports for that Saturday night's *Football Post*. As League matches tended to end between 4.40pm and 4.45pm in those days and our deadline was 5.05pm, you can imagine the pressure.

So you can also imagine the relief with which I packed into my overcoat pocket a mobile telephone for our adventure to Hillsborough on 15 April 1989. Not the kind of mobile telephone that would be recognised by today's generation, of course. This one, like all the early motor cars, was black. Colour apart, it looked very much like a house brick and weighed probably a few pounds more than a house brick. But I was assured that, once charged up, it would last for the best part of two hours – plenty for a running report from a football match as Clough continued his lifelong quest for the one major trophy to elude him.

To make me feel even better that afternoon, I had the *Post's* keenest young pair of football photographers for company as I drove us towards the ground: Steve Mitchell and Richard ('Gordi') Denning. Both were skilled, young and eager. Both had badgered the Head of the Photographic Department, Alan Haughton, for more chances to share the 'star matches' with the incomparable Trevor Bartlett, who had built-up a wonderful working relationship with Clough. Competitive as they were for the title of our Photographer of Choice, I seem to recall that Steve and Gordi even tossed for the choice of ends!

But before that, as usual, I got lost on the way to the ground. It happened in every major city. I was always deeply embarrassed, always aware of eyes rolling skywards among my passenger(s); always making excuses that: "I've been too busy to check my maps ... and I never can remember how I found this ground last year." It had been a joke in my previous life when I was playing village cricket for Sutton-on-Trent in the Trent Valley League and struggled to find flat fields in Notts and Lincolnshire. Now it was more serious; I even missed a kick-off at Millwall one day, sparking fears back in the office that the pickets had finished me off!

So it was as well I had given us extra time to reach Hillsborough. And suddenly pavements over-flowing with red shirted drinkers told us we must be close to our venue. Sure enough, it loomed like an impressive starship; one of the jewels of the English football industry in the age of massive hillsides of terraces, few seats and (post-Heysel) huge wire fences above the perimeter walls to prevent supporters invading onto the playing surface.

With the ground in view, I parked in a side-street and we walked the last couple of hundred yards past lots of supporters whetting their thirsts as they prepared to yell their hearts out for their heroes. It so happened that these were Liverpool supporters; but they could have been any club's on any Saturday afternoon in those days. All the top clubs had a section of 'support' that arrived ticketless, waited until the kick-off whistle was due and then charged the turnstiles. The clubs were aware of the situation. So were the police. Indeed, so were the Government who had responded to Heysel and the sport's many associated troubles by suggesting all spectators be given identity cards. It was dismissed by folk like me as a typical Civil Service response: when faced by a problem, try to hide it in red tape. Treating the miscreants as criminals – for they were truly terrorising huge parts of the law-abiding community – would have been a rather more effective response. But they seemed to be treated as special cases – in much the same way that motorists who kill are rarely labelled murderers – and were invariably free to carry on sinning at the next match.

And so to this match; this latest Titanic battle between the two Super Reds of the time (Alex Ferguson was then barely over the starting line at Manchester United)… It can now be said that within six and a half minutes of the kick-off, the killing of 96 Liverpool supporters began. How they died – precisely how and why they died – remains something of a mystery, more than 20 years later, to their loved ones who feel they have never been told the truth, the whole truth and nothing but the truth by the police, the other emergency services, the football authorities and/or the holders of various inquiries into what has become known as The Hillsborough Disaster.

FA CUP HORROR

HEYSEL AGONY HAUNTS 'POOL

FIFTY-THREE soccer fans were were feared dead in an afternoon of horror at the packed Hillsborough ground in Sheffield this afternoon.

The Nottingham Forest-Liverpool FA Cup semi-final had been under way for only six minutes when hundreds of fans at the Liverpool end spilled on to the pitch.

Scores were injured as they attempted to escape a crush thought to have been caused as fans without tickets flooded into a gate at the Leppings Lane end.

The game got no further. It was officially abandoned at 4.17pm.

FROM TREVOR FRECKNALL at HILLSBOROUGH

●ABOVE: A fan is lifted clear from the crowd at Hillsborough this afternoon.
●BELOW: An advertising hoarding is used to

In all honesty, it is not all that surprising that there are still unanswered questions because those of us who were there still cannot believe what we saw; certainly I cannot. Here's what I dictated over my house brick phone for that afternoon's *Football Post* (which, remember had a 5.05pm deadline)...

The full report, dictated 'off the top of my head' with increasing incredulity, read:

Fifty-three soccer fans were feared dead in an afternoon of horror at the packed Hillsborough ground in Sheffield this afternoon.

The Nottingham Forest v Liverpool FA Cup semi-final had been underway for only six minutes when hundreds of fans at the Liverpool end spilled on to the pitch.

Scores were injured as they attempted to escape a crush thought to have been caused as fans without tickets flooded into a gate at the Leppings Lane end.

The game got no further. It was officially abandoned at 4.17pm.

The game was halted after only six minutes when Liverpool fans spilled on to the pitch and referee Ray Lewis took the two teams back to the dressing rooms.

The width of the pitch quickly resembled a casualty clearing station, with some supporters being stretchered away and hundreds of others being lifted to safety over the 10ft barriers.

More than 100 police, stewards and first aiders were involved in the operation.

But one Liverpool supporter ran the full length of the pitch to taunt the Forest fans at the other end before being apprehended.

The Forest supporters stood impassively while scenes reminiscent of those in the Heysel Stadium were played out.

At the height of the drama, at least one supporter had to be given the kiss of life in full view of those sitting in the Main Stand. There were loud cheers when the fan was brought back to life by a St John Ambulance Brigade member.

An ambulance was driven onto the pitch to take away the most seriously injured.

There had been no fighting on the terraces. All the indications were that the Liverpool supporters had originally sought to come onto the pitch to avoid a severe crush among them on the terraces.

After about 15 minutes, there were about 1,000 supporters on the pitch, many of them unconscious and the majority clearly dazed.

Advertising hoardings were used as makeshift stretchers as a second ambulance appeared on the playing area.

A police message relayed over the public address system pleaded with all spectators on the pitch to move towards the perimeter tracks so that the many injured could be more easily identified.

From the stands, it looked as if at least 100 people had been injured, many of them seriously. Uninjured supporters relayed unconscious friends away from the mayhem on the advertising hoardings.

At one stage there were more than 20 made-up stretchers running a shuttle service from the Liverpool end of the ground to first aid workers at the Forest end.

Sheffield Wednesday trainees were also involved in the rescue operation as police lifted more injured spectators from the crush on the terraces.

It was 20 minutes before some semblance of order was restored behind the Liverpool goal, by which time many terrace supporters had been lifted to the sanctuary of the seating area above.

But there were still 1,000 or more supporters on the pitch and it was feared that some were very seriously injured.

From the stands, it appeared that at least five supporters were stretchered from the Liverpool end with their heads covered by coats.

Half-an-hour into the drama, some 200 Liverpool supporters charged towards the Forest end, forcing police to turn their attentions from saving lives to keeping the peace.

Within minutes a thin blue line stretching the entire width of the pitch began to move forward in an attempt to clear the marauders from the pitch.

It seemed incomprehensible that even a minority should have the stomach for violence amid such tragic, tearful scenes.

Having reached the half-way line, the police stood firm so that there was a no-man's land of 60 metres between the mayhem and the Forest supporters, who throughout had greeted each arrival of a seriously injured supporter with sympathetic applause.

So moving were the scenes that more than one police officer was in tears.

Scores of Forest supporters who had been sitting in the stands closest to the tragedy, left their seats, stunned and bemused by the drama that was unfolding.

Instead of the cheers of a massive football crowd, all that could be heard for a while was the wail of a fleet of ambulances.

After 40 minutes, managers Brian Clough and Kenny Dalglish appeared on the touchline to be briefed by senior police officers. Both looked ashen as they returned to the dressing rooms.

The Liverpool half of the pitch was still covered by supporters and, more seriously, a corner at the other end continued to receive casualties.

**Steve Mitchell took this picture of a Liverpool fan showing Clough he still
had his match ticket ... "They just let everybody charge in."**

First-aiders were so overworked that up to a dozen firemen gave them
assistance.

Forest chairman Maurice Roworth and some of his fellow directors talked
with the Forest fans packed behind the goal at what had become "the casualty
station end".

It looked decreasingly likely that the match could possibly be played.

Despite repeated loud speaker announcements, Liverpool fans continued
to occupy half the pitch. Finally Dalglish asked over the public address system
for the crowd to cooperate with the police and the first-aiders "to get through
this without any more injuries or fatalities." Within minutes some of the
Liverpool supporters began to file quietly from the pitch, leaving it covered in
litter.

A Sheffield Wednesday official said that the problems appeared to begin
when a gate in the perimeter fence was either opened or broken down.
Supporters spilled through the gate immediately behind the goal which
Liverpool were defending.

Another public address message to supporters said: "A very serious situation has obviously arisen. Please remain calm." Even as the announcer was speaking, police rushed to quell another scuffle involving Liverpool followers.

It took more than an hour to clear the dead and injured from the ground, by which time police dogs were out in force to keep a distance between the Forest supporters, whose behaviour had been impeccable, and Liverpool fans who were still on the pitch.

Refreshments were brought out to the masses of policemen and the first-aiders who had handled a tragedy that revived sad memories of the 1984 disaster at the Heysel Stadium. The major difference was that this time there had been no fighting among rival supporters.

Seventy-one minutes after the referee had taken the players off, it was announced that the match had been abandoned. A police message urged supporters to stay in the ground until the authorities were certain that all casualties had been taken to hospital.

There was a remarkable reaction when some of the hundreds of policemen marched from the pitch to man the streets. They departed to applause from the Forest supporters but boos from followers of the reigning League champions.

Later reports suggested that the pitch invasion began after police opened a gate in the fence because they considered there were too many supporters in that terraced area.

England manager Bobby Robson was in the stadium. He left to the accompaniment of abuse from Liverpool fans.

Over the next three days, I received two death threats from people convinced my report was unfair to the Liverpool supporters. I had reported what I had seen and what I was told; that was my job. I had no more right to judge than I have three decades on; I remain a reporter of what happened and continue to await an official report on the day that satisfies all. Once I had finished dictating my eye-witness account, I set out in search of my photographer mates Steve Mitchell and Richard Denning. Steve had won the toss to take pictures of Forest attacking and therefore had been at the end were the tragedy took place. And it transpired that he had realised the seriousness of the situation well before anyone in authority.

Indeed, when he initially turned his back on play and began trying to haul suffocating spectators up and over the wire cages designed to keep "the animals" in, he was attacked by a steward, who tried to haul him away! It took barely seconds, however, for the steward to realise the screams were of agony and terror and not the baying of a rioting mob; and he joined Mitchell in the rescue operation while play was still going on.

To further confuse the early efforts, however, one young male supporter rescued by Mitchell responded by trying to run off with his camera. Only the fact that the piece of equipment was attached to a lead which had wrapped itself twice round Mitchell's thigh foiled the would-be thief. But Mitchell still had to break-off from trying to haul another fan to safety to turn swiftly and kick the would-be thief to make him let go.

Little wonder that we who had a panoramic view from the safety of the Main Stand would see everything yet hardly believe anything that was unfolding in front of us.

While Mitchell went off in search of Denning in the Press Room inside the Main Stand, I walked around the ground. Around 6.30pm, I happened across Chairman Roworth. He solemnly told me that the death toll was up to "70-something and they're still counting." He went on: "I am so proud of the dignity with which our fans have behaved – but don't quote me; I don't want to be appearing to draw comparisons. Not yet, anyway…"

As he headed for the dressing room area, where both teams were still ensconced, I began to look for a short cut towards the Press Room. Big mistake! I opened a door to what turned out to be a gymnasium and was horrified to see what appeared to be rows of bodies laid out on the floor. I closed the door hurriedly and followed in Roworth's footsteps. Busy as the authorities were, I remain astounded that there was no guard on that door.

Close to the entrance to the dressing rooms, I happened across the FA Secretary Graham Kelly. He knew me to be a journalist from my visits to Wembley to cover England matches that involved a growing number of Forest players through the 1980s – and, of course, from the disciplinary furore that had followed Clough clouting those fans at the QPR Littlewoods Cup tie. Eerily, given the chaos of the afternoon and evening, we were the only two people visible for what seemed miles.

"Good evening Mr. Kelly; what on earth can we make of this?" I said.

"There will be an official statement in due course," he said, voice as flat as his expression. He was clearly as numb as me and everyone else around the now silent ground, which was at last devoid of supporters.

Almost as he spoke, the Liverpool team coach cruised to a standstill and their players filed out of the dressing rooms door and skipped up the steps for the journey home. Some were smiling. One appeared to be carrying a partially-consumed bottle of wine.

"I saw nothing," said Mr. Kelly in answer to my unspoken question, eyes suddenly wide like a startled rabbit caught in headlights, but sufficiently sharp-witted to almost run away from the scene. I mentioned this little cameo to the policeman who came to interview me on behalf of the commission of inquiry set up into the disaster weeks later; but I imagine it was deemed inconsequential. What it indicated to me was that the Liverpool players had no idea of the magnitude of the tragedy when they left the ground.

Back in the Press Room within the Main Stand, I reunited with Denning and Mitchell; and discovered that the police were to hold a Press Conference at 7.30pm – at the HQ in the centre of Sheffield. It was probably the only way they could have got the media out of Hillsborough that evening. We went, as did about six times the number of journalists who had been at Hillsborough at kick-off time; and we were far from the only ones to gasp in dismay when the extent of the tragedy was announced. The death toll was over 90. It was the deadliest disaster ever in a British sports stadium.

Among the additional reporters in the media melee was Tony Donnelly, the *Evening Post* chief reporter who had heard about the unfolding drama on the radio in The Bluebell, the pub across Forman Street from the office, and had driven up to Sheffield off his own initiative. What a pro! Instinctively he took over the police / human interest aspects, leaving me to concentrate on getting the views of the football community for Monday's newspaper.

I finally got home about 1am, to a fearful rollicking from my wife Gill, who tearfully complained: "You could have phoned me and let me know you were all right." I agreed and apologised; though I wasn't "all right" at all. I couldn't get those lifeless bodies out of my mind. I was in despair that the sport I had loved virtually all of my life had been swamped by lawlessness.

"Oh," she added, "and Barrie wants you to phone him no matter how late..." So I called the Editorial Director, whose praise about the job I'd done was somewhat conditional: "I'm told you didn't actually use the words 'body' or 'dead' anywhere in your piece." I'm not sure whether I responded or not; but, whether I had nor not, my mind – my country bumpkin's brain – steadfastly refused to accept that I was watching so many excited young people had indeed lost their lives at a football match.

Next morning, I got a call from Carol Parker, Clough's secretary: "We wondered if you were coming down to the ground ... The Boss is asking how you are..."

Clough was direct as ever: "You're going to say you're fine, we're all going to say we're fine, but none of us is fine. So there's a psychiatrist across in the executive boxes for any of the club's players and staff to go and talk to; and he's there for you, too, if you feel it would help to talk about Saturday...."

"That's very kind of you Brian," I said, genuinely astonished (not for the first time) that he was dealing with a situation so broadly rather than leaving it to the massed ranks of his directors (and, for that matter, the people he still referred to as "your f***ing bosses"). I left my options open but never did get round to trotting across to the other side of the City Ground and seeking out the psychiatrist. I daresay it was far from the only mistake I made through this episode.

To further emphasise that he considered me part of the team, Clough invited me to go with the players to visit injured Liverpool supporters in Sheffield hospitals on the following Wednesday.

But the master manipulator of the media added this caution: "Don't flaunt the fact that we're going. Don't flaunt the fact you're a journalist. We are not doing it for the publicity. We are doing it for the people who are in hospital. You make sure you treat them with respect and not as an excuse for – what do you call it – a scoop."

With news media staking out the main entrances to the two Sheffield hospitals tending the most seriously injured, and the Forest players determined not to be spotted, the loyal bus driver Albert negotiated parking spots adjacent to side entrances; and we were smuggled in.

I almost wrecked the compassionate operation, I'm ashamed to confess. This is how…

In one of the High Dependence Units, I found myself talking to the brother of a young man who had been in a coma since he was crushed against the cage constructed to stop fans invading the pitch. With typical dark Scouse humour, the brother said: "I keep telling him he better wake up soon. If he doesn't he'll have to start supporting Everton." When he asked me – a bespectacled 30-something – what I did at Forest, I confessed that I was a journalist who wrote about them in the local paper. "Will you send me a copy of what you write about this?" he asked. "Of course, give us your address," I said, taking out my notebook. Faster than my shorthand ever worked, a nurse swept between us: "You're not a footballer. You're an imposter. Security!" I was escorted out to rejoin my presumed colleagues, who were locked outside the Main Entrance. So I then had the job of slipping away from them unnoticed and making my way to the secret spot where Albert was waiting to whisk us back to Nottingham.

As luck would have it, Clough himself did not make the trip: "It'll do the players good to not have me around. The last thing I want the visit to do is create a fuss." So it was just as well nobody realised that the imposter (me) was even remotely connected with the Forest players. Next day, I had this piece on the front page of the *Evening Post*…

> Like one family coming together, the footballers of Nottingham Forest met the injured and grieving of Liverpool.
>
> There were handshakes, hugs, consoling words – and, above all, a bond of friendship that completely overwhelmed traditional concepts of inter-club rivalry.
>
> Twelve Forest players, plus coach Liam O'Kane, slipped quietly into two of the Sheffield hospitals which have tended the injured since the Hillsborough disaster claimed 95 lives.
>
> Forest were the innocent bystanders at Saturday's tragedy. But the players could not stay away; could not distance themselves from the suffering of fellow football folk.
>
> They were determined to show Liverpool that they were not – are not – suffering alone.
>
> Eight of the players had been on the pitch when Britain's worst sporting tragedy began: Steve Sutton, Des Walker, Terry Wilson, Steve Hodge, Tommy Gaynor, Neil Webb, Nigel Clough and Lee Chapman. Steve Chettle and Franz Carr had been among the Forest squad at the FA Cup semi-final, while Gary Fleming and Colin Foster had shared the country's disbelief at the television pictures. Their unanimous insistence was: "We do not want a publicity pantomime."

Indeed, the only time they showed ebullient emotion was when a hospital administrator told them they need not talk to waiting reporters. They applauded him.

There was plenty more emotion as they spent more than four hours wandering from ward to ward – from the critically ill in Intensive Care to the luckier ones who are about to be allowed home.

First stop was the Royal Hallamshire Hospital. Then came the Northern General Hospital.

All of the patients were teenagers. All had followed Liverpool regularly. All had been at the ground early to seek a good view of the action. All had been crushed as latecomers surged in minutes before kick-off.

The visitors from Nottingham talked with anxious, exhausted relatives. They took some of the floral tributes that have poured into the City Ground.

They signed autographs for patients and staff, left Forest ties and pens – and earned this tribute from a Northern General administrator: "You were brilliant."

Liam O'Kane said: "I think the players were a little worried about what they would be able to say, but they were superb.

"The lads talked to parents, they tried to talk to two young fans who were in comas, and they talked to a young girl who just half-an-hour before we arrived had opened her eyes for the first time since Saturday.

"The injured youngsters are being so well looked after. We are all glad we went. We spent four hours in the wards. We could easily have spent another four."

And on the largely silent journey back down the M1 with those 13 men who were as much in love with football as those supporters from Liverpool, I'm sure I was not the only one thinking: "There but for the grace of God…."

Not that there was any more time for quiet contemplation. There was never any thought that the Football League would call a pause in the fixture programme to encourage the sport to deliberate seriously on (a) how it had got into this disastrous mess and (b) how to rejoin the human race.

Indeed, there was such a swift start to the discussion among football's officialdom about when the re-arranged FA Cup semi-final should be played – and where – that I was reliably informed Clough's first instinct had been to tell his directors: "If Liverpool want the Cup that much, let them have it."

When I checked this with Clough, his eyes seemed blank – devoid of all emotion – as he said: "You know me well enough to know that I never query officials' decisions. I'm waiting for them to make a decision." What he went on to say, off the record, I tried to articulate in my *Football Post* columns on Saturday 22 April. My "Editor's View" piece sought to merge my views with those of virtually everyone I talked with at Forest and Notts. After all, I remained conscious that my thoughts carried no more weight than the average spectator's; and the average spectator was an animal in the minds of the political folk who would take all of the important decisions that would have to be taken to lift The National Game away from this horror. This is what I wrote …

Football Post, Saturday, April 22, 1989   5

BY *FOOTBALL POST* EDITOR TREVOR FRECKNALL

Humanity is needed

UNDERSTANDING is what football now needs most.

There was not a lot of it about at Hillsborough last Saturday while 95 supporters were being crushed to death.

In the days that have followed, hearts have instinctively ruled minds numbed by grief and disbelief; and thoughts have gone no further than the dangers of fences, the safety of seats and the vital need for a disaster fund.

But once the numbness eases, the thoughts have to go much deeper and the actions much further.

The dead Liverpool supporters deserve that much.

The fact that 400,000 watch League matches on most Saturday afternoons *demands* that our national sport be accepted back into civilisation.

It will not be easy. For almost two decades, this nation of ours has been almost brain-washed into believing football is populated by thugs, vandals and drunks.

The Prime Minister's insistence this week on pushing ahead with identity cards for all football spectators perpetuates this myth (though even the Government's statistics relating to arrests refute it).

Woefully inadequate

But Mrs Thatcher is merely the latest among many to believe that legislation will cure all of football's ills.

So far all have been wrong. All of the 'cures' accumulated over the years seemed to conspire to contribute to the deaths and injuries at Hillsborough.

The streets along which police insisted we all travelled through Sheffield were woefully inadequate. It took me 90 minutes to get from the specified M1 exit (at noon) to the ground; it took barely 15 minutes to drive back in the evening.

The turnstiles could not cope with the late surge of ticket-holders (and non-ticket holders) — begging the question of how many computer terminals will be needed to process 54,000 of Mrs Thatcher's identity cards.

The police, who have been given increasing crowd control powers outside and inside grounds, took an arbitrary decision to open a huge gate at the Leppings Lane end.

The officer in question adopted the routine line that it would be better to have the masses in the ground than in the streets.

And it was this same simplistic philosophy that led to the broader tragedy of Hillsborough — that 54,000 were never told they were spectators of death.

Initially jeered

This was why the Nottingham Forest supporters, caged at the opposite end of the ground, initially jeered their Liverpool counterparts, whom they thought were merely staging a pitch invasion.

In the absence of a loudspeaker announcement, Forest chairman Maurice Roworth, some of his fellow directors and coach Liam O'Kane went out to give the harrowing news by word of mouth.

But they were unable to spread the word before the early taunts had prompted a faction of Liverpool supporters to charge towards the Forest fans in what looked like fury but was probably — hopefully — no more than furious frustration.

This stampede forced a number of police men and women to revert from striving to save lives in order to form a thin blue line across the pitch to keep the peace.

It was horrendous. I stood and watched it all. A week later, I still cannot comprehend that I saw 95 people die.

I do know that I saw strapping policemen sobbing pitifully amid the hopelessness.

I do know that I saw supposed hooligans using advertising boards as makeshift stretchers for teenage supporters whose limbs flopped like rag dolls.

I do know that I heard supporters of both clubs applauding the rescue efforts.

Inferiority complex

I do know that St John Ambulance heroes and heroines strove to revive stricken supporters in extremely hostile circumstances.

And I do know that supporters of both clubs now have a mutual reason for striving to rescue our national sport not only from the despair of Hillsborough but from the depths of the depression into which it has been ground over the years.

I trust that supporters of other clubs share those wholesome motives — and that football itself will have the confidence to shed the inferiority complex that has enveloped it.

It was, I believe, this inferiority complex that stopped the truth emerging over the public address system at Hillsborough.

They were afraid to tell the 54,000 that there had been multiple fatalities because they did not trust the 54,000 to stay in the ground and keep the streets clear for ambulances.

They'd been conditioned to "cage the animals" and they instinctively treated them like dumb animals.

What they had forgotten was that those cages were full of football's pets; packed with people from all walks of life in love with the sport.

If — no, *when* — those people are treated like humans again and considered humane, then we shall know those 95 Liverpudlians did not die in vain.

Safety officers

And that does not mean simply installing seats and tearing down fences for their once-a-fortnight visit to the ground (though that's a start).

It means finding them space to park, offering them a refreshment service before and after the match, enticing them to the ground for other activities (social or sporting) on other days and nights, and generally becoming a focal point in society.

None of that can happen overnight. It cannot happen at all without the help of councillors who currently see their roles as safety officers in only the restrictive sense — nor without the support of MPs whose vision is equally narrow.

But the footballers of Liverpool and Nottingham Forest have discovered this week just how important the game is to the masses.

They have been stunned by grieving relatives and injured youngsters telling them: "The game must go on."

It is to be hoped the politicians who have visited those Sheffield hospitals have got the same message. And that they act by accepting football is part of English life and contribute in full towards helping it back from the leper status they have imposed upon it over recent years.

My "Forest Notes" sought to focus on how difficult it was for the players and staff at the City Ground to focus on mundane things like football. For example, nobody had felt able to really celebrate the news that Nigel Clough had been selected to make his England debut…

And Neil Webb, as articulate for his *Football Post* columns as he was creative in midfield for both Forest and England, made the valued contribution, reproduced opposite…

Meanwhile, the Saturday after the Hillsborough Disaster found Sod's Law taking Clough back to the ground where he first made his name. As the centre forward for Middlesbrough, his hometown club, he scored 204 goals in 222 matches, a rate that modern strikers would consider impossible. As befits the return of the cavalier, his Forest disciples won a thriller 4-3.

Nigel sat-out England's 5-0 win over Albania in a World Cup qualifier on Wednesday night 26 April 1989 but Forest were the best-represented club, by Pearce, Walker and Webb. The goals came from Peter Beardsley (two), Gary Lineker, Chris Waddle and, two minutes from time, young substitute Paul Gascoigne. The inevitable question for super-gaffer Clough was whether he was going to be tempted to take the young Geordie, who apparently was seeking a more successful club than Newcastle United. "He's certainly got all a top footballer's attributes," said Clough, whose spies had obviously done a Peter Taylor-like job. "Unfortunately, from what I hear, those qualities include a thirst for this kind of stuff." He waved his glass. "So no thanks. I've got enough

Hard not to be affected

THERE has not been much appetite for football talk at the City Ground this week.

They've kept telling themselves that life must go on; that not all planes were grounded after Kegworth and Lockerbie; that the trains kept running after Clapham and Peckham.

But thoughts have ceaselessly focussed back on the 95 who died at Hillsborough, the families who mourn, the hundreds who were injured physically and emotionally, the club and city of Liverpool…

The Littlewoods Cup, so joyously won at Wembley a fortnight ago, should have taken pride of place at a dinner in the Jubilee Club on Monday night.

The dinner was cancelled. The cup has spent the week in a cupboard.

Credit

Nigel Clough finally joined Stuart Pearce, Des Walker, Neil Webb and Steve Hodge in the England squad for next Wednesday's World Cup qualifying match against Albania at Wembley.

It was an occasion that called for more pride. Yet the last thing the young centre forward expected was congratulations.

Forest's under-18s drew 3-3 at Swindon on Wednesday night in the first leg

of a pulsating Midland Youth Cup final and the reserves defeated Sheffield United 2-0 in the Central League on Thursday night at the City Ground.

They were magnificently professional. A credit to the game which those Liverpool fans at Hillsborough loved so dearly.

But cups and points are suddenly put into perspective alongside deaths and injuries; and players find themselves guiltily wondering whether they should be performing again. Of course they should, but…

Helpless

It's not that they are ashamed. They have no reason to be; at worst, they were the innocent onlookers at Hillsborough.

It's simply a case of a sadness, a helplessness, enveloping all; a disbelief that a sunny day made for football should have spawned such a disaster.

Ninety-five people died for the game they loved. Not one, so far as can be ascertained, died as the result of violence. Certainly, not one died as the result of inter-club violence. Crazy, wasn't it?

Now, it's as crazy for football folk to feel guilty by association. But that is easier said than done.

Private

It will be eased, though, by the very people with most reason to feel bitter — the injured and the mourning people of Merseyside.

I was privileged to be an observer when Forest's players visited them in their Sheffield hospitals this week. I was an unwelcome observer, I hasten to add, because the players wanted the visits to be private.

"I shan't know what to say to them," said one of the players quietly.

They did know what to say, though, because they were all football folk; there was an instant, instinctive bond between them.

It is a bond that will be strengthened by the events of Hillsborough and will help the players get back to what will pass for normality … performing with pride in pursuit of success.

Because those Liverpool fans would not have expected the game to be played in any other way.

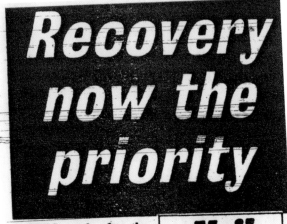

Recovery now the priority

Neil Webb *writes* **EXCLUSIVE**

A FULL week after the tragedy of Hillsborough, there are still no words to describe the sorrow I feel for the people who lost their lives on their way to watch the game I love.

The Liverpool players have been brilliant, visiting the injured in hospital and the bereaved in their own city.

We too, have spoken to the relatives and the casualties in hospital; and I would like to think those meetings were mutually beneficial.

The visit to Sheffield certainly helped we Forest players to come to terms with football's worst disaster; and I hope and pray that the injured youngsters we visited will come through.

There are still people who are not out of danger, skilfully though they are being tended in hospitals, and their relatives have lovingly gathered around them.

The priority is for them to recover. Then we can start to consider the question: Why did it happen?

I have never actually stood in a cage at a football ground; and, like everyone else in football, I await the results of the official inquiries into what happened at Hillsborough.

Perhaps all-seater stadia are the answer; though I cannot be sure because it is impossible to think rationally and clearly amid the visions of what happened on a sunny afternoon, that should have been full of good football.

What I do know is that our stadia are far behind those in other parts of the world. But now is not the time to think of buildings. The people of Liverpool fill our thoughts and prayers.

of that sort of problem." Oh how we laughed.

And then Forest were back at Wembley for the Simod Cup Final against Everton, who were already in the FA Cup Final and awaiting the winners of the Liverpool v Forest rearrangement. By now I was a welcome passenger on the Forest team coach. As befits the man who was in charge of everything, Clough told me exactly where to sit – in the seat immediately behind him and Ron Fenton ... right next to John Lawson! And there wasn't a word about strikes or politics or even a sacking. Hillsborough had put our differences into stark perspective; we shook hands and got on with our different lives.

19

Forest win "by an inch" at Wembley

. . . .

Everton 3 Nottingham Forest 4 (after extra time)

NO FOOTBALL follower requires much more information than a scoreline like that to tell her/him that this match was an epic. It attracted an attendance of 46,604, all of 30,000 fewer than had watched Luton lose to Forest in the Littlewoods Cup Final three weeks earlier; and not all of the comparable indifference was due to this match being the Final of the Simod Cup, the competition introduced for First and Second Division clubs to compensate them (somewhat) for the blanket ban from European football in the wake of the Heysel Disaster. It also gave a statistical insight into how the Hillsborough horrors had turned a significant per centage of people away from The National Game. Whether any of the missing thousands tuned into it on television and regretted not being there, I am not sure. But I do confess that it gave me pause for thought.

My initial reaction to Hillsborough was that I didn't ever want to walk into a football ground again. I said as much to Patrick Barclay, the immensely thoughtful and respected national newspaper football correspondent (who was with *The Independent* at the time) when we bumped into each other at an M1 service area on the night of the tragedy. It was between 9 and 10pm. Neither of us had eaten since breakfast (so, as I habitually had two Benson & Hedges tipped cigarettes and a coffee for breakfast, no food had passed my lips since Friday suppertime). Yet neither did we have the appetite for food. A chat over coffee brought us to the conclusion that football as we knew it was dead. Worse, we agreed that it had committed suicide through its leaders' unwillingness or inability to (a) properly identify the problems and (b) take the hard decisions as to how to deal with them.

As if to justify our doom-laden thoughts, Hillsborough changed nothing immediately: the Government reaction to the disaster was to intensify its insistence that all supporters be forced to carry identity cards. As if that would have saved the 96 innocents who arrived early and behaved impeccably at Hillsborough yet had the life literally crushed out of them!

Yet here we were on 30 April 1989, in the most iconic stadium in the world, seeing a celebration of everything that had made football The National Game. Even the fact that it was in a sideshow of a competition was transcended by the manner in which both sets of players, both unwitting victims of Hillsborough in purely football terms, set aside all mournful thoughts and produced a gem of a confrontation. It was packed with all the things that Our National Game should be about. There was no *Evening Post* on May Day – Clough was amused and bemused that my Tory bosses were so respectful of a Socialist celebration – but when we resumed service on 2 May, my euphoria was undiluted by the wait. Here's how my report sought to put the action into perspective:

> Forest rolled back the years to become the first club ever to win two major English cup finals at Wembley in the same season (never mind the same month).
>
> The Littlewoods Cup holders rolled back the memories to 1953 … They twice came from behind to defeat Everton 4-3, just as Blackpool beat Bolton Wanderers in the FA Cup Final that belonged to Stanley Matthews.
>
> They rolled back the memories to 1966 … Garry Parker went on an even longer scoring run than Geoff Hurst had for his World Cup clincher.
>
> They rolled back the memories to pre-1977 as the unfenced supporters – and there were 30,000 Nottinghamians among the crowd – celebrated a glorious match without so much as putting a toe on the hallowed pitch.
>
> They – team and fans alike – transformed the fourth Simod Cup Final into a celebration of everything that has kept football in its historical place as our No.1 Sport through the turbulent years.

The report went on to catalogue how the fortunes had swung … Tony Cottee put Everton ahead on 9 minutes. Parker equalised on 33. Graeme Sharp restored Everton's lead on 48. Parker's 60-yard surge and shot restored parity on 69. Steve Sutton pulled off a stunning save from Cottee, hurling himself to his right, 2 minutes before full-time. Into extra time, Lee Chapman chipped Forest 3-2 up on 92 minutes. Cottee headed an equaliser on 102. Sutton made an acrobatic double-save to foil Sharp and Cottee with 5 minutes to go. Chapman slid home the winner at the end of a lightning move by Webb, Clough and substitute Carr on 118 minutes. The Sutton saves prompted Clough to sum-up: "We won it by an inch."

Two-goal hero: Garry Parker against Everton in the Simod Cup Final.

As if that wasn't enough, the back page blazed…

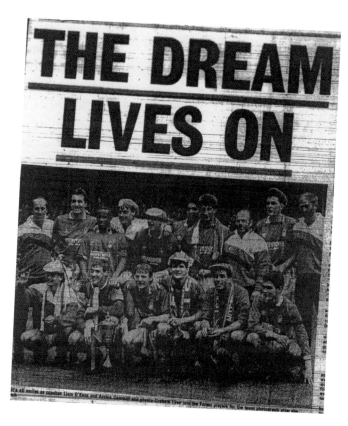

The headline referred to the fact that Forest could still scoop all three knock-out trophies in this unbelievable season. Our celebration picture illustrated how Clough acknowledged the extent of the team effort that had gone into the successes so far. With the 13 players were coaches Liam O'Kane and Archie Gemmill plus physiotherapist Graham Lyas. The full line-up in the picture taken at Wembley by Steve Mitchell is (from left): Back – O'Kane, Tommy Gaynor, Franz Carr, Lee Chapman, Terry Wilson, Des Walker, Garry Parker, Gemmill, Steve Chettle, Lyas. Front – Steve Hodge, Steve Sutton, Stuart Pearce, Brian Laws, Neil Webb and Nigel Clough.

The black arm bands were worn as a mark of respect to those who were killed and injured at Hillsborough. The smiles were those of young men who had grown up dreaming of playing football and coming to terms with a second Cup Final victory at the old game's most famous ground, something no other team had previously achieved in the same season.

Garry Parker, scorer of two of the goals against Everton – one after a lung-bursting run over the sapping turf – summed-up the Forest confidence when he told me: "We're thinking of leaving our boots at Wembley." And why not? After all, the FA had now decreed that the FA Cup semi-final against Liverpool would go ahead on the following Saturday at Old Trafford, with Everton again waiting to play the winners at Wembley in the Final on 20 May.

Clough quickly reminded us why not: "We've got a League game against Millwall tomorrow night. I wouldn't want us to lower our standards …" Forest duly won it 4-1.

One last point about the 1988-89 Simod Cup … It was no manager's highest priority. But Clough was far from the only astute thinker to use it to keep players in a mind-set of playing two matches a week in the belief that it would stand them in good stead when the ban from European competition ended. And Forest did not enjoy an easy route to success. For example, in their first tie on a chilling wet night at Stamford Bridge, Chelsea took them to extra time before folding 4-1. These were their results in the earlier rounds:

Date	Opponents	Venue	Result	Scorers
Jan 10	Chelsea	Away	4 – 1 aet	Chapman, Gaynor, Pearce (pen), Parker
Jan 24	Ipswich Town	Away	3 – 1	Hodge, Pearce, Crosby
Feb 22	Crystal Palace	Home	3 – 1	Webb 2, Pearce

Note the common denominator among the scorers: was there ever a more rampant left back? And by this time, Stuart Pearce had perfected the technique of firing his free kicks from the edge of the penalty area through the smallest of gaps in defensive walls created by little team-mates like Steve Hodge leaning heavily on an opponent at the crucial moment. This is how set-piece training was used in the post-John Robertson era. Naughty – but it worked frequently.

As for the purity of Everton v Forest football, it did not last. Their next meeting was the following November in the 1989-90 League Cup. Everton were so incensed to lose 1-0 (to a Lee Chapman goal) that they trashed the dressing room before they stomped out of the City Ground.

"Leave it," Clough ordered the cleaners, who had been accustomed to some nasty sights but none as bad as this.

With the cleaners clearly wondering if they had heard him right, he smiled and added: "They're back here on Saturday. Let them use their own pig-sty."

Sure enough, Everton returned to get changed in their own muck on 25 November 1989. They lost again, too. 1-0 again. And this time it was even more frustrating – a Nigel Clough penalty. It was conceded in the 62nd minute when full back Neil Pointon tripped Gary Crosby with no hope of getting the ball. It was called a professional foul and I still have Pointon's candid quote in the notebook I used that season:

"I was doing my job as a defender. End of story. I slipped as Crosby broke away. I saw Neville [Southall, the man-mountain of an Everton goalkeeper] advancing. It looked as if he was going to chip Neville so I just brought him down. I had to stop a goal and if I'd had to leave the pitch because of it, that would have been fair enough."

The match referee, George Courtney, one of the most-respected in the world at the time, was happy to stop on his way to the car park to answer the question: *Did you consider sending Pointon off?* "Not for one moment," he said. "I follow the FIFA guidelines and four or five years ago it would have been a sending-off offence. Now it's what's known as ungentlemanly conduct and that is a bookable offence."

And had Everton complained about the state of their dressing room? Courtney smiled and said: "I was aware of a special pressure around this game after what happened the other night." And then he was gone – presumably on his way to the Diplomatic Corps!

Not one Everton player complained about the mess, either. It was a case of "getting your own back."

20

Let Liverpool have the FA Cup

· ·

LIKE VIRTUALLY every other human being, Clough clearly had reservations about the 1988-89 FA Cup competition continuing after the horrors of Hillsborough. Throughout his career in football, his basic rule with journalists was: "Whatever I say is on the record unless I specifically tell you otherwise." He went off the record with me – and, I suspect, with other journalists he could trust – in the days before the re-arranged match against Liverpool to talk about his "no-win" situation; a dreadful place for a control freak to find himself.

He confessed to me that his instinct was: "If they want the Cup that badly, let them have it."

I winced; and, recognising that he sounded much harsher than he intended, he explained: "No game of football can compensate those poor souls who lost their lives and were crippled. Let's knock the competition on the head for this year and let the trophy stand at Anfield as a kind of memorial…"

I tried very hard to persuade him that was such a compelling, compassionate argument that it deserved to be written.

"F*** off," he snapped.

"Why?" I asked.

"Because the FA won't change their minds now all the tickets for Old Trafford are sold. And I've got to get my players in the frame of mind to win a football match that I reckon none of us wants to play. All we want to do is respect those poor souls who never left Hillsborough and those you saw in the hospitals the other day."

"They're cracking quotes, Brian," I tried again. "Real humane feelings…"

"I'd deny them – and make sure they were the last you ever wrote," he said, his drawl slightly quieter than usual; his tactic when he was making his most serious points.

"All right," I surrendered. "What line do you want to take?"

"The f***ing football one … We've won two games already this week … We only beat Everton by an inch … We've got the Cup bug … If you've quoted them accurately, the players want to go back to another Final … That sort of thing. Now let me get on with my work."

Hard though he and his staff worked to get the right players in the right frame of mind, the semi-final itself always seemed to me to be the equivalent of a phony war. Liverpool won 3-1 with John Aldridge snaffling two goals and Brian Laws nudging one into his own net.

Neil Webb, my *Football Post* columnist and the most in-form England playmaker at the time, summed up the hollow feeling afterwards: "We've put a smile on people's faces this year but we just didn't have it today."

Clough simply hopped onto the team bus and ordered Albert to drive him home. For the second time in days, he simply could not find the words; an absolute rarity for the master of the one-liner.

Even so, it's worth recording that Forest finished that traumatic season third in the First Division; though all that most people remember of the League drama is Arsenal snatching the title from Liverpool with two late goals at Anfield in the last match of the season.

Matches were coming so thick and fast and it was sometimes difficult for me and Webb to get together to compose his *Football Post* column. One week, the only opportunity came during a Forest Reserves' match re-arranged for a Thursday evening. Webb popped

up to the Press Box at half-time and was quite happy to sign autographs for astonished fans while he dictated his thought for the week, as you can see from this photograph (which, by sheer coincidence, includes John Lawson beside Webb's right elbow.

Imagine Stephen Gerrard or Frank Lampard doing a similar favour for a local reporter during a reserve match at Anfield or Stamford Bridge these days, and you get an idea of how the status of England's best footballers has changed in the last couple of decades…

By then, I had become piggy-in-the-middle as Webb pondered what to do when he ran out of contract at the end of the season. Clough had been telling me for weeks that Webb was going to Manchester United. The master manager even had the name of the Nottingham taxi driver who had driven the midfielder to a rendezvous in the North West around the middle of the winter and relished passing on the news in a phone call to the City Ground. Webb continually played a straight bat to all my questions: "I'll decide when the time is right…" Clough became increasingly frustrated at my inability to "do as good a journalistic job as a taxi driver." What made the situation even worse was the fact that I'd given a part-time job to Webb's wife, Shelley, who had left a reporter's job in Reading when he made the move from Portsmouth to the City Ground in 1985.

WAGS had not been invented in these days; and Shelley was quite happy to give a wife's perspective for every Saturday's *Evening Post* – a God send, as columns go, considering our deadlines had all gone before football matches kicked-off. We needed something fairly timeless to give our readers; and the thoughts of Shelley Webb became so successful that I believe she relaunched her journalistic career off the back of her features for the *Post*. Clough cast me as their friend, and therefore his enemy, in this particular battle.

Webb proved Clough – and his cabbie spy – correct by signing-on for Alex Ferguson in the summer of 1989. Clough valued him at £2.2 million. United were happy to go to a Tribunal and were ordered to pay Forest £1.5 million. Webb handled the pressure so well that he scored on his debut against Arsenal. Alas, he snapped an Achilles tendon playing for England shortly afterwards and was never the same creative driving force again.

My search for a new *Football Post* columnist was not eased by a furious Clough reminding all contenders that he was an avid reader of the tabloid that we rushed out as soon as the Saturday afternoon results were in. So imagine my surprise when Nigel Clough volunteered. Once I got to know him, which he made easy by his open manner, I was not surprised to discover he had vibrant views of his own. Folk who knew him better said he had inherited his Mum's ability to take other people's feelings into account. Allied with his Dad's conviction that he was always right, he had the perfect strength of character to survive in professional football.

As for the team, Clough signed Republic of Ireland midfielder John Sheridan from Leeds United for £650,000 but seemed to take an instant dislike to him.

"What's wrong with him, Brian?" I asked after Sheridan had played well in a reserves' match during his brief spell at the City Ground without earning a call into the first team.

"He smells," said Clough so quietly that I was sure I'd misheard him.

"You what?" I asked.

"He smells," whispered Clough, leaning closer to me so that there was no confusion.

It was only his choice of soap. But the master-manager had made up his mind. Sheridan had to go. He was sold on to Sheffield Wednesday two months into the season for £500,000 (and was to repay them by scoring the winning goal in the 1991 League Cup Final against Manchester United).

Sheridan wasn't the first midfielder to be given a pretty instant Clough cold shoulder: Gary Megson had been treated similarly a few years earlier on the perception that he did not trap the ball as efficiently as Clough demanded. So Garry Parker was moved from the left wing into Webb's No.8 shirt, and the flowing football demanded by Clough carried Nottingham Forest to Wembley again towards the end of the 1989-90 season.

21

Captives: Mandela and the young Keane

● ●

NELSON MANDELA came closer than most footballers to loosen the League Cup from Forest's grasp in 1989-90. Not a lot of people know that, including the icon himself who emerged from 27 years' imprisonment on Robben Island on 11 February 1990 and went on to become the President who unified South Africa, which had been violently divided by apartheid. By coincidence, ITV were contracted to show the first leg of the League Cup semi-final between Forest and Coventry City from the City Ground on that same Sunday afternoon. It was a soaking, shivering winter's day but 26,153 supporters braved the elements … only to be warned over the Tannoy that the kick-off would be delayed until ITV had shown Mandela's first steps to freedom. The problem was, nobody either in South Africa or the United Kingdom had the slightest idea when that might be. Within minutes? Hours? Today? During darkness?

Clough was incandescent at the thought that his players were being side-tracked. He stormed up the corridor from the changing rooms towards his office and shouted to nobody in particular: "How long has yon Mandela been in prison?"

"27 years," came a chorus from awed on-lookers.

"Surely the bugger can wait inside for another 90 minutes then," Clough went on.

He put this argument, forcibly, to the man in charge of ITV's match coverage, an innovative young executive called Greg Dyke, who was destined to achieve fame in many of broadcasting's higher echelons as time went on. The manager of Coventry City, a former Chelsea defender called John Sillett who tended to be as forthright as Clough, lent his support. The up-shot was that the match kicked-off only three minutes late.

But it was a characteristically bold move by Clough to put Forest and the fans foremost in all considerations. Over many previous years, he had been ITV's ace rent-a-mouth in their uphill battle to wrest an audience from the BBC in the decades before Rupert Murdoch created the all-powerful Sky concept. But there was no hint of mixed loyalties as he laid into the television folk in his office.

The gist of his rationale was: "Television channels throughout the world are hanging around for Mandela. ITV is the only one that can show this match. And you'd better get on with it or it'll be your fault if the rain-soaked fans give us a riot."

With the Hillsborough Disaster not yet a year old, it was hard to ignore his argument. Not that Dyke was impressed. He called me on the following day to complain that I had made a story of it! With expletives deleted, the quote I was able to use from him was: "It was just one of those extraordinary things. How often does a guy get released after nearly 30 years in jail? It's just ironic that football was affected. It seems to cop for everything these days."

Not that Clough's ploy ended there. He also made sure that the somewhat tyrannical organisers of the competition, the Football League, were aware of why the kick-off was delayed. This led to Forest escaping a fine of up to £200,000 – which they could not afford despite their recent successes – for not starting the match on time.

And after Forest squeezed a 2-1 advantage, he sparked instant discussion as to whether ITV would screen the second leg from Highfield Road. He murmured in that quiet, super-sarcastic way of his that he was "surprised they've packed up all their stuff and not said, 'See you next week' ... Maybe we've upset them in some way."

The decision was taken out of ITV's hands a few days later when Oldham Athletic beat West Ham United 6-1 in the first leg of the other semi-final, rendering their return match pretty irrelevant. And so the cameras moved into Highfield Road to cover a goalless draw of great drama. Forest hung on – and Clough gave the credit to coaches O'Kane and Gemmill, claiming they had changed his mind about what team to send out over a drink on the eve of the match.

It was his way of explaining why he had not selected a little Icelandic winger, Thorvaidur (Toddi) Orlygsson, a 23-year-old law student signed from Akranes for £150,000 in December 1989. Little Toddi was the intended replacement for Franz Carr, a small but leggy winger so swift that Clough often suggested we (Trevor Bartlett and myself) take him to the Old Market Square in Nottingham and "prove he can catch pigeons". We were up for it. Sadly, Franz didn't fancy the prospect of going all his length on pigeon droppings in front of hundreds of Nottingham's shoppers and limping back to the City Ground to "a rollicking from the Boss for getting injured". Whenever we reached this point, Clough would smile and acknowledge: "The little bugger's got a point. But that doesn't change the fact that he could catch pigeons."

He never made that prediction on behalf of Orlygsson, who made 15 starts during the second half of the season, was substituted three times, and went on as a sub three times. Hardly earth-shattering stuff! But Clough was all set to launch the inconsistent lightweight on the left wing at Coventry until the coaches argued that Terry Wilson would be a stronger option. Wilson, a lean and lanky Scot, was a midfielder who had put in several sterling shifts in the centre of defence alongside Des Walker when Colin Foster was injured. So that put him ahead of Orlygsson when it came to the first question Clough always asked about a player: "Can he win a ball?" And they were on a par regarding Clough's other two criteria: "Can he pass a ball? Can he trap a ball?"

So Clough slipped Wilson into the No.11 shirt but played him in the centre of midfield with Parker operating out on the left wing from where he had been mightily effective in the previous season.

The above is an extremely rare exception to the rule Clough applied to most differences of opinion: "We sit down and talk about it and then agree I was right in the first place."

The following is a unique example of him repaying me for a favour that saved my life…

It began shortly after Forest booked their place in the Final against Oldham. A determined young lady who had been employed to publicise National No Smoking Day in and around our fair city decided she needed only one ally – a former smoker by the name of Brian Clough.

He wanted nothing to do with her … "I'm busy enough doing my job without doing hers as well. Tell her to f*** off," he'd whisper every time she appeared near the club's general office before sloping back to the sanctuary of either his private office, the chairman's room or the changing rooms. Usually there would be a stampede of staff to obey his every order; but even the brave females among the office staff were too gentlemanly to tell this attractive female to be off.

Eventually she was spending as much time as me hanging around in the hope of catching a minute with the mercurial manager. Which gave him an idea… "Why don't you offer to write a feature for her?" he asked.

"Because I've got all on writing my sports stuff without getting involved in features again," I said. "Besides, we've got our own feature writers."

"Aye but if you write about the downsides of being a smoker meeting sports people …"

"What downsides?"

"Well, you smell."

"What?"

"Like a f***ing ashtray."

"Thanks."

"If you didn't, the players'd find it easier to talk to you."

"You reckon?"

"Oh aye. Tell you what – give up smoking for a day, write about it, get her off my back and I'll make sure you get all the stories you want."

"Really?"

"One a day. The players call you Scoop don't they?"

"Your Captain does."

"There you are then – a scoop a day!"

"All right."

"Oh, and persuade the Commercial Manager to give up with you. He smells as badly as you do."

"Right."

Of course, as soon as I got out into the car park, I lit a cigarette to contemplate whether this was the most bizarre conversation I'd ever had. I concluded that maybe it didn't cap the "move your seat" moment; but that Clough had lacked nothing in candour. I couldn't even argue about whether I smelled: having smoked from the age of 13 to 45, I had long ago lost the sense of smell.

As I stood there, by one of those unaccountable coincidences, the Commercial Manager strolled into view, heading back to his office from his liquid lunch at the Trent Bridge Inn, the hostelry made famous centuries ago as the home of the man who created the hallowed Trent Bridge cricket ground. David Pullan was the Commercial Manager's name. He had been a cricketer – a wicketkeeper – with Yorkshire and Nottinghamshire. Now he was built more like a Weeble; a drawback to the social life led by one of the pioneers in the business of trying to sell more than match tickets to wealthy football supporters.

We already had a great working relationship through the Junior Reds' Club. This supporters' club exclusively for under-16-year-olds was an *Evening Post* initiative. In the wake of the Heysel Disaster, the climax (we believed, until Hillsborough) of a series of horrendous outbreaks of terrace violence and terrorism, the *Post* Promotions Manager Bob Britten quickly realised that football needed all the help it could get to win back the confidence of the public. Bob and I went back a long way – to the days when North Muskham Juniors were reaching Notts FA Shield semi-finals. Bob was the star inside right who went on to earn a trial with Forest. I was the nipper who would sit on the bigger lads' shoulders to hang the nets on the crossbars before watching the matches and biking off home to write my reports. Now we were suddenly junior executives, travelling in his company car to Watford, of all places, to find out how to attract youngsters into football grounds and, equally importantly, how to convince parents the mites would be safe.

There was a strong Nottingham connection at Watford's homely Vicarage Road ground. Elton John, the pop-star chairman of the club, was a nephew of Roy Dwight, the right winger who had been carried off with a broken leg in the 1959 FA Cup Final and had then watched his 10 Forest team-mates hang on to defeat Luton Town. Eddie Plumley, the forward-thinking club secretary (chief executive in modern terminology) came from our neck of the woods. So we were given full access to their well-established Junior Hornets, who had their own base in a cosy cottage near the ground.

Back at the office, Bob and I had little difficulty persuading the *Evening Post* hierarchy that we could boost our circulation now – and possibly in the future – by making constructive and responsible contributions to the agonising debate raging about how football could be made safer. Forest and Notts, plus Mansfield Town, who were also deep in the *Post's* circulation area at that time, were all sufficiently interested for us to go searching for sponsors. It says much about the era that local breweries happily provided the financial backing: Shipstone's for Forest; Home Brewery for Notts.

All the clubs needed to provide was a 'safe area' in one of the stands. This was no problem at Meadow Lane, where Notts never came close to filling the place even as they were completing their amazing climb back to the top flight for the first time in 55 years. It was a tougher proposition at the City Ground. So we had to ask Clough for his help without making him feel he was being blackmailed by the fact that we were creating Junior Magpies and Junior Stags come what may. Pullan was all for it; but Clough always said he was in charge of all decisions affecting everyone "from the laundry ladies downwards" – so a meeting was arranged.

"You won't let the little buggers get under my feet, will you?" was his first reaction. Assured that we would not, he went on: "Or distract my players?" Bob bravely suggested that players not involved with the first team on match days might do a little PR stint by signing autographs for the little ones before or after the action. There was an over-long pause; a sigh from the manager. Then, not for the first time, his reaction totally stunned me: "Aye, something for them to do while they're on the sick list, I suppose."

So all we needed was a little seated section in one of the Stands. To the consternation of a few season ticket-holders, who had to shuffle along, we were granted a slot closest to the rowdies of the Trent End in what was to become The Brian Clough Stand. These were the same Trent Enders whose wit had nicknamed our Duncan 'Hamilton Academical' … the same Trent Enders whose sinister creations included this version of the song, *Seasons in the Sun*:

> *We had joy*
> *We had fun*
> *We had Chelsea*
> *On the run*
> *But the joy*
> *Did not last*
> *Cos the bastards*
> *Ran too fast*

Woe betide anyone who laughed at this little ditty. It was a report, not a joke. But Clough quickly helped us restore peace by agreeing to huge signs being erected stating:

> Gentlemen –
> No Swearing Please
> *Brian*

It worked. To a motley man and spotty adolescent, the Trent Enders not only obeyed The Manager's requests to clean-up their language. They became vocally protective of the little ones, even envious when Clough let Forest's players kick footballs into the Junior Reds' section as they emerged from the tunnel. "Wish we had new balls like you," came the instant chant. You'd have required a heart of stone not to smile approval!

There was an inevitable hiatus. It occurred on the day we launched the *Evening Post* Junior Reds' Club by flying-in the first two members in Colonel Forman Hardy's helicopter. It landed on the centre circle an hour or so before kick-off. It had hardly touched down before Clough took off from the players' tunnel. "What's that f***ing thing doing on my pitch?" he screamed at Britten.

"You said we could fly the first members in," Bob replied.

"I meant into the car park," screamed Clough. "If that leaves any oil on my pitch... And look at it blowing the grass!"

"What grass?" asked Bob, eyes glinting, referring to how the City Ground resembled a cabbage patch for too much of each season.

Aye, all right," said Clough, suddenly smiling too. "But get him off before the referee sees it or we'll all knackered."

As the partnership flourished, Pullan and Britten even persuaded Clough to allow Junior Reds activities on the Forest training ground. And imagine the thrill for the little ones – and the parents who accompanied them – when Clough himself turned up to make the presentations.

As he went into the Jubilee Club to perform the task for the first time after a Friday first team meeting, Clough said: "They're not going to mob me, are they?"

"Of course not, Brian," I promised.

Of course they did. He loved it.

On the following night, after the first team match, he was still smiling about the bright, shiny faces that had brought smiles back to his marvellous but currently miserable game: "Them bairns, eh? They make it all worthwhile, don't they?"

Thereafter, the Junior Reds' Club wanted for nothing. More space in the stands? Have two sections of the Main Stand! A special room for half-time soft drinks (courtesy of Shipstone's, of course)? No problem – and the bairns were welcome to wait in the safety there until their parents collected them post-match. Advertising the Club at *Evening Post* Open Days around the suburbs? Players were primed to turn-up in pairs to smile sweetly and sign autographs. By this time, the kids' club had grown so big that it needed a virtually full-time organiser so Forest arranged for one of the most thoughtful members of the club's staff, Annette, to be 'mum' to all the bairns. It was a brilliant success.

There was only one restriction: "Once a year with 'em is enough for me," Clough asserted.

So on balance, I suppose, Pullan and I owed Clough a favour. And getting the No Smoking Day Tsarina off his back was it. "All right," chuckled Pullan throatily; and neither of us spotted the irony in the fact that he was dragging on a cigarette at the time. Tsarina herself was still sitting in the foyer between two office blocks at the City Ground. So we introduced ourselves, with Pullan still dragging on his cigarette, explained that Mr. Clough was rather busy with things like getting his team ready for another Wembley final but, as an ex-smoker himself, fully supported her worthy campaign. So he had asked us to help her publicity drive. She was so thrilled with our plot that I felt satisfied enough to relax with a cigarette as I drove back to the office.

I got back to Forman Street in time to go to the 3.30pm Editorial Conference at which Barrie Williams daily strove to decide what would be going in the next day's paper. Gone (with Mr. Snaith) were the days when news was allowed to happen and we all reacted accordingly.

Here was the era when Barrie brought in thought, planning, imagination, the concept of campaigns and made no secret of his desire for the biggest newspaper in the East Midlands to win awards as the best in the country.

As I was spending so long at the City Ground digging for the best nuggets, I tended to leave my conscientious and competent deputy, John Lucy, to attend Conference and add substance to Barrie's crystal ball. After all, my old club cricket conspirator was called Sports Editor now that I gloried in the title of Group Sports Editor. John's eyes fairly lit up any afternoon I suggested he catch an early bus home to his wife Janice in the wealthy suburb of Wollaton while I represented us at Conference; it was a tad like a schoolboy being excused detention at the end of a long, hard day.

I brought up the "No smoking" feature under 'anything else' at the end of the meeting. Barrie saw no irony in the fact that he was squinting through his own cigarette smoke as he said: "Yeah, fine, but we've got to use it on No Smoking Day."

"So Pullan and I've got to give up a day early," I said.

"Well, we could do with the copy a couple of days in advance," said the Features Fuhrer, Ian Scott.

"We'd better give up now then," I said.

"You're not giving up smoking," grinned Williams, rising from his chair to signal the meeting was over and making a point of offering me a cigarette as he passed me on his way to the door from the Conference Room, which (fittingly, some might cynically suggest) faced Nottingham's Royal Centre, focal point of the city's theatreland.

Oh yes I was giving up smoking – though I didn't even realise it at the time. My first move was to phone Pullan and sort out what to write in the feature I was going to have to complete in the next day or so. We fed our imagination in the Trent Bridge Inn that night and, eyes watering with as much laughter as smoke, came up with a heart-rending tale of how a 24-hour absence of tar (sorry, nicotine) played havoc with our nerves and yet sharpened our appetites so that we ate properly (i.e., healthily), cleared our heads so that we felt more alert and left us coughless so that we were able to sleep properly.

All I needed the next morning was a quick quote from a player to stick into the feature. Goalkeeper Steve Sutton was first out of the changing room door after training, so I asked him: "What would you say if I went 24 hours without a cigarette, Sutty?"

"That you died 24 hours ago," he replied, deadpan.

I tried again, explaining briefly why I was asking him. He rewarded me with a serious answer that stunned me: "Well pleasant though your company is, it is sometimes hard to spend time talking to you because you do stink somewhat. If your clothes didn't reek of smoke, you would find your job of talking to us a lot easier."

"Thanks Steve … Has the Gaffer been talking to you about me?"

"No more than the usual 'Watch what you say to that f***ing Frecknall'. Why?"

"Thanks Steve."

Off he went home to Radcliffe-on-Trent, the first village outside Nottingham eastwards along the A52 towards Grantham. Off I went back to the office to churn out the feature. Instinctively, I lit a cigarette to spark my thought processes while my computer terminal booted up – and then stretched my imagination as best I could. The finished article must have appeared on a Tuesday because it coincided with a reserve team match in the Central League at the City Ground. I'd woken up that morning at 6am as usual, washed and shaved while the kettle boiled, poured a cup of coffee and gone to my packet of Benson & Hedges tipped and box of Swan Vesta matches. The cigarette was in my lips and the match struck when I caught site of my reflection in the kitchen window. On impulse, I took the fag out of my mouth, held it in front of me and said: "Today is National No Smoking Day. Today I am going to make do without you."

I put the cigarette back into the packet, stowed fags and matches in my jacket pocket and set-off for the office. I was surrounded by smoke. John Lucy at the desk to my left smoked a pipe. Des Lowe, sub-editor and golf corresponded at the desk immediately in front of me, smoked untipped Senior Service cigarettes. George Bramley, the long-serving Deputy Sports Editor, smoked fags. Even before lunchtime, I was shaking. And I felt so hungry that I could have believed my stomach had been scoured. Chewy sweets helped for a while but I was in a dream-like state.

Normally I would light a cigarette while I set-up my computer to begin a story. Now that 'trigger' was unavailable, I had no way of sparking the 'intro' to the story from my brain – my pounding brain – to my fingertips.

With more relief than usual, I set off from the office to the City Ground … to discover my "fags fairy story" had been well and truly rumbled. Far from going through the agonies of withdrawal symptoms, my co-conspirator Pullan was unconscious. He had slipped from his bar stool at the Trent Bridge Inn the previous evening, bumped his head on a brass pole on the way down and been taken to the Queen's Medical Centre, where doctors were fairly confident he would come round soon. He made a quick and full recovery; but was never in shape to even reach for a fag on this National No Smoking Day. I didn't know whether to laugh or cry.

I was certainly lost for something to do while I waited for Forest to finish training and for someone – usually assistant manager Ron Fenton – to give me the team selected for the night's reserve match. My smoking mate John Robertson had long gone to Derby County, on his way to life with Martin O'Neill, first in insurance and then in football management. My new smoking mate, Ron, the Jubilee Club manager, was an excellent conversationalist as well as a fine chef but, alas, a smoker. So when he lit up almost as soon as we sat down, I made my excuses and went to hide in the office foyer.

Clough appeared presently, on his way from the changing rooms to his office. "How are you?" he nodded in passing, not pausing for a reply.

"Bloody awful, Brian," I replied. "This no-smoking business is making me ill."

He froze in mid-stride. "Is it today? Are you really doing it? Blow me! Come and have a drink."

"I'd rather have a reserve team," I ventured, wanting only to get home and steal a sleep to escape all the pangs for a while.

"A drink first," he insisted, taking me into the Chairman's Room. While he poured out my Scotch and ginger, he chanted the team I wanted and indicated I could use the phone in the corner of the room. Job done, I quite enjoyed the extra dizzy feeling that a treble Scotch bestowed on my nicotine-starved brain.

Driving the 25 miles home was as weird as trying to start a story. Four or five times, I took my cigarette packet out of my pocket. Two or three times, I actually put a cigarette to my lips. But I resisted the temptation to light-up. The afternoon sleep gave me a couple of hours' respite but I felt so awful when I woke up … sweating, shaking, light-headed, endlessly hungry … that Gill felt it would be dangerous for me to drive back to the match on my own. She had gone through the agonies of giving up smoking a few years earlier. Although she never smoked half as many as my 40 or more a day, she understood what I was going through by going cold turkey.

At half-time, secretary Carol came up to us in the Press Box: "He wants to know how you are."

"Dreadful," I said and meant it; and tottered down the steps rather dizzily to join Clough in his office.

"Have you really gone all day without a cigarette?" he asked, holding my gaze.

"I have," I said.

"Blow me," he smiled (because Carol was within earshot and he always strove to curb his language in front of his ladies). "Have a drink." He also gave me a story but to this day, I cannot remember what it was. And as we went our separate ways to watch the second half, he shouted: "I'll make sure you get a story for every day you don't smoke."

He did, too. Sometimes they came straight from the Gaffer's mouth. Some were so outrageous that I'd be almost rolling around laughing and he'd be growling: "Stop f***ing laughing and start writing!"

One of the "fillers" (for Clough knew so much about my job that he even knew the word for "little stories") that he gave me related to the signing of a teenager from the Republic of Ireland.

"He's got every chance of doing very well," drawled Clough while the smartly dressed young man listened, "providing he doesn't go down the same road as me and a compatriot of his known as Mr. Best."

As slightly embarrassed coughs and giggles rumbled around the Chairman's Room, Clough went on: "It's far too easy in this game to have a drink. Everybody wants to buy you a drink. And then all of a sudden, you actually need a drink."

He turned to his new signing and concluded: "The trick for you, young man, is to draw the line before you need a drink."

The young man in question was Roy Keane, 18 years old and on the brink of a career in which he was to play 123 games in a fading Forest team before moving in 1993 to Manchester United, with whom he spent more than 12 gloriously successful years. By an amazing coincidence, his original signing ceremony took place during the interval of a Forest home match against Manchester United, of which there will be more in the next chapter.

Here is how I reported the signing in the following Saturday's *Football Post* (complete with spelling error emanating, I submit, from nicotine withdrawal symptoms) ...

In fact, the youth tournament was in the Netherlands. Keane scored the winning goal in the final, nerveless from the penalty spot at the end of a tense shoot-out; and was instantly promoted to the first team squad. Thus Clough was on the way to creating another legend.

Keane has frequently taken time to thank Clough for allowing him to nip back to Ireland each time he felt homesick

AS IF beating Manchester United 4-0 wasn't enough at the end of the week in which they retained the Littlewoods Cup, Forest also had time to plan for the future.

They signed 18-year-old midfielder Roy Keane from Cobh Ramblers in the Republic of Ireland — for £10,000.

Keane will be playing for his country in the European Youth Championship finals in Budapest next month.

But before then, he has a date with Forest — at a youth tournament in West Germany startiung on May 23.

● Keane is pictured being welcomed to the City Ground by Forest assistant manager Ron Fenton watched by (from left) Cobh chairman John O'Rourke and secretary John Meade plus Forest chief scout Alan Hill

in the early days. What he probably doesn't know is that he worried the manager with his choice of decor in his early weeks in the Forest apprentices' lodgings behind the Bridgford End Stand.

"He's turned everything black," said Clough, obviously astonished and mystified after popping over for an unscheduled inspection while the apprentices were out training … "the furniture, the walls, the curtains. It's like the Black Hole of Calcutta. You don't think he wanted to join that team in black across the river, do you?" Clough's eyes were wide and sparkling. If there was one thing he enjoyed more than a player showing individual character, it was him finding out about it.

Certainly none of Keane's forthright performances suggested he ever had second thoughts about whether he should be giving his all to Forest, even if it did prove to be ultimately in a lost cause. Neither did he have any doubt about his role: "The Gaffer said to me before most matches, 'Your job is to win the ball and pass it to another player in a red shirt. I've made a career out of it."

He did, too: he won every honour available to a club footballer after he moved to Manchester United with Clough's career at its fag-end (if you'll excuse the pun).

22

Carry this trophy out of Wembley for me

· ·

GIVING UP smoking saved my life. My medics assured me of that 11 years later, in 2001, when I had a couple of heart attacks, needed a stent in a blocked artery and discovered all my arteries seemed to be 20 years older than me. Alas, giving up smoking also effectively ended my stint as a football reporter. Each spring morning after that No Smoking Day of 1990, I rose, went to the kitchen cupboard where I had stowed a half-full packet of Benson & Hedges, took one out and told it: "I got by without you yesterday. I'm going to get through without you today." But the one thing I should have done was have a word with the No Smoking Tsarina to obtain help. I didn't; just as I had never talked through the Hillsborough horrors properly with anybody, even the psychiatrist kindly offered by Clough.

Even now, with time aplenty to contemplate, I cannot fully explain the feeling of desolation that led me to decide I could no longer cover Forest. I told Ron Fenton first because, like Peter Taylor before him, he had frequently been the club mouthpiece when Clough himself did not want to talk to me. I came to regard Ron as a trustworthy friend and nothing ever happened to change my opinion of him. He understood the pressures; and he obviously did a good job of explaining to Clough that I was not really deserting him because there was no backlash from the manager.

Promising me a story for every day I did not smoke had fired his imagination quite brilliantly. And one of his gems made a hero of the oldest smoker in his back-up team. The driver of the team coach, Albert Kershaw, was grey haired, balding, a skinny, chain-smoking and sallow shadow of the man he used to be … but he was first on the Clough team sheet for the 1990 League Cup final against Oldham Athletic.

Clough came up with the line to celebrate his 55th birthday on 21 March. We at the *Post* had been on our usual mission to get a picture of him celebrating with a birthday cake.

He agreed to pose on one condition – "that yon Sports Editor comes on the picture with me."

"You don't want me spoiling the picture, Brian," I protested, laughing.

"I do, you know. You tell me that you're 10 years younger than me. But nobody will believe that. You'll make me look 10 years younger than you. It might even get me a new contract. Can you send a copy to each of my Directors?"

"You know why I'm ageing so fast, don't you?" I ventured.

"No but you're going to bore us all by telling us, aren't you?"

"It's because of my working hours – I can't really start work until you stop playing."

He stopped shuffling furniture to prepare for the picture, looked hard at me, and asked: "So what time do you get home from a night match?"

I shrugged: "It depends … 2am, 3am, with the milkman."

"F*** me!"

It didn't excuse me from the line-up: me sitting in front of the cake, Clough leaning on my left shoulder, Fenton leaning on my right shoulder, club secretary Paul White standing behind me looking somewhat bemused by it all. Some at the *Post* reckoned it was too close to illustrating to our critics that Forest in general, and Clough in particular, controlled us. I preferred to believe it was something of a triumph that we could now relax and celebrate together; something that nobody at the *Post* dared to even dream of when I had become Sports Editor.

Did I feel pressured? Well … I never got a slice of the cake. So make your own mind up.

As for the story about Albert being the only man on the team-sheet for Wembley, Clough reasoned: "You've got your picture. Let John [Lawson] have the Albert story first." Grrrrr!

The line he came up with was vintage Clough. Forest had won only one of the four League matches since they overcame Coventry in the League Cup semi-finals; and that was a dubious 1-0 success over Manchester City achieved when Gary Crosby headed the ball out of the palm of goalkeeper Andy Dibble's hand as he prepared to clear it, not knowing the winger was lurking at his shoulder.

So Clough came up with this message for the players to read in as much of the media as Lawson the freelance could interest:

> "If anyone thinks they have booked their ticket to Wembley yet, they can think again. The only bloke certain about boarding the coach for the Littlewoods Cup Final is our driver, Albert. He's definitely going. And if I survive long enough, I'll be there with him. But at the moment there are 13 places up for grabs on the team-sheet – and nobody is sure of a place. If anyone thinks they can hold something in reserve for a Cup Final, I strongly suggest they bring it out of reserve now and show me what they can do because you cannot turn it on and off in football."

He said more along the same lines; and then emphasised to me: "If I see that in the *Nottingham Evening Post* before I see it in the nationals, I'll know you can't be trusted."

The fact that I did not jump the gun provided further evidence to my critics at the *Post* that I was in thrall to Clough. Far be it from me to suggest jealousy was a factor here; but at a time when I was struggling health-wise, I could have done without the extra hassle.

It wasn't as if Clough's words had any magical affect on the players. Forest won only one of the remaining seven matches before the Cup Final.

Indeed, Clough was doubly incandescent after the 2-0 loss at Southampton in the last League match prior to the Wembley showpiece. Even the punnet of strawberries that Saints staff always presented to him – a tradition begun when Lawrie McMenemy was the manager at The Dell – were of no consolation to him.

"We only got one kick today and that was on the back of my Centre Forward's calf," he said as he clambered onto the team coach and slumped into his seat.

Before he was entirely settled, a policeman appeared on the steps into the coach. "Can I help you, Constable?" asked Clough, clambering to his feet again, elbowing his way past Fenton to meet the officer in the gangway.

"Yes Mr. Clough," said the young, fresh-faced PC. "Your coach was unlocked when I checked it just after 3pm."

"Thanks for pointing that out. Did you find somebody to lock it up?"

"Well I was uncertain as to whether you had had intruders so I carried out a search as a matter of priority and found alcohol in a large wicker basket, Mr. Clough."

"You found what?" gasped Clough, as aware of the nationwide ban on alcohol being transported to football grounds as he was of the false bottom in a kit skip that hid my Scotch, his vodka and the favourite spirits of the coaches, Company Secretary White and the ever-faithful Lawson.

"Alcohol, Mr. Clough. On your coach. In that recess," said the PC, pointing over Clough's shoulder to the hiding place for the skip, midway up the bus opposite the microwave on which Ron the Jubilee Club manager conjured the hot meals.

"Blow me," gasped Clough, leaning on the young PC's arm, guiding him back towards the door. "It seems you've got two choices now."

"Choices, Mr. Clough?"

"Aye. You can either take us all to your station and spend the night taking statements from all of us. Or you can leave me to sort this out."

By now the policeman was reversing, albeit unwillingly, down the bus steps with Clough shunting him slowly but inexorably. "Now," Clough went on as one of the policeman's feet reached the car park, "you're a young man who I daresay is coming to the end of his shift and is ready for a night out, probably with a girlfriend. You know enough about me to know I'm a disciplinarian. So rather than spend all night over all that paperwork, you could leave me to sort it out, confident that I will deal appropriately with the guilty party or guilty parties. How does that sound?"

"Well, Mr. Clough…"

"Look, Sergeant, you know I can't abide law-breakers."

"I do, Mr. Clough."

"Good lad – now you have a good night with your girlfriend and I'll get this sorted on the long way home. Believe you me, the culprit or culprits will pay!"

By the time he had finished talking, Clough had backed the policeman fully out of the coach. "Off we go, Albert," he said through gritted teeth, waving and smiling to the somewhat bewildered but utterly out-manoeuvred policeman.

"Not a word," he hissed to Lawson and me, eyes blazing, as he squirmed past Fenton into his seat by the window.

There was utter silence for the first several miles. Indeed, I don't think anyone dared to even breathe as the police motorcycle escort – mandatory for visiting teams in these days of rampant hooliganism throughout the football community – led the Forest bus away from The Dell and towards the motorway to take us onwards to "Oxford and The Midlands" as the signs proclaimed.

Presently, Albert took an elongated look in his rear view mirrors and broke the silence: "He's gone, Gaffer." A few more miles on, as if a mind-reader, he glided to a halt across the road from an off-licence. Off hopped a couple of the staff, returning minutes later with replacements for the victuals that had been confiscated by the policeman.

Clough had kept his promise to the eagle-eyed young policeman that the culprits would pay for the crime. Those whom he deemed responsible for leaving the coach unlocked had to buy the alcohol. Before Albert eased us past Oxford, we were all dosing like contented newts.

It transpired in the following days that this was not the first time the Forest team bus had been at odds with an officer of the law. A few seasons earlier, before I was a welcomed passenger, it had been caught in a traffic jam on the A1 into North London after the squad had lunched at South Mimms *en route* to a match at Tottenham Hotspur. As the minutes ticked away with no indication that traffic was beginning to move, Clough became increasingly agitated.

Eventually he asked: "Albert … why is there nobody in that lane to the left?"

"Because it's the hard shoulder, Gaffer."

"What's that for?"

"Use by the emergency services, Gaffer."

"Get in there, Albert."

"But …"

"This is an emergency for us, Albert. Get in there!"

Within minutes of Albert obeying, the sound of a siren and the sight of a flashing blue light brought him to a halt.

The police motor cyclist had hardly got to the open door of the bus before Clough greeted him: "Good afternoon, officer. Am I pleased to see you!"

"Aah, Mr. Clough," said the officer, obviously unaware he had been halting the Forest bus, "you do know you shouldn't be here, don't you?"

"Of course I do, young man – I should be at White Hart Lane."

"No, what I meant Mr. Clough, is that this lane should be kept clear for emergency vehicles."

"This is an emergency for me," responded the manager. "If I don't get this lot to White Hart Lane in the next 30 minutes, we're going to disappoint 40,000 or so people."

"I know that, Mr. Clough. I support Spurs myself."

"Good lad – we all have our crosses to bear. Now, as you obviously know the way to White Hart Lane, would you be good enough to clear the way for us."

And he did! Instead of booking Albert for encroaching onto the hard shoulder, he replaced his helmet, manoeuvred his motor cycle to the front of the bus, put on his lights and siren – and led Albert through the congestion so adeptly that Forest avoided, albeit only by a couple of minutes, a fine for handing-in their team sheet late to the referee.

Clough was so grateful that, as he shook the young policeman's hand, he made a mental note of his number. And he made sure that the policeman had tickets for "yourself and your mates" in the Main Stand for the next match Forest played at Tottenham.

This episode was why every Forest trip to London thereafter was timed so that they had an hour to spare in case of unexpected delays. On the Sunday after the Southampton defeat, 29 April, Forest went to Wembley without any such dramas or traumas and retained the Littlewoods Cup by defeating Oldham 1-0 with a goal by another of Clough's dubious discoveries, Nigel Jemson. He was a policeman's son from Preston. "Far too full of himself," said Clough of the young striker's lack of modesty and shyness at one stage in an unforgettable 'pot-kettle' moment.

But, as with the Southampton match, the coach journey home was immeasurably more memorable for me than the match had been. As he climbed on, last as ever, Clough asked "The Company Secretary", as he called Paul White, to switch seats with me. Baffled, I dutifully perched on the front nearside seat, immediately behind the door, instantly fearing I was to be evicted at the first railway station. So imagine how I felt when Clough plonked the newly-won Cup on my knee and said: "Wave that to our supporters, please."

"Whaaaat!?!" He went back to his normal seat. The huge wooden doors of Wembley swung open, Albert eased the coach out into the throng … and thousands wondered who the hell that was in the Forest bus holding the trophy they had just retained.

As we crawled away from the environs of the ground and along the A41 towards Watford, avoiding the car park known as the North Circular Road, my pride swelled by the minute. Until we became stuck outside a Tube Station thronged by Forest fans who really knew their team…

"Albert! Albert! Albert!" they chanted. "There's only one driver Albert, one driver Albert!"

"What are those beggars singing?" asked Clough.

"My name, boss," chuckled the old driver.

"In that case, old man, you're sacked. You're far too famous."

As soon as we reached the M1, Clough suggested "The Company Secretary" and "The Sports Editor" resume their usual positions. And after the usual meal cooked by Jubilee Club manager Ron, he even suggested that I go through the curtains to the players' compartment and gather my quotes.

The only other occasion he had sent me back there was after a defeat that had particularly disappointed him. "Go and sit beside The Captain and blow as much smoke as you like over all of them," he had ordered.

The trip from Wembley was a much happier experience. "Your smell's definitely going," said Sutton. And the quotes flowed in the back half of the coach as lavishly as the spirits in the front half.

I was back in my seat by the time Albert surprised me by turning off the M1 at Junction 24 and heading for East Midlands Airport. The usual turn-off point was at the A52 junction so that Clough's chauffeur could meet him in one of the hotel car parks and whisk him westwards to his home while the team headed east to Nottingham. Now, as we pulled up outside the doors leading to Departures, Clough rose from his seat, collected the trophy and lumbered out of the bus. He took the trophy through the doors into the main hall of the airport, to the mystification of all and sundry on this April night, before returning to his seat – pausing only to say to me and Lawson: "Not a word about this. This is for Sadler."

It was his way of providing *The Sun* columnist, John Sadler, with a Tuesday exclusive (for which he would be handsomely paid) about this Littlewoods Cup win being his passport back into Europe. He had good reason to be optimistic. The blanket ban on English clubs was coming to an end. All of the vibes had been that whoever won the League Cup would be welcomed into the UEFA Cup.

Oh, we of too much faith! At the season's end, Aston Villa were given England's only UEFA Cup spot, having finished runners-up to Liverpool in the First Division while Manchester United qualified for the Cup-Winners' Cup by beating Crystal Palace 1-0 in a replay of the Final.

It was the second time in three years that he threw his passport away in disgust. The first occasion was when the Forest directors refused to let him talk to the Welsh FA about becoming the part-time manager of their national team early in 1988. Cynics said he was managing Forest part-time anyway, leaving many of the training sessions to O'Kane, Fenton and Gemmill; so it would have been no skin off the club's nose if he'd popped away to Cardiff for the odd week. And there is no doubt that, in the absence of European club competition, he would have relished the chance to upset the natural order at international level much as Jack Charlton was doing with the Republic of Ireland. But the Forest leadership put its collective foot down.

"I might as well throw my passport away," said Clough, though he quietly enjoyed the knowledge that the club continued to value him so highly.

"That'd make a good picture," I ventured.

It was only after Steve Mitchell took it that I realised that, as ever, Clough had had the last laugh – by insisting on a copy of the *Football Post* being uppermost in the waste basket …

But back to 1990 … After their miserable run between the League Cup semi and final, Forest consummated the Wembley win over Oldham in style in their next League match. They smashed Man United 4-0 at the City Ground. It was such a comprehensive thrashing that, within minutes of the final whistle, manager Alex Ferguson had got his troops lined-up behind him and marched them stern faced along the main corridor from the changing rooms to the double doors through which I had made my undignified exit, prompted by Clough's boot, all those years earlier. Among them was Neil Webb, looking and feeling even more humiliated than I had felt in 1978.

Down the side corridor in the Chairman's Room, Clough was not in the mood to celebrate. "If we'd done our jobs in the third round, we might be heading for the FA Cup Final instead of them – and yon Ferguson might be back in Scotland by now."

This was a reference to the third round FA Cup tie at the City Ground the previous January. All the pre-match talk focussed on speculation that Ferguson had been such an under-achiever since his arrival from Aberdeen in November 1986 that another early exit from a prestigious competition would end his tenure at Old Trafford.

The Trent End, still smarting from losing a highly popular midfielder to United, greeted the appearance of the Junior Reds' corpulently-padded mascot DJ Bear with a rousing chorus of: "Are you Webby is disguise?"

United scored (57 minutes, according to the notes I still have from the season) when Stuart Pearce – decisive Captain Psycho of all people – got too far under a hopeless-looking long lob towards the Forest goal and a hopeful young striker called Mark Robins was able to leap above him and head the ball past Steve Sutton. Wembley winner Jemson had an "equaliser" disallowed by a linesman's decision with two minutes left. And, to all intents and purposes, Clough's FA Cup hoodoo had struck again.

Except the man himself saw it differently. He stormed out of the City Ground in record time and never spoke about the tie … until he was musing on the 4-0 League win four months later. It was immaterial in his view. All that mattered to him was: "We could have seen yon Scotsman off that day. Now the f***er'll be around for years."

"Can I use that, Brian?"

"Do you think I want him to think I'm at all concerned about him? F*** off!"

So I did. But this time without his boot up my backside.

Postscript

What happened next

· ·

I TOOK redundancy from the *Evening Post* in February 1992. It was only then that I realised just how drained I was. Eventually I exchanged the publicity-savvy football scene for athletics, a sport which to this day seems shy of the full glare of publicity although it contains almost as many news-worthy characters as The National Game. Oh, and I never smoked again. A year to the day after I stopped, I gave the half-full packet of Benson and Hedges to a friend. She lit one – and it was so dry that it flared up and singed her eyebrows. Cynics would claim it was the nearest I got to hot news while I worked in athletics.

Within days of my departure from the *Post*, Clough had found time to send two of his players to my home to make sure I had not suffered the same involuntary fate as his mate Lawson at the hands of my "f***ing bosses". His lovely secretary Carol and my *Football Post* columnist Nigel Clough both phoned separately to ask: "Is there anything you want us to do?" There wasn't, I assured them. I was spent, I explained.

On reflection, there was something: I wanted Clough to walk away from the pressures, as I had, so that he and Barbara could enjoy the years of relaxation together that they deserved for their undoubted devotion. He didn't. He stayed loyal to his post-Derby pledge to Barbara that he would never resign again. He had taken Forest back to Wembley for the 1991 FA Cup Final, in which they lost after extra time to Tottenham Hotspur who featured Paul Gascoigne in a kamikaze role; and in 1992 both the Full Members' Cup[8], in which they beat Southampton, and the League Cup, in which they lost to Manchester United as Alex Ferguson's philosophy began to bear more fruit.

In 1993 Clough took Forest down to Division Two and retired. Only he could have been worshipped so unreservedly in defeat, as this picture graphically illustrates…

---

[8] By now the Full Members' Cup (formerly sponsored by Simod) had become the Zenith Data Systems Trophy.

The burghers of Nottingham rewarded him with the Freedom of the City and a statue in the Old Market Square, which many considered too little reward far too late for the benefits he had brought to this fair city. And he had certainly earned more retirement time than he actually had with wife Barbara, sons Simon and Nigel and daughter Elizabeth ... more time for moments like the one he allowed photographer Trevor Bartlett to share on the day he announced his retirement in April 1993. No words are required to express the contentment he finds in this cuddle with his two-year-old grand-daughter Susannah. Bartlett's exclusive snap, taken in the garden of the Clough home in Derbyshire with the rest of the world's media locked out in the road, covered half of the *Post's* front page on 28 April 1993. It also illustrated the trust and respect Bartlett had earned from Clough over the years.

Clough had often said, particularly at times when he felt ignored by Board members seeking to balance the books: "These non-football folk don't realise, you know, what it takes to get a set-up like this one this far. Maybe they will eventually. I just hope I live long enough to see this lot back where I found them."

His morose wish came true. When Brian Clough died on 20 September 2004 Nottingham Forest were fifth from the bottom of the second tier of English football, one place lower than when he had become their manager.

As he would have reflected: "What a game, eh?"

The Clough chronology

· ·

BRIAN HOWARD CLOUGH, born in Middlesbrough on 21 March 1935, was a legend several times over before he became Manager of Nottingham Forest. Between the start of the 1953-54 season to July 1961, he scored 204 goals in 222 games for Middlesbrough. When he was sold to Sunderland for £55,000, his prolific form continued at Roker Park: 54 goals in 61 League games. But his playing career was ended prematurely by a knee injury suffered on Boxing Day 1962 – though, with typical stubbornness, he battled on until November 1964 before acknowledging he would have to retire. He joined the club's coaching staff but always felt he was born to lead rather than obey.

And so...

1965. Became Manager of Hartlepool United. Spent Saturday mornings before home matches driving around in a bus with a loud-hailer urging shoppers to "come and watch the best League side in town". Particularly enjoyed causing havoc in Stockton High Street ... "It's the widest street in the world, you know," he would reflect decades later when drink made him sufficiently mellow. "Just was well with you at the wheel of a Corporation bus," fellow north-easterner Ron Fenton (who succeeded Taylor as his assistant) would venture. "Behave," Clough would caution, pointing his index finger at Fenton to emphasise that the mellow moment had passed and the Gaffer ruled. He and Taylor lifted Hartlepool from 14th in Division IV at the end of the 1965-66 season to fifth in 1966-67.

1967. Became Manager of Derby County. Won Division II (equivalent of Championship) title in 1968-69. Became the youngest manager to win Division I (equivalent of Premier League) title in 1971-72. Reached European Cup semi-finals in 1972-73; went to his grave convinced refereeing decisions in Turin had cost him a victory over Juventus and a place in the Final.

1973. After a massive fall-out with Sam Longson, his chairman at Derby County, he moved to manage Division III Brighton and Hove Albion in November and surprised many by staying to the end of the season.

1974. Spent 44 days at Leeds United; alienated 'star' players who had performed under Don Revie; received so much compensation to leave (£100,000), he said it set him up financially for life.

1975. Replaced Allan Brown as Manager at the City Ground on 6 January with Forest sixth from the foot of Division II. They finished the season 16th; record under Clough: P17 W3 D8 L6 F16 A23 Pts 14.

1975-76. Peter Taylor, born in Nottingham on 2 July 1928, arrived as Assistant Manager. Forest finished the season 8th in Division II: P42 W17 D12 L13 F55 A40 Pts 46. Won Anglo-Scottish Cup[9], defeating Leyton Orient in the two-leg final – the triumph, Clough always reflected, that gave them the appetite for future silverware. He'd explain: "You can teach footballers how to play. That's easy. But they have to learn how to win. The first trophy is always the hardest to win."

1976-77. Forest finished third in Division II – P42 W21 D10 L11 F77 A43 Pts 52 – and were promoted behind Wolverhampton Wanderers and Chelsea thanks to Bolton Wanderers imploding in their last two matches.

1977-78. Forest won their opening match in the top flight 3-1 away to Everton, led the table for most of the season and clinched the Championship for the first time in their history: P42 W25 D14 L3 F69 A24 Pts 64. They also won the League Cup, defeating Liverpool 1-0 after extra time in a Final replay at Old Trafford after 0-0 draw at Wembley. It was the first time the same club had won both the League Championship and League Cup in one season. Clough was Manager of the Year after winning a then record 4 Manager of the Month awards. Kenny Burns was voted Sportswriters' Footballer of the Year and Midlands Sportswriters' Player of the Year. Peter Shilton was the Professional Footballers' Association Player of the Year. Tony Woodcock was the PFA Young Player of the Year and the Division I Managers' Player of the Year. John Robertson scored the ITV Goal of the Season. The Forest squad released a record titled: "We've got the whole world in our hands"; nobody argued.

1978-79. Forest took the European Cup by storm, eliminating holders Liverpool in the first round and clinching the trophy with a 1-0 win over Malmo in the Final. The goal was scored by Trevor Francis, who had become Britain's first £1 million footballer when he joined from Birmingham City in February. Forest also retained the League Cup, defeating Southampton 3-2 at Wembley in a pulsating Final, and finished League runners-up (8 points behind Liverpool): P42 W21 D18 L3 F61 A26 Pts 60. Building began on the City Ground's Executive Stand (so-called because it was to incorporate the club's first executive boxes for businesses to hire).

1979-80. Forest retained the European Cup, defeating Hamburg 1-0 in the Madrid Final, having added the European Super Cup with a two-leg triumph over Barcelona. They were

---

[9] The Anglo-Scottish Cup was a competition for clubs in the English and Scottish Leagues

surprisingly defeated in the League Cup Final, also 0-1, by Wolverhampton Wanderers. Forest finished 5th in Division I (12 points behind champions Liverpool): P42 W20 D8 L14 F63 A43 Pts 48. These achievements were despite Tony Woodcock being transferred to FC Cologne and Trevor Francis suffering a severe Achilles injury in May that prevented him from playing in the European Cup Final.

1980-81. Forest dipped into the European transfer markets for the first time, signing midfielder Raimondo Ponte from Grasshopper Zurich and defender Einar Aas from Norway but went out in the first round of the European Cup, 0-2 on aggregate to CSKA Sofia of Bulgaria. And they made a little more unwanted history when they became the first club to lose the European Super Cup Final on the away goals rule: they beat Valencia 2-1 at the City Ground but lost the second leg in Spain 1-0. To complete a hat-trick of frustration, Forest lost the World Club Final 0-1 to Nacional Montevideo of Uruguay in Tokyo. Forest finished seventh in Division I (10 points behind champions Aston Villa) – P42 W19 D12 L11 F62 A44 Pts 50 – and missed a UEFA Cup place on goal difference.

1981-82. Little went right. Forest finished 12th in Division 1, 30 points behind champions Liverpool: P42 W15 D12 L15 F42 A48 Pts 57. They had been knocked out of the FA Cup in the third round by Wrexham of the Third Division and out of the League Cup in the quarter finals at Tottenham. Peter Taylor departed at the end of the season, citing health problems.

1982-83. Taylor stunned the football world by becoming Derby County manager and was branded a "snake" by Clough when he lured John Robertson down the A52. Clough set about rebuilding his two teams, in the backroom and on the pitch. In as Assistant Manager came Ron Fenton, born in South Shields on 21 September 1940, who played as an inside forward for Burnley, West Bromwich Albion, Birmingham City and Brentford before managing Notts County 1975-77 while Jimmy Sirrel tried out the hot-seat at Sheffield United. In as coach came Liam O'Kane, born in Derry, Northern Ireland, in 1948, who had played in Forest's defence 1968-76, and was to stay at the City Ground until 2005. Clough sold Peter Shilton to Southampton for £325,000, a record for a goalkeeper, and replaced him with Dutch international Hans van Breukelen for £200,000. Despite a catalogue of injuries (Aas was cruelly forced into early retirement by an injury) Forest finished fifth in Division I, 33 points behind Liverpool: P42 W20 D9 L13 F62 A50 Pts 49.

1983-84. Forest suffered the trauma of awful refereeing decisions in the UEFA Cup semi-final second leg against Anderlecht (it emerged years later that the Belgian club had bribed the referee, who had died in a road accident in the meantime). Van Breukelen returned to Holland and was replaced with one of his countrymen, Hans Segers from PSV Eindhoven. By finishing third in Division I, within 6 points of champions Liverpool and 3 of surprise runners-up Southampton – P42 W22 D8 L12 F76 A45 Pts 74 – Forest qualified for Europe again.

1984-85. In a season remembered primarily for the deaths of 39 Juventus supporters at the European Cup Final against Liverpool in what became known as The Heysel Stadium

Disaster, Forest went out of the UEFA Cup, 0-1 to FC Bruges of Belgium in the first round. Transfers included Viv Anderson departing to Arsenal, and Dutch giant Johnny Metgod arriving from Real Madrid along with winger Franz Carr from Blackburn Rovers. Despite losing the first League match to be shown as it happened on TV, 1-2 at Tottenham, Forest finished 9th in Division I (26 points behind champions Everton): P42 W19 D7 L16 F56 A48 Pts 64.

1985-86. Out went defenders Paul Hart, Jim McInally and Kenny Swain, midfielders Steve Hodge and Steve Wigley and, most disappointingly for Clough, striker Peter Davenport in Forest's drive to balance their accounts. In came defenders Ian Butterworth and Stuart Pearce from Coventry City, midfielder Neil Webb from Portsmouth and winger Brian Rice from Hibernian, while Robertson returned to the fold. A friendly against PSV was lost 0-4; and Forest fans talked in awe for years about the skills of a dread-locked young giant called Ruud Gullit (who was so unknown at the time that, to March 2010, he was still referred to as Rudd Hullit on Forest's official website). After going unbeaten in their last 12 matches in Division I, Forest finished the season 8th (20 points behind champions Liverpool): P42 W19 D11 L12 F69 A53 Pts 68.

1986-87. Out went Butterworth. In came central defender Colin Foster from Division 4 Orient. Forest led Division I until early November but finished 8th again (21 points behind champions Everton): P42 W18 D11 L13 F64 A51 Pts 65. At 21, Nigel Clough was Forest's joint top scorer with 14 goals.

1987-88. The young side, playing with fearless fluency, won the Football League Centenary Tournament; reached the FA Cup semi-finals, losing 1-2 to holders Liverpool (who in turned were sensationally defeated 1-0 by Wimbledon in the Final); and were third in Division 1 (17 points behind Liverpool and 8 behind Manchester United): P40 W20 D13 L7 F67 A39 Pts 73. Forest Reserves won the Central League title for the first time.

1988-89. Steve Hodge returned home from Tottenham for £550,000. Segers moved to Wimbledon, giving Steve Sutton a long-awaited chance to play in goal. Brian Clough was fined a record £5,000 and banned from Football League touchlines for the rest of the season by the FA after thumping Forest fans who invaded the pitch at the end of a League Cup win over QPR. In between becoming the first club to win two Wembley Finals in the same season (the League Cup 3-1 against holders Luton Town and the Full Members' Cup 4-3 against Everton), Forest were the opponents when 96 Liverpool supporters died in the Hillsborough Disaster and lost the replayed semi-final 3-1 at Old Trafford. Forest again finished third in Division I (12 points behind Arsenal, who pipped Liverpool on goal average by winning the last match of the season 2-0 at Anfield): P38 W17 D13 L8 F64 A43 Pts 64.

1989-90. Forest went out of the FA Cup, 0-1 to Manchester United in the third round, but retained the League Cup by defeating Oldham Athletic 1-0 in Wembley's first all-seated Final. They finished 9th in Division I (25 points behind champions Liverpool): P38 W15 D9 L14 F55 A47 Pts 54. Clough received an Honorary Arts degree from the

University of Nottingham and assured all around him: "If anyone wants to see my O-levels and A-levels, I'll get my medals from upstairs and put them on the table."

1990-91. Clough got closer than ever before to getting his hands on the only major trophy to elude him, the FA Cup. Mark Crossley became only the second goalkeeper (after Wimbledon's Dave Beasant) to save a penalty on this great occasion but Tottenham Hotspur won 2-1. Forest finished 8th in Division I (29 points behind champions Arsenal): P38 W14 D12 L12 F64 A50 Pts 54. Awarded the OBE for services to football, the man the fans already called Sir Brian tried to keep his feet on the ground: "My wife says it stands for Old Big 'Ead."

1991-92. Clough broke the club transfer record pre-season, paying Millwall £2 million for striker Ted Sheringham. In November he sold Garry Parker to Aston Villa for £650,000. Two more Wembley Finals: Forest beat Southampton 3-2 to win the Zenith Data Cup (as the Simod Cup was now called) but lost to a Brian McClair goal for Manchester United in the League Cup Final. Forest finished 8th again in Division I (29 points behind champions Leeds United, managed by Howard Wilkinson of blessed Notts County memory): P42 W16 D11 L15 F60 A58 Pts 59. Roy Keane was named Young Player of the Year ("Barclay's Young Eagle" as the sponsors titled him). Stuart Pearce and Nigel Clough were in the England squad for the European Championships in Sweden.

1992-93. The first year of the Premier League coincided with the end of The Clough Phenomenon. Des Walker went to Sampdoria in Italy pre-season; and Sheringham was sold to Tottenham (and finished the season as the League's top scorer). These two deals were totally out of character for the manager who always prided himself on the strength of the "spine" of his team. Forest finished bottom of Division I and were relegated: P42 W10 D10 L22 F41 A62 Pts 40. With relegation inevitable, Clough announced his retirement, was given the Freedom of the City of Nottingham and was replaced at the City Ground by Frank Clark (as he had always insisted he should be).

Clough's full record with Forest in League matches was:
P 759 W 331 D 208 L 220 F 1103 A 840 Pts 1075

Brian Howard Clough died on 20 September 2004, surrounded by his loving family. As his body gradually succumbed, he had had far more than enough time to tell all how he wished to be remembered:

> *"I want no epitaphs of profound history and all that type of thing.*
> *I contributed;*
> *I would hope they will say that.*
> *And I would hope somebody liked me."*

Uniquely, he was liked, even loved, by so many in the rival cities of Derby and Nottingham that the stretch of A52 dual carriageway between the two is now officially called Brian Clough Way.